√ e·
c·

235.2
21.5cm

D1058380

SAINTS: THEIR PLACE IN THE CHURCH

SAINTS

Their Place in the Church

by PAUL MOLINARI, S.J.

Preface by CARDINAL LARRAONA

translated by Dominic Maruca, S.J.

SHEED AND WARD : NEW YORK

FOREWORD TO THE AMERICAN EDITION

Since the publication two years ago of the original Italian edition of this book, the Second Vatican Council, in a special chapter on the Dogmatic Constitution on the Church, has dealt with the problem of our relationship to the Church Triumphant, and in particular to the Saints (Chapter VII, "Eschatological Nature of the Pilgrim Church and Its Union with the Church in Heaven").

In council for the purpose of studying herself to make herself better known to mankind, the Church has felt the need to express her awareness of the vital union she has in Christ with all who are His, and of her special union with those who as members of the Church in Heaven are perpetually united to Him. It is from this deeply felt need that Chapter VII of the Constitution on the Church derives, the chapter that is specifically concerned with the union between the Pilgrim Church and the Church in Heaven. This is the first time in the history of the Church that this doctrine, so intimately related to her life and therefore to her practices from the very first centuries of Christianity, has been set forth positively and systematically by her supreme teaching authority.

In view of this ample conciliar treatment of the problems we had already discussed, the question arose whether it would not be advisable to rewrite our study for its publication in America, or even to turn it into a commentary on Chapter VII of the Dogmatic Constitution "Lumen Gentium." On reflection, however, we decided to leave the book in substantially the form it had in the original Italian and in the German and Spanish translations.* This decision rests, on the one hand, on the fact that in our opinion no full scientific commentary on the conciliar teaching can be published unless and until the Acts of the Council, in particular the Acts of the Theological Commission, have been made generally accessible. Only then will it be possible to write the detailed history of this chapter and to examine each sentence, and sometimes each word, in the light of the conciliar interventions and against the background of the discussions both in the Theological Commission and in the special Subcommission which was responsible for this text.†

On the other hand, even in its present form, the book is a theological commentary on the conciliar Constitution. A comparison clearly demonstrates that there is a perfect harmony between the teaching and practical proposals contained in Chapter VII of the Constitution and our own study.

PAUL MOLINARI, S.J.

Rome, 27th April 1965
Feast of St. Peter Canisius

---

* The only major difference between the American and the other editions is that the scientific apparatus of the present volume has been considerably reduced.

† Editor's note: We should point out in this context that Fr. Molinari is a Peritus attached to the Theological Commission of the Second Vatican Council and that he has served as Secretary to the special Subcommission which was responsible for Chapter VII of the Dogmatic Constitution on the Church.

PREFACE

The Reverend Paul Molinari, S.J., author of the book we have
the honor of presenting, is the faithful and conscientious
Postulator for the Causes of the Servants of God who were
members of the Society of Jesus. In keeping with this sacred
trust, he has achieved distinction as a theologian dedicated
to promoting the development of hagiography in several of
its different aspects. He offers us in this collection a revised
and expanded version of several of his essays—certainly, a
most timely work. It is a deep, organic, and comprehensive
synthesis of theological reflections on the function of the
Saints in the Church (Part One) and considerations on the
nature, spirit, and limits of the honor paid to the Saints (Part
Two); these two theological sections are followed by some
solid and valuable reflections on the extreme tendencies encountered in the cult of the Saints (Part Three).

It would be pleasant, perhaps even useful, to present a
synthetic summary of the contents of the book in order to
offer the reader in advance a concrete idea of its doctrinal
depth and richness. I will limit myself to stressing briefly its
principal merits and value and to pointing out those aspects

which make it truly useful, practical, and timely both in the present atmosphere of the Council and outside it.

The doctrine is *solid* and *comprehensive*: no theoretical or practical question which is the subject of theological, apologetic, ascetical or liturgical discussion, or which has been advanced regarding the Saints and their cult even in the most recent literature, has escaped the author's attention. It is, moreover, perfectly elaborated to the last detail and supported by an exhaustive bibliography.

The exposition is clear and careful: it demands concentrated attention on the part of the reader because it is packed with meaning and at times closely wrought; but the effort will be well rewarded because the argument is sound, pleasing, and convincing.

In the area of doctrine and movements which are at once theoretical and practical (for example, the spheres of spirituality, the liturgy, and social organizations) a condition develops which is rather like that which accompanies the flowing of great rivers: even though the current is following its course strongly, surely, and majestically, stagnant backwaters are to be found along the banks. This phenomenon holds true even for the literature concerning a contemporary event of paramount importance, namely, the Council. The calm, serious words which concluded Pius XII's last discourse, prepared but not delivered by him, entitled "The Personality, Thought, and Work of the Supreme Pontiff Benedict XIV" (Pius XII, *Discorsi e Radiomessaggi,* vol. xx, pp. 453–472), made unmistakable reference to those theories not in accord with solid theological doctrine, and to certain practices and tendencies, which would cause the honor paid to the Saints to deviate from the true mind and directives of the Church.

Father Molinari's work is a timely contribution to the exposition of the Church's doctrine, enriched and illustrated by

the developments of her teaching authority (e.g. those concerning the Mystical Body), and by the gains in breadth and
depth of modern theology. From a practical viewpoint, Father
Molinari provides us with a solid aid for safeguarding the
vital force of the cult of the Saints, which, if lived according
to its true spirit, represents a strong apologetical argument for
the Church's holiness. It constitutes, moreover, an apt means
for increasing, deepening and renewing in the hearts of the
faithful a sense of the Mystical Body; it enables us to realize
the power of our Head, who is wonderful in His Saints and
triumphant in His Martyrs; it gives us an appreciation of the
beautiful doctrine of the Communion of Saints, which includes
intercession and assistance, and is a source of incentive and
consolation.

We hope that the book will reach the wide reading public
it so richly deserves and benefit that public in full measure.

I am writing this Preface on the Feast of St. Ignatius
Loyola, who from his earliest years had a vivid realization of
the salvific power deriving from contact with the Saints. May
Vatican Council II, among so many other salvific fruits, effect
an intensification of our fraternal relations with the Saints,
relations of cult, imitation, and confidence which will draw us
closer to Christ, the King and crown of the Saints.

ARCADIO CARDINAL LARRAONA
Prefect of the Sacred Congregation of Rites

Rome, July 31, 1962

CONTENTS

Foreword to the American Edition   v
Preface by Arcadio Cardinal Larraona   vii
Introduction   xiii

PART ONE: THEOLOGICAL REFLECTIONS ON THE
FUNCTION OF THE SAINTS IN THE CHURCH

   I. The Dogmatic Significance of Catholic Doctrine on the
      Saints, Viewed in the Light of Tendencies and
      Advances in Contemporary Theology   11
  II. The Apologetic Function of Canonized Saints   22
 III. Considerations of a Practical Order   32

PART TWO: THEOLOGICAL CONSIDERATIONS
ON THE NATURE, SPIRIT AND LIMITS OF THE
HONOR PAID THE SAINTS

   I. General Considerations on the Nature of the Vital
      Relationships Existing within the Mystical Body 49
  II. The Cult of the Saints and Our Progress towards the
      Fullness of Christ   54
 III. The Cult of the Saints and the Perfection of Our
      Progress towards Christ and the Father   76
  IV. The Necessity of the Cult of the Saints   95

xi

PART THREE: REFLECTIONS ON THE EXTREME
TENDENCIES ENCOUNTERED IN THE CULT OF
THE SAINTS

I.   Minimalistic Tendencies   109
II. Maximalistic Tendencies   139

Appendix I: On the Possibility of a Communication between
                    Wayfarers and the Saints   150
Appendix II: The Saints in the Church according to the
                    Recent Dogmatic Constitution "Lumen
                    Gentium" of the Second Vatican Council   160

Notes   176
Index   235

INTRODUCTION

Last year I published in the periodical *Gregorianum* (42
[1961] 63–96) an article entitled, "Theological Reflections
on the Function of the Saints in the Church." As the title
indicates, I did not aim to attack the problem in its full complexity, but simply to expound what seem to be the principal
ideas according to which our thought must be oriented if we
wish to arrive at an adequate understanding and appreciation
of the Saints and their function within the community of the
Church. In doing so, I thought it useful to draw attention to
the fact that the advantages to be had from modern theological trends—specifically the doctrine of the Mystical Body—
had not yet been sufficiently applied to the study of the phenomenon of the Saints. This article, limited though it was,
was well received and evoked an interest which was followed
by requests both for further elucidation and for explanation
of points which I had purposely left unconsidered in the
article. More urgently, because they penetrated to the very
heart of the matter, some stressed the need for clarification of
the entire question of the "cult of the Saints." It is a fact
worthy of note that whereas, on the one hand, contemporary

society is exhibiting a lively and increasing interest in the Saints—an interest manifested at times, unfortunately, in exaggerated and unwholesome devotions—on the other hand, ideas and opinions are being disseminated which undermine the importance of their cult. This observation constitutes an added reason for a study, with a view to proposing some theological reflections that might direct the attention of scholars to the urgency of this problem which is awaiting further study and development. It seems to me, in fact, that there is a real lacuna in this area. That there are no studies which treat this problem systematically is, in my opinion, the cause of that ignorance which finds external expression in both exaggerated forms of devotion to the Saints and disdainful opposition to their cult.

I set about the task of preparing an article on this subject. The complexity of the topic; the need of incorporating all the different aspects in a clear and systematic exposition of the Church's traditional doctrine; the opportuneness of treating the problem by descending to the deepest roots which manifest not only the liceity and utility but also the wealth and even the necessity of a genuine cult of the Saints; and, finally, the urgent need for a clear demarcation of the limits of this cult—all these demanded such lengthy treatment that, as the work progressed, the limits of an article were exceeded. When my work was completed, it was suggested that I combine the original article and the newly prepared material into a single volume. The reflections made in the original article were the basic premises from which one must proceed, and from which, in fact, I did proceed, in the study of this aspect of the problems relevant to the Saints. Those reflections laid down the fundamental theological principles on the basis of which we can understand who the Saints are, what their function is, and consequently what relations should prevail between them and us.

This assembling in one volume of what were originally conceived as articles will explain to the reader the absence of the treatment of other aspects of the problem of the Saints. If at the outset I had proposed to write a book, I would have followed a different course and would have attempted to touch upon every aspect of the problem, giving an organic and systematic presentation, and including even other considerations which do not bear directly on the cult of the Saints.

This I could not do, and yet there are both intrinsic and extrinsic motives which justify the presentation of this study whose specific scope is the "cult of the Saints"; so I venture to present my work for publication. I hope that it will serve as an invitation to some scholars to treat what I have attempted to expound more profoundly, and as an incentive to others to consider the many aspects which still await study and evaluation, for the good of souls and of the Church.

Rome, Feast of St. Robert Bellarmine, May 13, 1962

PART ONE

Theological Reflections on the Function of Saints in the Church

Anyone capable of viewing the past few decades with a comprehensive glance must acknowledge a singularly arresting phenomenon: the growing interest in sanctity and the Saints.

The number of canonizations and beatifications have noticeably increased during recent pontificates, to the extent of assuming vast proportions. Various publications had already called attention to this fact in one form or another[1] when an article on recent canonizations in the *Nouvelle Revue Théologique* made this penetrating observation:

> The great American sociologist P. A. Sorokin asserted, just a decade ago, that the stream of sanctity was beginning to dry up because—in his opinion—modern civilization leaves no role for Saints to fulfill.
>
> This opinion is certainly contradicted by the facts as reflected in the canonizations and beatifications of the Catholic Church. Never in the course of history have so many Saints and Blessed been raised to the honor of the altar. In this respect, the pontificate of Pius XII has been the most fruitful on record.[2]

The complementary article on recent beatifications underscores this fact:

3

A total of 1,194 persons have been beatified in this way (according to the canonical procedures followed since 1634). But the rate of beatifications is being accelerated to such an extent that the vast majority of the present Beati have attained to the glory of the altar in comparatively recent years.

The number of persons beatified between 1951 and 1960 so far exceeds the sum total of those enrolled among the Blessed between the years 1662 and 1852 that a single decade has witnessed more beatifications than did two centuries. One should bear in mind that 93% of all the beatifications were promulgated during the last century.[3]

The official documents promulgated by the Supreme Pontiffs on the occasion of these events—the Bulls of Canonization, Decrees of Beatification, and Allocutions—constitute a precious and inexhaustible treasure by which the Supreme Teaching Authority has expounded fundamental principles concerning Christian perfection and virtue. The depth and breadth of teaching presented authoritatively in such documents represents a source of major importance for any study of the many problems of spiritual theology.[4]

The interest in the Saints which the teaching Church has manifested is matched by an equally extensive interest on the part of the faithful. Their devotion towards certain persons now elevated to the altar shows how deeply sympathetic a rapport exists between the faithful and the activity of the Holy See and the Teaching Authority of the Church.[5] We must acknowledge, on the other hand, that this very same spontaneous devotion of the faithful—quick to notice, understand and appreciate almost intuitively the hidden sanctity of certain persons—is what draws attention to, sustains, and prepares the way for what then becomes the Church's activity in the processes of Beatification and Canonization.[6]

A factor contributing to this complex phenomenon—and in

a sense its effect—is the output of studies and hagiographical works of various kinds,[7] ranging from those of a rigorously scientific character to a veritable deluge of biographies directed to the body of the faithful at large. These popular biographies, unfortunately, have not always been written in accordance with those sound theological, historical, psychological, and literary norms which ought to regulate this work, so important in the life of the Church today.

Mention must also be made of how this keen interest in the Saints and their lives has been the occasion of countless writings and monographs, continuously endeavoring to approach and analyze, with ever-increasing accuracy and objectivity, the many problems involved in the lives of the Saints. These studies delineate the character of various Saints in the light of ascetical and mystical theology, medicine, psychology, history,[8] iconography,[9] and even graphology.[10]

This interest in the lives of the Saints is not restricted to the field of literary productions of a spiritual and religious character. The attention of novelists and other secular authors has been so captivated by the phenomenon of sanctity that they have based works on the pattern of sanctity and presented various Saints as their central characters.[11]

We have presented these general observations and remarks —with no pretext of treating any of them exhaustively— simply to substantiate the validity of our initial assertion that during the past few decades the phenomenon of sanctity and of the Saints themselves has been the object of an ever-increasing interest which has now assumed noteworthy proportions.

A confirmation of this can be seen in the fact that the motion picture industry has not remained insensitive to this development or unconcerned with it. We are not referring to the Catholic studios which have treated a few of the Saints with a purely spiritual and apostolic intent, since this is not at all surprising in view of the interest noted above. Much more significant is the fact that even those studios which ordinarily are not concerned with the screen presentation of questions and problems on such a lofty moral level as those pertaining to the Saints have nonetheless produced several noteworthy films on these very themes.[12] The fact that those whose concern is primarily economic have ventured to produce such films indicates that they have recognized that subjects of this type supply a demand and meet an interest on the part of the public.

The enthusiasm with which films of this type have been received by both critics and public is a confirmation of what has been said about the timeliness of this topic. At the same time it is a manifestation of that response evoked in the human heart by a vivid, real, and concrete presentation of that ideal of goodness and perfection to which man is basically oriented and destined.

We must not, however, blind ourselves to the fact that this rebirth of interest in and devotion to the Saints, though sustained and encouraged by the Supreme Authority of the Church, has nonetheless been viewed with indifference or displeasure by certain Catholic theologians. Motivated by laudable ecumenical preoccupations, but insisting exclusively on some aspects of dogma to the detriment of others, these theologians have failed to embrace the varied manifestations of our faith.

Here and there within the ranks of the Church are found currents of thought which advocate reducing the cult of the Saints to a minimum because this practice is considered a marginal element that could be eliminated without serious danger—or even with profit—to the purity of faith and the effectiveness of our apostolate. At times a different attitude is taken, and the cult of the Saints is classified as an expression of an exaggerated "Latin devotionalism." These critical opinions, naturally, are not expressed and formulated in clear, categorical terms, since the teaching of the Church on this subject is so explicit that condemnation would follow close upon the heels of any denial of this doctrine. They either lie just under the surface of certain movements which place an exclusive emphasis on selected truths or are manifested by certain practical courses of action.

At this point we should like to consider briefly the opinion of some modern theologians who maintain that honor paid to the Saints might easily deflect the attention of the faithful from the unique Mediator, Christ, who should be the center of all honor and devotion. This will also give us an opportunity to touch upon the attitude of some modern theologians who—under the pretext of favoring union with Protestants—fail to maintain a balanced appreciation of all the integrating elements of our faith, omitting those which they consider accidental in the interest of establishing rapport and understanding with non-Catholics on matters deemed essential.[13] We might mention, in this context, that bent of mind encountered here and there which has reached the point of banishing images and statues of the Saints from our churches.

As is well known, these tendencies have on various occasions been the object of criticism. One of the last documents prepared by Pius XII, and posthumously published, clearly and unequivocably branded these opinions as alien to the genuine spirit of the Church.[14]

We are not denying, to be sure, that in practice there have been, and still are today, deviations or exaggerations in the forms which devotion to the Saints has assumed.[15] Such lamentable aberrations have served as weapons in the hands of critics. But one would be guilty of a serious error if he could not discriminate between certain forms of practice, which are not guaranteed by the Church, and that doctrinal richness inherent in the dogma of the Communion of Saints. In other words, we deplore the fact that a lack of discrimination has led to a depreciation, rather than a protection, of that many-splendored reality and complex of doctrines which go to make up our faith.

This observation brings us to the heart of our subject. It is our conviction that these erroneous tendencies would not gain currency and would not be mingled with certain exaggerated attitudes which give rise to deviations in the expression of devotion, if the theology underlying true cult and solid veneration of the Saints were better known, more rigorously elaborated, and more deeply appreciated.

We must admit with all honesty that very little, if anything, is said about the Saints either in scientific treatises of theology or in oral dogmatic teaching. For the most part, the Saints are mentioned in passing when there is question of distinguishing adoration paid to God from the honor paid to Mary (hyperdulia) or to the Saints (dulia). Again, in the treatment of virtue or the infallibility of the Church in canonization processes, the Saints are mentioned briefly.[16] It would seem that what come in for consideration when the Saints are mentioned are simply certain aspects derived from a nucleus of theological truths which have not been sufficiently analyzed or examined in depth. In our opinion, sufficient treatment is not allotted to the Saints, despite their important function as vitally effective members of the Mystical Body. As a consequence of this failure, in large segments of both clergy and laity, even where true devotion to the Saints is accorded a place, there is no vital awareness of the full theological richness from which devotion can and should draw inspiration. A second consequence of this failure is the frequent difficulty, even among good Catholics, of understanding the relations which should prevail between the Saints and ourselves.

If the increasing devotional interest in the Saints is to have a solid foundation which will guarantee its orthodoxy, there is a definite need for a deeper study of the theological bases of this phenomenon such as I described in my Introduction. Prejudices and objections, in my opinion, will then fade away and, above all, certain neglected dimensions of Catholic teaching will be revealed in clear detail.

We know from the history of theology that there have often been circumstances, situations, and historical exigencies that have necessitated the clarification of certain elements in the complex deposit of our faith and have thus precipitated more profound study. It should cause no astonishment if the contemporary circumstances of increased interest in this problem of the Saints should occasion a deeper analysis of a subject as rich as that of the role of the Saints in the Church.

It would seem that what has been a frequent occurrence in the historical development of theology has been repeated in the case of the doctrine of the Saints: often, out of a group of teachings essentially and intrinsically interrelated, only one was developed and assimilated while the others remained temporarily in obscurity. This should not be surprising, since every age and every generation must appropriate the riches of revelation and dogma in a vital manner corresponding to the circumstances proper to itself. It is the constantly changing nature of the challenge that causes this appropriation to be realized not according to pre-established plans or theoretical schemata but rather as a vital development which is not always regular or homogenous. We can with good reason maintain that in scientific theology and in the consciousness of the faithful today great strides have been made in penetrating into certain dogmatic truths which by their very nature are intimately connected with the theological doctrine of the Saints; but there has been no explicit clarification of the connection. This modest contribution of ours is intended as a partial remedy for the deficiency and will deal with the following points:

(1) The dogmatic significance of Catholic doctrine on the Saints, viewed in the light of tendencies and advances in contemporary theology;

(2) The apologetic value of this doctrine;

(3) Considerations of a practical order.

I. THE DOGMATIC SIGNIFICANCE OF CATHOLIC DOCTRINE ON THE SAINTS, VIEWED IN THE LIGHT OF TENDENCIES AND ADVANCES IN CONTEMPORARY THEOLOGY

Modern man's cast of mind is such that he esteems, stresses, and has a deep attachment to, the concrete, the existential, the vital, the personal. He is less inclined to engage in considerations of an abstract or essentialist nature—however necessary these remain—and feels instead the need and desire to embrace whatever has practical importance and personal significance. Consequently the interest of theologians and of the faithful has been directed in the fields of dogma and theology to the reality of our concrete historical order. This mentality penetrates into every area of theology: the supernatural vocation of the human race in this concrete order of divine Providence; the history of our salvation; the Person, Life, and doctrine of Jesus Christ as presented in Sacred Scripture; the transcendental and central place He occupies in the actual creation willed by God in the life both of mankind and of each of us in particular; our vital contact with Christ in the Church, His Mystical Body; the ontological unity of the human race in Christ, its Head; created and uncreated grace as personal participation in the life of the Trinity, in Christ; His sacraments as means of personal encounter with Him; and so on.

This orientation and emphasis in the domain of contemporary dogmatic theology finds its counterpart in the tendencies of current moral theology. The stress placed on the subjective aspect of our responsibility for personal decisions is a clearly observable phenomenon. A similar emphasis is given to the totality of our moral life, which, in terms of a christocentric orientation, is conceived and presented as an intimate personal relationship between the God-man and ourselves. In this same context, attention is directed to the function of infused charity, the "bond of perfection" and ontologico-psychological root of the intimacy and union between God and His sons in Christ. Finally, our social responsibility has been recognized as an essential part of our supernatural, Christian life.

This same predilection for the concrete, the practical, the existential, the vital, and the personal, can be observed—and in a certain sense even more conspicuously—in the field of contemporary spiritual theology.

The very stress placed on the unity between dogmatic, moral and spiritual theology is in itself a clear indication of the desire to see theory penetrate into practical life. There is a keen desire to make explicit the practical implications of dogma for the spiritual life and, conversely, a demand for a solid dogmatic foundation to support spiritual practices. The same holds true for the liturgical life, prayer, and private devotions. It is no cause for astonishment, then, that so many theologians have set themselves the common goal of presenting the classical doctrines of spirituality in the light of the new dogmatic trends. As a consequence the doctrine of Christian perfection and of the path we must follow to achieve it has been reformulated. Perfection is now expressed entirely in terms of union and of identification with Christ, Head of the Mystical Body; for Christ, by means of His grace, His sacraments, and His inspirations enables us to share in His vivifying and sanctifying life, His apostolic activity, His prayer, work, and sacrifice, His Passion, resurrection, and glory.

If we now ask ourselves in what measure these fruitful orientations have influenced the contemporary theological concept of the person and function of a Saint, our reply must be rather pessimistic. We do not deny that all, or practically all, the substantial elements of the doctrine presented above can be found at least implicitly in the common concept of a Saint. But it would seem that very few theologians or laymen have incorporated these new theological tendencies explicitly and systematically into their vision of the problem of the Saints. This is rather strange, if not incomprehensible. For actually, one who has first-hand knowledge of the writings of the Saints and has tried to penetrate into their teaching and uncover the radical motive forces of their entire lives cannot avoid the conclusion that what constituted the nucleus of their experience and their spiritual vision is precisely the same thing that is of such vital concern to modern theology. In all the Saints we find this ardent desire for union with Christ Jesus. In the life of every Saint there is evident a strong emphasis on the need for a noble, unconditional self-surrender to Christ motivated by deep personal love, and of self-abandonment to a life wholly inspired by a living, effective love.[17] In every Saint one finds a deep sense of responsibility for the building up of the Body of Christ which is the Church. Everywhere, in brief, we find a feeling for what is concrete, existential, vital, and personal in our relations with God and men.

Long before our time, Saints throughout the ages—guided

by the Holy Spirit, who imparts to them a rich interior penetration of the truths of our faith—sensed and lived that which
we, by means of slow process of study, have gradually realized
must become once more a living reality, both in theology and
in the practice of the spiritual life. While on the one hand this
proves the soundness of contemporary theological and religious positions and explains, at least in part, the pre-theolog-
ical interest in the Saints, on the other it enables us to
understand the importance that a sound, objective, theological
consciousness and presentation of the person and function of
the Saint in the Church can have, and actually does have,
both for theology and for the religious life of the faithful.
Since we have thus focused attention on the convergence of
modern orientations and the basic vision that inspired the
lives and teachings of the Saints, it seems apposite to propose
a theological description of a Saint.

We would, then, tentatively suggest a theological description of a Saint, combining the elements of the classical concept
with contemporary theological orientations. In doing so, we
must restrict our description to the canonized Saints; for it is
in those actually declared by the Church to be Saints that we
most assuredly find all the elements essential to sanctity.

A canonized Saint is a member of the Roman Catholic
Church who:

(1) has welcomed, and corresponded unconditionally with,
the invitation of God in such a way that he has lived a life of
ever-increasing perfection in union and conformity with Christ,
by means of the heroic exercise of charity and the other Christian virtues;

(2) because of this life, confirmed by subsequent miracles,
has been proposed by the infallible teaching authority of the
Church as a person particularly pleasing to God, who, pre-

cisely by means of the miracles performed, has manifested His intention that the Saint be considered, by the other members of the Mystical Body:

as a mediator and intercessor "through Christ, with Christ, and in Christ," for all those who have not yet reached the goal of their journey towards the full glorification of God in heavenly beatitude;

as worthy of religious veneration proper to a creature;

as visible proof of His providential action in the Church, and therefore an illustrative norm of typical and truly Christian life.

In this theological description of a canonized Saint we perceive that there are two principal ideas, intimately connected, which are the source of all the other qualifications expressed in the definition: first, the idea of the union and conformity of the Saint with Christ; and second, the idea of his social or ecclesiological importance.

The significant contribution made by the application of modern theological categories to the lives of the Saints, and the study of their existence in the light of those principles, will become evident when we discuss the significance and implications of their eminent union and conformity with Jesus Christ. On this basis we will be able to present a unified and luminous picture in which the fragmentary remarks about the specific qualifications of a Saint will be given their proper setting and relative importance. We have in mind specifically the Saints' titles of mediator, intercessor, and model. The ecclesial dimension of such titles will be seen to stand out in bold relief.

The phrase "eminent union and conformity with Jesus Christ" signifies that the Saints participate most intensely in the life of the Incarnate Word; that is, in the life which He, as Head of the Mystical Body, communicates to His members.

Such an abundant sharing in the life of the Head means in turn that the Saints are not only members, but members eminently active in the Mystical Body.

At this point it is well to recall that the expression "Mystical Body of Christ," as is clear from the developments of modern theology, is not a pure metaphor or simple figure of speech devoid of all correspondence with reality;[18] rather, it refers to an ontological reality so profound that every good work accomplished by one member of Christ's Mystical Body has repercussions on the entire Body and consequently on each individual member. From this it should be clear that the Saints, in virtue of this union among all the members of the Body, are, ontologically speaking, the most outstanding benefactors of the entire Church and of humanity in general.

As we continue to develop this concept further, we will arrive at various familiar aspects, but we will view them now as deriving from a central root and consequently as intimately interrelated.

The beneficent action of the Saints as pre-eminent members of the Mystical Body is not exhausted by the contribution they make to other members through their virtuous and meritorious activity. But in virtue of the "Communion of Saints" (that is, of that intimate, living and vital union among the members of the Church Militant, Suffering, and Triumphant) they continue even in heaven to benefit the other members, no longer by gaining additional merits but by interceding for them (though the merits they acquired on earth continue to exercise their influence upon the Church throughout the ages). This means that, because of their distinguished union and conformity with Christ, the prayers which they in heaven address to the Most High in behalf of those who have not yet reached the final goal of the beatific vision are especially efficacious.

From this one can see how Catholic teaching concerning

the meritorious activity and the intercessory mediation of the Saints in no way detracts from the merits and mediation of Christ. It is evident that the power of the Saints depends entirely upon, and derives all its efficacy from, the very union of these members with Christ the Head.[19]

This comprehensive teaching enables us to recognize the reasonableness and the theological suitability of the position which the Saints occupy in the worship of the Catholic Church. What the Church intends and practices with regard to the Saints is in reality either an act of acknowledgement, praise, and thanksgiving to God for what He has effected in His Saints—"Blessed be God in His Saints"; or it can be an act of veneration (one proper to creatures) towards the Saints themselves, due to them because of their pre-eminent union with the Word Incarnate, Head of the Mystical Body. It should be quite clear in view of this relationship that the veneration of the Saints does not in the least subtract from the theocentric character of Catholic worship; on the contrary, it constitutes a more diffusive glorification of God inasmuch as He is admired, honored, and praised under a new formal aspect, that is, in so far as He is working in His Saints.

The fact that the Saints are pre-eminent members of the Mystical Body particularly dear to God enables us to understand more clearly why the Church proposes them as models for Christian living and teaches that their spiritual life constitutes a safe norm for anyone aspiring to a life of full union with God. With respect to this, it is worth noting that although the exemplarity of the Saints has figured in the Church's vital activity—in fact, it is perhaps the aspect stressed most insistently by preachers and spiritual writers—there is a dimension of this very aspect that has not been equally appreciated as far as its theological import is concerned, though it can make a major contribution towards our understanding of the

function of the Saints in the life of the Church. We refer to
the fact that no sufficient explanation has been advanced to
account for the large number and amazing diversity of types
of Saints throughout the ages; nor has any reason been advanced to explain why the Church continues to canonize
Saints.

The evident reason—and consequently the one frequently
adduced—is that the wealth of Christ's sanctity is so incomprehensible (Eph. 3.8) that even the persons most like unto
Christ, namely the Saints, can do nothing more than participate in and reflect that sanctity in a very limited manner.
With good reason has the observation been made:

The universal example of sanctity given by Jesus is differentiated
and specified in a considerable number of types of sanctity, of
vocations to one or another state in life, of programs corresponding to determined conditions in which various groups of the faithful are living. Each type or program is not a "part" of the sanctity of Jesus; rather, it is a way of placing the sanctity of the Lord
within the reach of a determined category of the Faithful. The
eternal law that was resplendent in our Lord's sanctity becomes,
in this way, translated into diverse tongues so that it may be
better understood and put in practice by all. Every vocation is
complete and perfect in its own kind, because it is simply a
manifestation of the plenitude and perfection of Jesus Christ.[20]

But what might be stressed more emphatically is precisely
the fact that the Providence of God continues to raise up in
every age a diverse array of Saints as living models teaching
us how we can unite ourselves to Him efficiently and concretely in the varied circumstances and vicissitudes of human
society.

When one surveys in a theological light the history of salvation as realized in the Church, the providential plan and intention of God are revealed and the function of the Saints

in the Mystical Body can be comprehended at a more profound level. It is, then, most astonishing to find some who still maintain that the Catholic doctrine concerning the Saints is merely a marginal aspect of its teaching, or even a totally expendable adjunct.

The profound considerations which have followed from reflection on the providential function of the Saints within the life of the Church can be illustrated from the writings of Father Karl Rahner. He characterized the Saints as initiators and creators of new styles and new forms of Christian living.[21] The peculiar forms their lives assumed have been revealed to be authentic models of Christian sanctity, and in this respect they continue to be developed in the Church as legitimate imitations of the perfection of Jesus:

The history of Christian perfection (of that perfection which pertains to every Christian because every one of us has been sanctified and called to perfection) is, on the whole, a unique history; for the eternal is not characterized by endless repetition. It is for this reason that the history of the Saints reveals ever new and unforeseeable phases, and that (even in the perennial imitation of Jesus as a perfect model) the notion of perfection must be rediscovered anew by every Christian. In this task lies the particular function of the canonized Saints for the good of the Church. They are the initiators and the creative prototypes of the forms of perfection that occur during a determined period. They realize a new style of life; they demonstrate that a specific form of life and action is an authentic possibility; they teach experimentally that one can be a Christian in a new way; they accredit a specific type of perfection as authentically Christian. Their influence, however, does not wait for the moment of death before making itself felt. Rather is their death the seal of the task which they, during their lives, had within the Church, in their capacity as creative models. Their continued existence signifies that this possibility has been translated into actuality in their exemplary lives and will remain henceforth as a recognized style of Christian living indelibly impressed on the Church's countenance.[22]

In this sense one can understand how the Lord, who guides and rules the development of His Mystical Body by using the hierarchy which He Himself instituted and permanently assists, accomplishes this same growth by influencing directly and in a hidden manner the souls of His Saints, leading them to penetrate and actuate—according to times and circumstances—in ways that are ever new, the riches of Christian life. His Holiness Pius XII, in the Encyclical *Mystici Corporis,* expressed this concept in the following terms:

Moreover, He conferred a triple power on His Apostles and their successors, to teach, to govern, to lead men to holiness. This triple power, defined by special ordinances, by rights and obligations, He made the fundamental law of the whole Church.

But our Divine Saviour governs and guides His community also directly and personally. For it is He who reigns within the minds and hearts of men and bends and subjects to His purpose their wills even when rebellious. "The heart of the King is in the hand of the Lord; whithersoever he will, he shall turn it." By this interior guidance the "Shepherd and Bishop of our souls" not only watches over individuals, but exercises His providence over the universal Church as well, whether by enlightening and giving courage to the Church's rulers for the loyal and effective performance of their respective duties, or by singling out from the body of the Church—especially when times are grave—men and women of conspicuous holiness, who may point the way for the rest of Christendom to the perfecting of His Mystical Body.[23]

The question arises as to how God's providential action on the Church through the twofold agency of the Hierarchy and the Saints is co-ordinated harmoniously in the divine mind.

The answer is provided by the fact that the Saints are considered as pre-eminent members of the Mystical Body only when the Hierarchy, in virtue of its teaching and ruling office, has recognized the genuineness of the Holy Spirit's activity in them. Before making this solemn pronouncement the Hierarchy subjects the life and virtues of each candidate to an attentive examination and judges whether God has placed His seal of approval thereon in the form of at least two unquestionable miracles. The supreme and infallible act of canonization crowns this lengthy, painstaking process.[24]

From all the dogmatic principles and theological considerations expounded above, one can understand easily how authentically Catholic is the profound joy of the Church and of those whose "minds are in harmony with that of the Church,"[25] when the canonization of a Saint is declared. They find in this fact a confirmation of their faith, inasmuch as they perceive therein a visible proof of God's continual presence and action in His Church and of her perennial vitality and sanctity.[26]

This idea that the presence of God in the Church is rendered visible in His Saints leads us to consider another theological aspect, namely the important function which canonized Saints exercise in the field of apologetics.

II. THE APOLOGETIC FUNCTION
OF CANONIZED SAINTS

From the advent of Protestantism, Catholic apologists have
drawn upon the sanctity of the Church and of its Saints in
particular to construct an argument for the truth and genuineness of the Roman Catholic Church.

The *argumentum ex notis Ecclesiae* (argument from the
characteristic traits—the "marks"—of the Church) is commonly proposed in this generic form:

The true Church, founded by the express desire of Christ,
must be endowed with the distinctive characteristics of unity,
holiness, catholicity, and apostolicity.

Observation and analysis reveal that the Roman Catholic
Church alone is graced with these distinctive qualities.

Therefore, the Roman Catholic Church alone is the true
Church, founded by the express desire of Christ.

During the last few decades serious difficulties have been
raised against this argument by some Catholic authors. As is
well known, the popular Louvain theologian, Gustave Thils,
in his work, *Les Notes de l'Eglise dans l'Apologétique depuis*

la Réforme,[27] has conducted an extensive scientific examination of the origin and historical evolution of this argument, and at the end of his research the conclusions he drew with respect to the possibility of using this argumentation today were rather pessimistic and negative.

According to this author, since contemporary Protestantism has undergone such a notable change from what it was at the time of its origin, we can no longer construct an argument based on scriptural texts which would be accepted by all Christian communions, any more than we can rely on other common foundations which are presupposed by the "argument based on characteristic traits."

Moreover, Thils maintains that as a consequence of the extension and application of this argumentation to the Orthodox Church the definition of the individual characteristic traits has become more complicated and diversified. Various apologists propose their own definitions, with the result that the scriptural foundation of these marks can be called into question and their discernibility is seriously compromised. The confusion which has in fact resulted from continuous additional specifications, distinctions, and subdistinctions renders this form of argument practically useless inasmuch as a distinguishing characteristic, by definition, is a quality essentially connected with the Church, and at the same time:

> better known than the Church itself;
> easily discernible by all, even the uneducated;
> proper to the true Church alone;
> inseparable from that Church.

Obviously we do not intend to enter into the discussion raised by the arguments advanced by Professor Thils; much less do we intend to pronounce on the merits of his position, since such a question is outside our limited scope. We have noted Thils' observations simply in order to place the problem in proper perspective. Within this framework, the reader can more accurately appraise the value of our contention that the Saints have an apologetic value for the Church.[28]

There is no need to belabor the fact that we are concerned here only with the "characteristic trait of holiness" and that, within this limited frame of reference, we will further restrict our discussion to a single aspect, one which, however, we consider primary.

Our observations will be divided between two points:

(A) Unsatisfactory definitions and interpretations of holiness as a distinctive characteristic;
(B) Suggested definition and interpretation of holiness as a distinctive characteristic.

A. UNSATISFACTORY DEFINITIONS AND INTERPRETATIONS OF HOLINESS AS A DISTINCTIVE CHARACTERISTIC

Several points must be made clear at the outset of this discussion: first, holiness in the context of the present argument is to be considered apologetically and not dogmatically; secondly, the holiness of which we are treating must be more visible than the Church itself, so that it will be evident to all, even the uneducated; finally, holiness in so far as it is a distinctive trait of the Church must be defined in such a way as to apply to the Roman Catholic Church alone. With these criteria in mind, we can understand quite easily why the following interpretations of the "mark" of holiness—though dogmatically legitimate and correct—serve no practical purpose in the present discussion:

(1) the holiness of the Church's origin and institution;
(2) the holiness of its faith and doctrine;

(3) the holiness of the means which it offers to the
  faithful, above all, the holiness of the sacraments;

(4) the holiness of religious Orders and Congregations;

(5) interior holiness, whose full flowering is found only
  in lives that are fully Catholic.

But not even from the holiness of the members of the
Catholic Church—a holiness which is at times technically referred to as "passive," though the term is not entirely apt—
can we deduce a distinctive trait of the true Church without
introducting futher specifications. We know, in fact, that even
the true Church of Christ, according to the words of the
Founder Himself, contains "bad fish," "trees which bear no
fruit," "weeds," that is, members who are not holy and who
do not appear as such to others. We know, moreover, that
Sacred Scripture gives no indication as to the comparative
number of good and bad members.

Consequently, if the distinctive trait of the Church's holiness
must be explained in terms of the holiness of its members,
additional specifications are necessary. It is precisely for this
reason that Catholic apologists, with ever-increasing frequency
and insistence, have introduced into the traditional argument
the existence of canonized Saints within the Church. The proof
derived from the argument is usually expressed in this way: the
true Church of Christ must manifest itself and render itself
visible through the splendor of the heroic virtues of many of
its members. Now, the Roman Catholic Church alone is resplendent with the light of heroic virtue in many of its members. Therefore. . . .

But even this definition of holiness as a distinctive trait (and
the argument derived therefrom) fails to satisfy all modern
apologists. With good reason! Today it is becoming increasingly common to find apologists who are slow to deny that
there can be found in other Christian Communions men and

women who are distinguished in the exercise of Christian
virtues. This honest recognition obviously disallows this use
of considerations and irrefutable conclusions which can be
adduced from another source, namely dogma. Dogmatically,
in fact, we can demonstrate and maintain with certitude that
only the holiness that derives from the total integral Catholic
faith and is conformed to all the practices of the Church can
attain to complete fullness of Christian living.

But in our present discussion we are in the area of apologetics, in which the specific difference between the holiness
of one Christian communion and another must not only be
more discernible than the Church itself, but also visible, immediately manifest and obvious to the minds of all, even the
uneducated.

Consequently, it is not surprising that some of the more
recent apologists have constructed their definition of holiness
to include not only the heroic sanctity resplendent in the
lives of many of the Church's members, but also this eminent
holiness precisely in so far as it has been approved by God
by means of external signs or miracles.[29]

Though the argument in this form has been advanced here
and there,[30] it does not seem to have been proposed as yet
with its full probative force. We feel, therefore, that we will
serve some purpose if we make some new suggestions and
propose the argument more explicitly, thus rendering its probative force more evident.

B. SUGGESTED DEFINITION AND INTERPRETATION OF HOLINESS AS A DISTINCTIVE CHARACTERISTIC

With the reader's indulgence we will take as our point of
departure an incontestable and easily observable fact: no one
who surveys our contemporary Christian world can remain

unaware of the fact that there are countless Christian communions, each claiming to be the true and authentic Church founded by Christ. Nor can anyone be any less aware of the fact that among this array of communions one alone, namely the Roman Catholic Church, claims that God, throughout the ages and up to our own time, used miracles as the sign that He has placed His seal of approval upon her, singling her out as the authentic and true Christian community which, according to the will of our Lord, can lead all men to the heights of holiness. To substantiate such an astounding assertion the Roman Catholic Church presents an amazing array of men and women of every age, condition, race, nation, and time.[31] She points to them and makes a twofold claim:

First, that they are her most genuine and authentic children, inasmuch as in every condition and circumstance of life, in every action and decision, in every difficulty and doubt, they have completely and faithfully acted in accord with the faith, teaching, and practices of the Catholic Church, and that they are therefore, *par excellence,* the exemplary representatives of the specific holiness which she proposes as her ideal.

Second, that God has demonstrated abundantly, by means of the miraculous signs He has given to mark His approval of the Saints, that their form of life and holiness, which is typical and specifically proper to the Roman Catholic Church, is pleasing to Him in the highest degree and in every respect in accord with the will of His divine Son. We may conclude legitimately from this that the Roman Catholic Church, and she alone, according to the will of God, is the true Church which has the obligation and the power to guide mankind securely and completely to holiness and to life eternal; therefore, the guidance of the Roman Catholic Church ought to be followed by all men in all matters.

The force of this line of argumentation is that it presents God as inviting all mankind to membership in this Church, putting on His lips this message:

"Behold, and stand in wonder at, these men and women (the canonized Saints) who have lived within the Roman Catholic Church in perfect conformity with the faith, practices, and life which is typically hers. Behold the heights of holiness and perfection which they attained by drawing nourishment from this font. Behold finally the signs or miracles whereby I make clear to you that this form of life nourished by the Roman Catholic Church is the form of life which I desire and accept with approval. It is this form of life that I would have you embrace."

To complete our appraisal of this apologetical argument based on the canonized Saints of the Roman Catholic Church, we will add several further explanations.

(a) It is quite easy to establish that those persons whom the Roman Catholic Church proposes as Saints in her solemn canonizations are truly outstanding representatives of the holiness that is typically Roman Catholic.[32]

Before canonization, in fact, the lives of prospective candidates are subjected to a prolonged and meticulous examination by the Sacred Congregation of Rites.[33] (This fact is quite evident to anyone who has had access to the voluminous documentation of a single Cause.) In this examination particular attention is directed to ascertaining whether the person in question has professed integrally the faith and doctrine of the Roman Catholic Church; whether he or she has been perfectly obedient to the Roman Pontiff and to his representatives; whether he or she has been faithfully attentive in the observation of practices prescribed by the Church; in short, intensive research is done to determine whether the candidate, through the exercise of heroic virtues practiced according to the mind of the Church, can be proposed as an exemplary model. After such a painstaking process there cannot be the least doubt that the Roman Catholic Church proposes its Saints precisely as a living epitome of its teaching.

(b) But, as we have already stated, what constitutes the probative force of our argumentation is not the proposal of this holiness simply in itself, but precisely inasmuch as it has been confirmed and guaranteed by God through miracles.[34] Before there can be question of a canonization, two or more miracles are required, generally cures of organic disease which, in the opinion of doctors esteemed for their learning and experience, cannot be explained through the activity of natural forces. These facts are subjected to thorough examination and evaluated with utmost care. Afterwards, they may be studied in minute detail by any interested person, since every detail of the investigation is incorporated in the official documents of the canonization process.[35]

(c) Can it be said that such authenticated miracles are sufficiently recognizable to satisfy the definition of a distinctive characteristic, a "quality of the Church which is obvious and discernible even by the uneducated"? Without hesitation, we can reply affirmatively and refer our readers to the recent study of Father L. Monden, S.J., who has treated this question in his work on miracles, in which he weighed carefully all the relevant literature, grappling with various difficulties with complete candor, and presenting his resolutions of the problems most convincingly.[36]

(d) A scriptural foundation for this argument (the holiness of the Church confirmed by miracles) can be adduced from the famous Marcan text:

And he said to them, Go out all over the world and preach the gospel to the whole of creation; he who believes and is baptized will be saved; he who refuses belief will be condemned. Where believers go, these signs shall go with them; they will cast out devils in my name, they will speak in tongues that are strange to them; they will take up serpents in their hands, and drink poisonous draughts without harm; they will lay their hands upon the sick and make them recover. And so the Lord Jesus, when he had finished speaking to them, was taken up to heaven, and is seated now at the right hand of God. (Mark 16.15–16, Knox)[37]

In our opinion, an accurate and scientific investigation into the authenticity of this text[38] and a sober and objective exegesis of its meaning will demonstrate that it possesses solid probative force for the argument we have formulated.[39] But in order to reveal the full biblical foundation of our argument, undoubtedly we must have recourse to certain ideas basic to the entire Gospel; namely, to the fact that throughout the Gospel the holiness of our Lord's person, life, mission, teaching, works, and institutions receives continual confirmation on the part of God in the form of signs or miracles. From this biblical perspective, then, it will not appear strange that the holiness of the Church, which is radiantly incarnated in its Saints, has been distinguished by this characteristic throughout all the centuries, inasmuch as it has been constantly confirmed by miracles. Thus, it has been a standard lifted up for the nations, constantly indicating where Christ our Lord continues His salvific work today and always.[40]

(e) To complete our argument based on the distinctive characteristic of the Church's holiness as evidenced by the miracle-confirmed holiness of its Saints, it must be shown that such a distinctive trait is applicable to the Roman Catholic Church alone. The simple fact is that there is no other Christian communion which proposes any of its adherents as integral representatives of its faith, doctrine, religious practices, institutions, etc., and at the same time claims and proves that its faith, doctrine, religious practices and institutions, which have been incorporated completely in the lives of such adherents, have been confirmed from on high by miracles and thus demonstrated to be in perfect conformity with God's will, totally pleasing to Him, and consequently to be embraced and faithfully lived by all, through the imitation (in so far as is possible) of those who are its champions.[41]

(f) We have been trying to indicate the important function which the Saints can exercise in the field of apologetics. The considerations we advanced had as their aim a reappraisal of the classical argument of the "Marks of the Church" as this is usually presented in discussions with non-Catholics. We might observe, however, that even those who are already members of the Roman Catholic Church can find in the considerations we have presented additional support for their faith, motives for consolation, and inspiration during periods of spiritual crisis as well as in times of serene reflection.[42]

III. CONSIDERATIONS OF A PRACTICAL ORDER

It is our contention that the ideas expressed above demonstrate clearly that the continual existence of Saints in the Church constitutes a valuable source for an increased knowledge of dogma, apologetics, and spirituality. We feel that it is equally evident, however, that this treasure could be further exploited and its full value recognized, at least in certain of its dimensions.

The realization of the undiscovered possibilities that lie beneath the more commonly known truths about the Saints can serve as a point of departure for noteworthy developments in this field.

First and foremost, in our opinion, is the urgent necessity for a systematic *dogmatic treatise,* in which one could find an harmonious exposition of all the principles and considerations that bear upon this important section of our theology. The treatise we envision, *De Sanctis* (On the Saints), would have its logical point of insertion in the dogmatic treatment *De Ecclesia* (On the Church). Many feel the need for such a treatise keenly, and its realization is actually being effected by countless forces already making their presence felt. The scriptural bases which proclaim the providential function of the Saints in Salvation-History as it continues to be enacted in the Church and the rich documentation offered us by other common sources of theology have certainly advanced to the point where they can provide solid proofs for all that we have emphasized above. They could assure, moreover, the harmonious integration of this subject into the total picture of dogma and theology. The rearrangement of this subject matter into a single comprehensive treatment would offer the additional noteworthy advantage of collating and synthesizing all the disparate aspects of the subject now alluded to briefly and treated incompletely in different places.

On the level of *Apologetics,* in addition to the development of the argument from the Church's distinctive mark of holiness, scientifically documented publications on the miracles admitted or rejected by the Church in the processes of beatification and canonization would be extremely useful.

But the task most urgently awaiting serious study—a task which must naturally be undertaken in subordination to and close collaboration with dogmatic theology—seems to concern the renascent field of *spiritual theology.* It is faced with the challenge of filtering out from the vast flood of historical material the true doctrine of the Saints, in order to present their example, and to unveil their importance for the spiritual life of the Church. This must be carried out in accord with criteria that meet the rigorous demands of historical and dogmatic disciplines. In this context we might refer to the valuable material contained in the processes of beatification and canonization. This treasury has been woefully neglected until now, though Father Ludwig von Hertling called attention to it some time ago:

In every process a prodigious amount of effort is expended not only on historical and canonical questions but also on asceticotheological matters. There is no theological question which could not be illumined by interesting information found in the reports of consultors and, above all, in the observations of the "Promoter of the Faith" and subsequent replies thereto.

Unfortunately, this exceptionally rich material contributed in large measure by theologians of extraordinary competence has not been exploited by ascetical theologians and remains in the archives practically unused. Benedict XIV has indicated the path to be followed in this respect, but, up to the present, he has had few imitators. Public documents, such as decrees of Beatification and solemn declarations of Canonizations, are equally rich in the material they contain.[43]

This entire enterprise must be carried out all the more painstakingly in depth inasmuch as it endeavors to discover, reveal, and explain the internal and truly providential nexus that exists between dogmatic teaching and theology on the one hand and, on the other, the concrete, practical life of the Saints. If indeed it is true that the lives of the Saints have been nurtured and inspired by dogma, it is equally true that no one has understood as intimately as they the significance and value of Christianity; for, guided by a certain supernatural instinct, they have taken dogma and penetrated to its depths, then proclaimed it to all by translating it into practice, all the while bearing witness to its truth by their example.

This fact is undoubtedly the reason for the immense authority that the "Saints" enjoyed in the theological argumentation of former times. It is well known that Melchior Cano, O.P., in his classic treatise, *Locorum theologicorum Libri duodecim*, dedicated an entire section to the Saints—*De Sanctorum Auctoritate, quae sexto loco continetur, Liber Septimus*.

Spiritual theology, understood and elaborated in this way, not only could make precious contributions to dogmatic theology—and that from a strictly scientific point of view—but also would have ample opportunity for proposing to students sublime dogmatic and theological truths in a more vital, existential and personal manner, thus enabling them to see, reflected in the lives of the Saints, how these great truths can and must permeate our lives.

This brings us to what we might call the pastoral function which the Saints exercise in the Church. Since Christianity is a way of life—and thus much more than a mere philosophical, theological, moral, or ascetical system—the example of a life lived fully and integrally according to the Christian ideal, such as is offered by the Saints, has a particular, indeed a compelling, attraction, and thus serves as an apt instrument in our priestly apostolate. *Exempla trahunt* (examples exert a power of attraction).

But in order that the Saints may exercise this function they must be properly presented. Their personalities must not be used solely as the occasion and point of departure for abstract moralizing on virtue. We should not, by laying undue stress on the exceptional graces they received, insist exclusively, or even principally, on the extraordinary deeds and events that surrounded their persons. Rather, panegyrists and hagiographers should—with the aid of solid theological, historical, psychological and literary criteria[44]—develop fully the fundamental idea that the Saint was a human person like ourselves; that he lived in circumstances peculiar to his age and country, just as we are immersed in those peculiar to our own. What made him a Saint was the fact that, within his environment, he gave himself unconditionally to Jesus Christ and lived an integrally Christian life; a life of intimate union with the person of our King and Saviour.

Theological Considerations on the Nature, Spirit and Limits of the Honor Paid to the Saints

Our exposition of the fundamental concepts governing the function of the Saints in the Church has shed some light on the theology of sanctity and at the same time directed attention to the importance of the problem. It has also clarified the position which should be accorded to the Saints in the exposition of Catholic doctrine, not only in the area of dogmatic theology, but in the spheres of apologetics and spiritual theology as well. We must now dwell on an aspect of the problem which, because of its complexity and of the reactions it evokes in the minds of many, is in urgent need of clarification. We refer to the problem created by the *cult of the Saints*.[45]

Is it licit, is it fitting, is it necessary that the Saints should have a share in Catholic worship,[46] public as well as private? What is the nature of the honor directed to them? What is the spirit that should animate this honor? What are its limits?

There is an urgent need for a reply to these questions in order to meet a twofold series of difficulties: one of a doctrinal character, which leads many to advocate a lessening or even complete abolition of the honor paid to the Saints; the other of a practical nature, which sees in the deformations and exaggerations introduced at times into the cult of the

Saints an occasion for reiterating their stand against any honor
whatsoever being paid to the Saints.

To understand the origin and development of these difficulties, we must first establish a clear notion of what is
meant by the expression "cult of the Saints."[47]

What Is Meant by the Cult of the Saints

All our critical reflections on the greatness of the Saints
and their role in the Church could lead us to consider them as
inspiring examples and even induce us to draw upon their
merits in our approach to God. This, however, is a far cry
from directing to the Saints themselves expressions of admiration and honor, not to speak of invoking their assistance in
the form of intercessory prayer. The full exercise of the cult
of the Saints, understood in the strict sense of the word and
with all the implications of Catholic practice, is had when
we not only recognize their eminent greatness but also turn
to them directly to express sentiments of praise and esteem,
and to recommend ourselves to their protection by invoking
their aid and intercession.

Obviously, the specific and essential characteristic of this
whole series of acts lies in the fact that a person turns, with
humble submission,[48] *directly to the Saints themselves*—created
human persons—and not formally to God in so far as He is
living and working in them (which would be rather an expression of cult towards God Himself, considered under a particular aspect).

Now it is precisely in this direct reference to human, created
persons that the problematic nature of the cult of the Saint
lies, giving rise to the questions mentioned above. It is because of this direct application to creatures that many non-
Catholics view the honor paid to the Saints as a deviation

from true religion, which should have God as its unique object. Many oppose this cult of the Saints and consider it illicit and erroneous, because, by addressing ourselves to the Saints as intercessors, we seem to detract from the fundamental truth that Christ, the Word Incarnate, is our sole mediator.[49] Still others, not a few in number, repudiate the cult of the Saints by Catholics, because they recognize it as an expression of a basic doctrine which they refuse to accept: meritorious human action.

This opposition, however, is not restricted to non-Catholics: even among Catholics there are persons who find difficulty with the practice, maintaining that the cult of the Saints interferes with their intention of glorifying God in the highest degree possible, or interposes itself between themselves and Christ, whose life they wish to have as their model. As a consequence, they feel that honor paid to the Saints diverts them from their christocentric spirituality.

Such difficulties—of a doctrinal, conceptual, or spiritual order—naturally give rise to practical attitudes and even to deviations such as those to which Pius XII was alluding when he said:

For several decades, we have noted the rise of a movement aiming to remove as far as possible all images of Saints from our places of worship, and even curtail the veneration of the Saints. The churches which have been constructed and decorated in accord with this tendency are identifiable by a distinctive characteristic—a "cold iconoclasm" that renders them mute and devoid of beauty.[50]

On the other hand, it is certain that by the very fact that the cult of the Saints is directed to created persons definite dangers arise. We note with sorrow that in areas where proper instruction is lacking, exaggerated forms of devotion arise which are in fact deformations that obscure the theocentric and christocentric worship of the Church. His Holiness, John XXIII, cautioned the clergy against such abuses in his allocution of November 25, 1960. Saints and devotion to the Saints assume at times proportions which distort their proper role. Conscious participation of the faithful in the Eucharistic Sacrifice and other fundamental devotions—not sufficiently known or appreciated, and therefore not accorded a place in Christian living—are at times neglected or oppressed by unwholesome forms of devotionalism. Such sickly devotion quite often no longer has as its scope a more profound and sincere union with God by way of the aid and intercession of the Saints; rather, it is transformed into a wretched reliance upon the Saints in order to obtain every conceivable kind of help other than that which would contribute to a growth of true religion and Christian devotion. As a consequence of such deplorable ignorance and reprehensible attitudes, we find those traditional practices which consist in external manifestations in which the true religious spirit is smothered and distorted. This is why in certain churches and sanctuaries the center of devotion and religious service is no longer the tabernacle of the Lord, but quite often a statue or picture, before which can be found mounting tiers of candles and countless devotees pouring forth prayers that are often tainted by base self-interest.[51]

These two tendencies are diametrically opposed, but they share a common root: a failure to comprehend the true and authentic spirit of the cult of the Saints. The adherents of the first school of thought reject the cult of the Saints precisely because they fail to take into account the fact that the cult of the Saints, if practiced according to its authentic spirit, not only does not detract from, but rather fosters and amplifies, that religious movement of the Christian which they with good reason insist must be theocentric and christocentric. If those who follow the second tendency distort the cult of the Saints in a censurable manner, it is due to their ignorance of the fact that the cult of the Saints is of its nature subordinate to the worship of God and, both in its foundation and in its realization, absolutely and totally dependent upon God, the source of all holiness, and upon Christ the unique mediator.

When this fact is emphasized, it becomes clear that we must look for the solution in a study of the nature of the cult of the Saints, especially the spirit that animates it, and the limits imposed upon it by its very nature. This is precisely what we are trying to accomplish.

The scope of this present study is not to prove, by means of a positive, historical investigation, that the Church recognizes the liceity, the usefulness, and therefore a certain necessity for the cult of the Saints, and for this reason encourages and invites the faithful to practice this devotion. We presuppose this, since it can be easily established either by the authentic practice of the Church or by its official documents, especially the documents whereby it has at different times defended the cult of the Saints[52] or even recommended it.[53] We will simply note in passing that the supreme authority of the Church not only institutes special feasts in honor of the Saints, but also prescribes that they be celebrated by the universal Church with a special liturgical office, consisting of the celebration of the Eucharistic Sacrifice in honor of the Saint and a corresponding recitation of the breviary.[54] We might also note that the Church, through the concession of special indulgences,[55] not only approves but actually proposes to the faithful certain prayers and other pious exercises in honor of the Saints. Such approval is extended to veneration

of their relics,[56] their statues, and their images[57] as apt means
for assisting and promoting in the faithful a devotion to the
persons they represent.[58]

What we propose to undertake, rather, is a theological
investigation of the nature and authentic spirit of the cult of
the Saints. This will in turn lead us to understand why the
Catholic Church not only approves this form of devotion as
something that does not obscure the worship due to God and
to Christ, but also encourages it because, in its genuine form,
it enriches and completes Christian worship in its fundamental
orientations and characteristics—that is, in its theocentrism
and christocentrism. In fact, these are the two characteristic
and basic laws which, in intimate organic union, govern the
entire religious worship of the Catholic Church. We do not
deny that theocentrism and christocentrism are the unique
laws, the unique criteria determining our lives and our religious worship, and that anything impeding them must be
eliminated. In brief, every human relationship, every friendship, every manifestation of reverence and respect is to be
admitted only in so far as it fits into this framework and
promotes this orientation.

We cannot disagree on something as basic as this. We all
accept, with absolute conviction, the principle that the goal
which governs all our lives and activity as creatures is to
achieve the knowledge and love of God: to adore, praise,
thank, and invoke our Creator, so that we may live more
intensely a life of glorifying Him, finding in this activity our
happiness.[59] We agree wholeheartedly with the statement that
in our actual historical order, which is a supernatural one,
our end—the glory of God—is expressed practically in the
glorification of Christ, the Word Incarnate,[60] God-become-
man, and in the glorification of the entire Trinity, "through
Him, and with Him, and in Him." In other words, the aim of

our life is to adore the Father through, with, and in the Son, in the Holy Spirit;[61] such a life constitutes our supreme happiness.

We approach our question, therefore, by asking what is the most perfect and most comprehensive way to live a theocentric and christocentric life? Subsequently we will raise the question whether such a form of life makes the cult of the Saints not only licit but also fitting and even necessary. With this end in view, we will have recourse to the doctrine of the Mystical Body, that doctrine which—as we have seen above —provides the key to a balanced appraisal of the Saints and their function in the Church, and moreover makes evident the nature and depths of the relations existing among the members of the Mystical Body and between them and the Head. From this we will understand that christocentrism and theocentrism cannot be practiced in their fullness if, in our movement towards Christ and with Him towards the Father, we overlook those persons whom He has incorporated into Himself as members of His Mystical Body, especially if we disregard those who are His pre-eminent members, namely, the Saints.

This doctrine derives from the fundamental dogmatic truth that the Divine Word became man, like unto us in all save sin, in order that He might lead to salvation man in his total being: corporal and spiritual, individual and social. As a matter of fact, in explaining how Christ, applying to men the benefits of His Redemption through the communication of His Spirit, unites them to Himself and makes them sharers of His life, we come to understand that men, precisely because they are vivified by this same Spirit and sharer of this same life, are united among themselves in Christ and constitute by this very fact that vital organic structure, that humanly divine society, that Body of which Christ is Center and Head, and which through Him, and with Him, and in Him forms the total Christ, Head and members, the perfect new man in whom all is of Christ, just as Christ is of the Father.

This brief synthetic introduction will enable the reader to glimpse the lines along which our reflections will be developed. When we consider the general nature of this Body and observe the relations that exist between Christ the Head and the men incorporated into Him and vivified by him; when we then explain how these men, in virtue of the grace they have received but also in proportion to their free response and personal contribution, are living, life-giving members of the Mystical Body and enrich and complete both the Head and the members—then we will come to understand that the movement whereby we must tend towards Christ in order to glorify Him, the God-man, remains incomplete unless, in our relationships with Him, we include His members. Similarly, the movement whereby we tend towards God in order to glorify Him in union with Christ lacks its plenitude if we likewise fail to unite ourselves to the members of His Mystical Body. Finally, we will apply these considerations to the privileged case of the pre-eminent members of the Mystical Body, namely, the Saints.

We have inserted this introduction to emphasize that the problem of the cult of the Saints is not a question standing in isolation; rather, it is a question intimately connected with, and dependent upon, the basic conceptions of the nature of Christian living and of our relations with God and with Christ. Consequently, one can understand quite easily that opposition to the cult of the Saints or attitudes fundamentally opposed to it depend in the final analysis either on theological conceptions foreign to the Catholic conception of certain doctrinal points whose implications are far-reaching or on a deficient analysis and awareness of the implications of this same Catholic vision of the doctrinal truths in question. In fact, it is quite evident that there exists a bond of deep intimate dependence between our question and many fundamental doctrines: redeemed man's internal justification and sanctification; his free, personal collaboration with the grace of the Redeemer and therefore his merits; the nature of personal sanctity and its social effects; our supernatural solidarity; the communal, social, visible aspects of our life and of the cult in the Church founded by Christ; and many other doctrines as well.

Naturally, we do not intend to enter into a detailed discussion of all the questions to which we have just referred; but they must be touched upon in the course of any discussion seeking to place the Catholic doctrine on the cult of the Saints into the framework of the teaching on the Mystical Body, since all the problems alluded to above must enter into a comprehensive synthetic treatment.

We will divide our subject in the following way:

I. General considerations on the nature of the vital relationships existing within the Mystical Body;

II. The cult of the Saints and our progress towards the fullness of Christ:

A. In virtue of the completion which the members of the Mystical Body contribute to the human perfection of Christ the Head;

B. In virtue of the completion which the members of the Mystical Body contribute to the salvific work of Christ.

III. The cult of the Saints and the perfection of our progress towards Christ and the Father:

A. In virtue of the contribution which association with men makes to the perfection of the human knowledge and love of Jesus Christ for the Father;

B. In virtue of the contribution which association
with others makes to the perfection of our progress towards Christ and towards the Father.

IV. The necessity of the cult of the Saints.

I. GENERAL CONSIDERATIONS ON THE NATURE OF THE VITAL RELATIONSHIPS EXISTING WITHIN THE MYSTICAL BODY

The first major ecclesiastical document *ex professo* dedicated to a systematic theological description of the relationships that exist betweeen Christ and the persons redeemed by Him and duly united to Him—namely, the encyclical *De Mystico Jesu Christi Corpore deque nostra in eo cum Christo coniunctione* —achieves its stated purpose by recurring to the classical doctrine of St. Paul, according to which we are the Body of Christ.[62] Recourse to this doctrine, authoritatively enucleated and clarified, has served to cast into bold relief the total dependence upon Christ of all those incorporated into Him. He in fact is the Founder, the Head, the Sustainer, and the Saviour of His Body.[63]

Men are members of the Body of Christ, but only because He communicates His life to them, pours into them the power to feel and move; that is, He illumines them with an infusion of the light of faith; He sanctifies them with that grace without which it is impossible to perform a salutary act; He sustains them with a communication of His Spirit who is indeed the

49

soul, the internal principle, that vivifies and unifies the whole Body.

So full of grace and truth is He that of His inexhaustible fullness we have all received. (John 1.14–16) These words of the disciple whom Jesus loved lead us to the last reason why Christ our Lord should be declared in a very particular way Head of His Mystical Body. As the nerves extend from the head to all parts of the human body and give them power to feel and move, in like manner our Saviour communicates strength and power to His Church so that the things of God are understood more clearly and are more eagerly desired by the faithful. From Him streams into the body of the Church all the light with which those who believe are divinely illumined, and all the grace by which they are made holy as He is holy.[64]

The nature of this dependence is therefore so profound and so intimate as to entail a truly ontological bond that unites the members to the Body, and above all to the Head from whom they draw their life. Those who are incorporated into the Body belong to Christ, and they possess supernatural value in so far as He communicates to them His life. Certainly it is quite evident that this dependence upon Christ (and the consequent belonging to Him) is the fundamental quality that distinguishes every member of the Body of Christ precisely as such, and it is the attribute from which all other characteristics follow. In fact, it follows from this reality that all who are incorporated in Christ are united among themselves, precisely because they are united to Him as members of His Body and animated by the same principle. In other words, the relationship that each member has with the Head implies a relationship with the other members and cannot prescind from these. Thus, in treating of the vital bonds existing among the members of a single organism, one can easily understand how each of these, in virtue of the vivifying communication he re-

ceives from the Head, has an influence on the others, and how
all sustain one another and contribute to the well-being, the
development, and the perfection of the entire Body:

But a body calls also for a multiplicity of members, which are
linked together in such a way as to help one another. And as in
the body when one member suffers, all the other members share
its pain, and the healthy members come to the assistance of the
ailing, so in the Church the individual members do not live for
themselves alone, but also help their fellows, and all work in
mutual collaboration for the common comfort and for the more
perfect building up of the whole Body.[65]

In so far, then, as the Pauline teaching of our incorporation
into Christ enables us to understand clearly that the members
of Christ's Mystical Body depend upon the Head for their
entire life and activity, it also makes clear to us that the
members enjoy a vital union among themselves and therefore
are destined in turn to complement one another and thus constitute His Body. But by this very fact, in virtue of the life
that flows into them from the Head, they complete the Head
Himself and constitute together with Him and in Him the
total Christ:

This communication of the Spirit of Christ is the channel through
which all the gifts, powers, and extraordinary graces found
superabundantly in the Head as in their source flow into all the
members of the Church, and are perfected daily in them according to the place they hold in the Mystical Body of Jesus Christ.
Thus the Church becomes, as it were, the filling out and the
complement of the Redeemer, while Christ in a sense attains
through the Church a fullness in all things. (St. Thos., *Comm. in
Ep. ad Eph.,* Cap. I, lect. 8) Herein we find the reason why,
according to the opinion of Augustine already referred to, the
mystical Head, which is Christ, and the Church, which here below
as another Christ shows forth His person, constitute one new

man, in whom heaven and earth are joined together in perpetuating the saving work of the Cross: Christ, We mean, the Head
and the Body, the whole Christ.[66]

But we cannot terminate our reflections at this point. After
having insisted with good reason on the ontological union
existing between Head and members and among the individual
members—a union which has its origin in the single animating
principle—we must now avoid falling into the crude error
of considering the persons incorporated into Christ as if they
were members of His physical Body—that physical Body born
of the Virgin Mary, now in heaven at the right hand of the
Father, and on earth concealed beneath eucharistic signs.
Indeed, the Body which men redeemed by Christ constitute
in their union with Christ has this distinguishing characteristic:
each of its members—though all are truly animated by the
Head and therefore vitally linked with one another in the
sense we have just explained—nonetheless retains his own
proper personality:

In a natural body the principle of unity unites the parts in such
a manner that each lacks its own individual subsistence; on the
contrary, in the mystical Body the mutual union, though intrinsic,
links the members by a bond which leaves to each the complete
enjoyment of his own personality.[67]

That such a distinction is possible and actually maintained
is due to the fact that the transformation whereby a man
becomes a member of the Mystical Body of Christ and shares
in the life of the Head is realized in the most intimate depths
of the person himself. The power of Christ's grace lies precisely in the fact that rather than superimpose Himself upon
a person, remain external to him, and suppress his personality,
Christ preserves the distinction of personality, and by penetrating to the deepest roots of that personality, transforms,
ennobles, and animates it from within, enabling it to exist

with all that is proper to it as a person, as a living member of His Mystical Body.[68] It is from this that one can understand how, in contradistinction to every physical body, in which the members are, in the final analysis, destined solely for the good of the whole complex, the Mystical Body is on the contrary instituted for the good of each and every individual member, so that each, as a person, can achieve, in Christ, his greatest happiness and by that very fact increase the glory of Christ the Head and, in Him, of God.

For this reason, the internal structure effected under Christ the Head is most appropriately called the *mystical* Body of Christ. Such a distinction serves a twofold purpose: it contrasts the Mystical Body with a physical organism, and at the same time it sets off Christ's Mystical Body from a simply moral body in which the principle of unity is constituted solely by a common purpose which various persons, united under a social authority, seek to realize in unison. The Mystical Body, on the other hand—beyond the multiple bonds of a social, juridical, and hierarchical character—is, as we have explained above, united to Christ and in itself possesses a single vivifying and animating principle, the Holy Sprit, who confers on it a unity incomparably superior to the unity existing within any physical or moral body.[69]

By way of conclusion, we might say that the Mystical Body is neither a physical body nor a merely moral body, but an absolutely unique body that unites—in an eminent way—the most typical qualities of each type: its members are indeed both members and distinct persons; therefore they must live their relations with Christ the Head and with the other members in a manner proper to persons. This must be achieved within a structure that is not only animated by the same Spirit, but is also—in accord with the will of Christ—hierarchically, juridically, and externally organized.

II. THE CULT OF THE SAINTS AND OUR PROGRESS TOWARDS THE FULLNESS OF CHRIST

A. IN VIRTUE OF THE COMPLETION WHICH THE MEMBERS OF THE MYSTICAL BODY CONTRIBUTE TO THE HUMAN PERFECTION OF CHRIST THE HEAD

The general considerations of the nature of the Mystical Body and our insistence on the fact that men incorporated into Christ become members but remain distinct persons give us the proper orientation for a resolution of our problem. Their membership in Christ signifies that they belong to Christ, that they live in Christ, and Christ lives in them.[70] Their distinct personality signifies, however, that they are not simple recipients of the divine presence, nor are they vitalized in the way in which the members of a physical body are; they can and must freely and consciously actuate their "existence in Christ" by making a contribution proper to their unique personality. This contribution is transformed and utilized by Christ for the creation of the *Novus Vir Perfectus*—the new and perfect man.

54

This twofold truth entails a twofold consequence. First, each member of the Mystical Body fulfills his role as a member in so far as he freely opens his heart and corresponds with the internal action of grace which invites him to acknowledge and glorify Christ, God-made-man, and to be inspired to an unconditional self-surrender on account of His love. Secondly, in so far as he responds to this love and accepts the sublime grace offered to him whereby he can freely participate in Christ's life, consciously conforming himself to Him, allowing himself to be moved and guided in all things by the same spirit that animated Christ's life, a person places at the disposal of Christ all that is his unique possession, so that Christ may vivify, elevate, and incorporate it into the lifestream of His Mystical Body.

In this way, every man who corresponds to God's invitation, by surrendering and offering himself to the God-man, is elevated and rendered capable of fulfilling the function for which he has been called to be a member of the Mystical Body. He is given the power to contribute all that is his unique possession, so that Christ Himself can live and actuate in him those human possibilities that He could not live in His single individual human nature.

By consciously taking hold of this grace and giving himself to the God-man, man receives a communication of the divine life that makes him a member of the Mystical Body and enables him to contribute to the realization of Christ's intention to draw men to Himself. What is Christ's aim? That the entire human race and every individual person may be united to Him and supernaturally vivified by His grace; for then man can offer to God "through, with, and in Him," the most perfect and complete human glorification—that is, the glorification given by the *Novus Vir Perfectus,* the total Christ, Head and Members.

It is precisely in order to realize this intention that the Divine Word, by becoming a member of our human race through His Incarnation, wishes to transform humanity into His Mystical Body and make each human person a member of that Body. Herein we can perceive a marvelous manifestation of God's immense Goodness which elevates men to such a sublime dignity. For in each member Christ lives and works in such wise that these human members are not only mutually complementary, but precisely because they constitute His Mystical Body, they complete Christ Himself in so far as they form together with Him the total Christ, Head and Members.

Nor should our reference to a completion of Christ and His work by the members of His Mystical Body occasion surprise, since we are only using an expression drawn from the encyclical *Mystici Corporis*. It should be evident that the completion of Christ effected by His Mystical Body is not a completion of the divine perfection of the Person of the Word, nor of the Incarnate Word in so far as He, our Redeemer and unique Mediator, is the cause of all grace, fountainhead of all justice, vivifying source of all our supernatural activity; rather, the completion affects only His humanity.[71] It should be equally evident from our preceding exposition—but we wish to emphasize the point in order to preclude any misunderstanding—that if men can contribute something to this completion of Christ, this is due solely and exclusively to the fact that Christ Himself confers upon them that power on which their existence and activity as members depends radically and entirely. This growth and development, therefore, though it must be attributed to men inasmuch as they freely abandon themselves to the action of Christ and draw their vitality from His life, has as its ultimate cause, and derives all its efficacious value from, the fact that it is Christ Himself who pours His grace into men and transforms them with His life; and this

he does with the intention of giving them the power to contribute to His fullness, so that He may constitute with them
the total Christ, Head and Members.

These clarifying observations, which we have made in detail
in order to delineate clearly the meaning of our considerations
and preclude any erroneous interpretation, lead us to re-
emphasize the fact that our ability to understand how a completion of Christ is possible depends on our understanding of
the implications of the reality of the Incarnation; that is, on
our appreciation of the concrete significance of the expression
Verbum caro factum est (the Word became flesh) and what
is implied in this fact that Christ became "like unto us in all
things, sin excepted" in order to make us sharers of His life
and members of His Mystical Body. The reason why Christ
can be completed—and consequently the reason for our union
with Him and in Him, together with other men—is that the
Word, becoming Incarnate, assumed a single, individual nature, which was necessarily limited and capable of completion.
In other words, by becoming man like ourselves, the Word
subjected Himself to the laws deriving from the metaphysical
constitution of man, who, as a spiritual-material, personal-
individual being, has all the characteristics of the wealth and
unique perfection of personal existence, but also simultane-
ously is characterized by the distinctive marks of the limitations and perfectibility of individual existence.

If, then, by reason of his metaphysical make-up every man,
inasmuch as he is an individual being, can and must receive
from other men and be completed by them; so, too, the man
Jesus Christ, inasmuch as He is truly man and therefore an
individual human being, can and must receive from other
men and be completed by them. If, by reason of this same
constitution, a man cannot, as an individual, live all the
concrete modes in which the specific perfection of human

nature can exist, and can realize the maximum of human perfection only in union with other men, mutually complementing one another, then not even the man Jesus Christ, inasmuch as He is an individual being, can realize by Himself, in His humanity, all the concrete modes in which specific human perfection can exist.

What is unique in the case of the God-man is that He, by making men sharers in His life, lives not only in His individual human nature but also, through the communication of His Spirit, in those human persons who freely open themselves to His grace and give themselves to Him, and thus become members of His Mystical Body. It is, therefore, the prerogative of Jesus Christ, living both in His own human nature and in the persons who constitute His Mystical Body, that He can live all the concrete modes in which, according to the designs of Divine Providence, human perfection should exist. In this way, Christ brings it about that the entire assembly of men vivified and united by Him to constitute the total Christ, Head and members, realize the ideal of human perfection by complementing one another. In this sense, then, the human perfection of the total Christ, Head and members, as well as the perfection of the glory that is offered to God, is fuller and richer than the perfection of the individual man, Jesus Christ, and of the glory He offers God. From this one can appreciate the sublime dignity of the living members of the Mystical Body, called and rendered capable of making a real contribution to the plan of God, through their voluntary co-operation; for through the contribution of their unique personal qualities they enhance the human perfection of the total Christ and render greater and more perfect glory to God, "through Him and with Him and in Him."

Nor should this diminish our esteem for the sublime perfection of the individual human nature of the Word Incarnate.

The fact that this nature was full of grace and elevated to the highest dignity of being hypostatically united to the Person of the Word does not alter the fact that it is, and remains in all its properties and vital manifestations, a single, individual human nature, and therefore limited.[72] On the other hand, we would not wish to be misinterpreted and accused of lacking reverence for the mystery of the Incarnation or the humanity of our Lord. Quite the contrary; it is precisely in ascertaining the consequences to which He subjected Himself by becoming Incarnate that the depths of His love for us are revealed and the sublime dignity to which He has elevated those who respond to His invitation is made manifest. Indeed, His love was so great that it led Him to become man in order that He might be able to communicate to His fellow men the inexhaustible wealth of His life. By uniting us to Himself He enables us to receive from His Person what He alone can give, the power to return His love from the depths of our unique personalities; that is, to give ourselves freely and lovingly, with all that we are and have, to the Word Incarnate, God-made-man. By this gift we offer to Him the unique riches of our personalities, so that He may vivify them with His grace and make them His very own. Thereby we become members of His Mystical Body and contribute, "through, with, and in Christ," to the fuller and more perfect glorification of God offered by the total Christ, Head and members.

The considerations we have proposed up to this point, in which we have endeavored to present the aim, effects and consequences of the Incarnation and of our incorporation into Christ, should be sufficient to make one conclusion quite evident: the concept of Christ—of that Christ who must be the goal of the christocentric movement whereby we rise to the Most Holy Trinity—if it is to be an adequate concept, must embrace Christ in all His reality and fullness. This means that it must encompass not only Christ in Himself, in so far as He lives and works in the individual human nature hypostatically assumed, but also Christ in so far as He is vitally united to His Mystical Body and to the individual members in whom He lives and works by means of His Spirit; for these persons, vivified and appropriated by Christ, actually fill out His humanity.

From this we may draw an obvious conclusion: we cannot live our union with Christ fully and perfectly—that is, we cannot know and love, honor and praise Him fully and perfectly—if we restrict ourselves to the historical Christ and fail to unite ourselves to the members of His Mystical Body in whom He is now living and working. Moreover, just as the human perfection of Christ and the glory He offers the Father are not diminished but rather enriched and brought to a greater fullness by the fact that He lives and works not only in the individual human nature which is hypostatically His but also in the human persons who are His mystical members, so too our union with Christ—that is, our knowledge, love, and praise of Him—is not diminished but on the contrary rendered fuller by the fact that we unite ourselves in knowledge, love, and praise, not only to Christ Himself but also to all His members.

However, as we have explained above, though these members belong to Christ and live by His life, they do not become identified with His Person, do not become united with Him in such a way as to cease to be human persons. They are, and ever remain, distinct persons. Consequently, our relationships with them can and should be realized in the usual way in which persons are united with one another; namely, through direct contacts which are based on mutual knowledge and externalized in explicit manifestations of mutual love, honor, admiration, and praise, as the occasion may demand. These direct personal relationships whereby we manifest honor and admiration for certain members of the Mystical Body are entirely proper, because the honor paid is merely an acknowledgement of the generous response these persons made to Christ, enabling Him to fulfill in them the perfection of His total humanity and the glory He offers to the Father in it.

We have repeatedly insisted on this aspect because we believe that it constitutes one of the two points on which the solution of our problem turns. Sufficient emphasis has been given to the other cardinal truth; namely, that if men are elevated to a life as members of the Mystical Body and complement the Head, this is due to their union with Christ and must be attributed to the grace He confers on them. Therefore, the ability to contribute to the fullness of the Head derives fundamentally and entirely from Christ Himself, whose precise intention is to vivify men and unite them to Himself in order to appropriate what they are and what they possess as distinct persons. This appropriation by Christ of the persons incorporated into His Mystical Body, and, on their part, this union with Him, is what guarantees and explains the fact that our relations with other members of the Mystical Body—direct relations at that, because they are persons capable and deserving of such direct contacts—do not involve acts on our part which subtract in the least from Christ or diminish in any way our union with Him. Rather, we are doing something that makes our union with Christ more fully real; for in uniting ourselves to those who live by His life we are in fact uniting ourselves to Him also, inasmuch as He is living in His members.

The observations made up to this point make it unnecessary to emphasize that the homage we pay to the members of the Mystical Body, manifesting love, admiration, and praise for the greatness that is theirs in Christ, has characteristic qualities

essentially different from those proper to the worship we pay
to the Head.[73] In the prayers we address directly to Christ, the
Person of the Word Incarnate Himself, the specific characteristic is that of recognition and consequent love, admiration
and praise for His infinite and transcendent greatness as God
and as God-made-man.[74] Homage to Him therefore contains
explicit expression of the honor and love due to God and to
God alone. In other words, we render Him the homage of
adoration. In the homage we pay the created persons elevated
to the dignity of members in the Mystical Body of Christ, on
the contrary, we offer the honor and praise proper to those
who live by the life of Christ and in whom Christ Himself
lives; but since these remain always created persons, all their
dignity derives fundamentally and radically from Christ Himself.

It should be equally evident that the manner in which we
pay homage to the members is not equal in all cases. It varies
not only according to the state and condition in which the
members are found, but also in proportion to the intensity
and perfection of their incorporation in Christ. The manner
in which one turns to those members who are indeed united
to Christ but are still in a period of probation, and therefore
capable of either defection or a growth in perfection, differs
from the homage paid to members now in heaven, indefectibly
united to Christ. In the first instance, the acts with which one
enters into direct contact with those persons esteemed as intimately united with Christ but still on earth are, to be sure,
acts replete with reverent respect and Christian love, and at
least implicitly containing admiration and praise. Generally
speaking, however, this admiration and praise—for obvious
reasons stemming from their condition as wayfarers—will not
be expressed formally and explicitly. With respect to the mem-

bers in heaven, on the other hand, since they have already crowned an earthly Christian life by embracing death heroically and arriving at their final goal,[75] they now enjoy a status of immutable superiority owing to their glorious and eternal union with Christ.[76] There is no reason, therefore, why we should refrain from expressing openly the acts of admiration and praise which are their due.

What we have said naturally applies to all members of the Mystical Body who have attained their glorious goal and now belong to the Church Triumphant. It is particularly true of those whom the Church, with infallible assurance, declares to be in heaven eternally united to Christ; for these are pre-eminent members of His Mystical Body, inasmuch as they opened their hearts to the divine call without reservation and lived a life of ever more perfect union and conformity with Christ through the heroic exercise of charity and all the other Christian virtues.[77] Now that they are in heaven their function as members does not cease; on the contrary, they continue to complement the work of the Head in a far more vital manner. It is truly meet and just, then, that we should direct our acts of admiration and praise towards these members whom we call the Saints. And because they are *persons* who contributed the riches of their unique personalities to the building up of the total Christ—in virtue of the life that was poured into them by Christ the Head—we turn to them directly.

These acts which with good reason we address to the glorious members of the Mystical Body of Christ constitute the honor paid to the Saints. In technical language this honor is called the cult of dulia, a cult subordinate to that offered to Christ and to God, because in turning to the Saints as human creatures, we pay tribute to a greatness which, though personal, nevertheless derives from Christ.

B. IN VIRTUE OF THE COMPLETION WHICH THE MEMBERS OF THE MYSTICAL BODY CONTRIBUTE TO THE SALVIFIC WORK OF CHRIST

Our consideration of the Saints as pre-eminent members of the Mystical Body has led us to acknowledge that they contribute to the greater perfection of the total Christ in an outstanding degree. We deduced from this as a logical conclusion that it is appropriate for us to unite ourselves to them in order to intensify our union with Christ and thereby render our glorification of God fuller and more perfect, "through, with, and in Christ." It is evident, we trust, that the explicit acts of love, admiration, and praise addressed to the Saints do not violate or detract from the fundamental law of Christian cult but are in perfect accord with it.

There is an additional consideration which adds to and re-enforces the motives for honoring the Saints. We refer to the fact that the function of the members of the Mystical Body is not exhausted by their completion of Christ's humanity (of which we have been speaking) but extends beyond this. When the Divine Word became Incarnate, joining Himself to the human race so that we might share in the riches of His life, He did not wish to give us merely the possibility of completing His human life of loving glorification of the Father, as members of His Mystical Body; rather, it was and remains His wish that by participating in His life of divine love which is expressed in loving activity among men,[78] we should collaborate and co-operate with Him in His task of erecting the supernatural framework of His Mystical Body, to the greater glory of God. In brief, He wants us to be associated with His salvific work, contributing to it by applying His redemptive merits to individual human persons. By living and working in His members, through His Spirit, He extends and prolongs His life and activity among men through time and space. His aim is to live in His members those concrete forms of existence, activity, and love which His individual nature could not realize, and in this way complete His salvific work, develop it, consolidate and amplify it extensively and intensively.

Since men are not, however, mere recipients of the divine presence, or vivified by Christ in the same way in which the members of a physical body are animated, Christ is able to live and work in men for the building up of His Mystical Body only in so far as they, in accordance with their dignity as persons, freely open their hearts to His grace, consciously associate themselves with His life, share in His love, and offer themselves to Him. Conversely, only through such a loving surrender to Christ can man offer his personal contribution to the supernatural good of the entire human race and to the greater glorification of God. The salvific work of Christ, therefore, will be completed, the structure of His Mystical Body will be consolidated, developed and extended by the persons who have become members of that Mystical Body, in proportion to their willingness to allow themselves to be animated by the love which Christ has for man, sharing in it through the communication which the Incarnate Word makes of His Spirit. But this sharing must be effected in a personal manner, in so far as the members enable Christ to realize in them His active, salvific love in new forms and modes, consonant with the existential forms proper to their personalities:

Christ is in us through His Spirit, whom He gives to us and through whom He acts within us in such a way that all divine activity of the Holy Spirit within our souls must also be attributed to Christ. (St. Thos., *Comm. in Ep. ad Eph.*, Cap. II, Lect.

5) "If a man hath not the Spirit of Christ, he is none of his," says the Apostle, "but if Christ be in you . . . , the spirit liveth because of justification." (Rom. 8.9–10)

This communication of the Spirit of Christ is the channel through which all the gifts, powers, and extraordinary graces found superabundantly in the Head as in their source flow into all the members of the Church, and are perfected daily in them according to the place they hold in the Mystical Body of Jesus Christ. Thus the Church becomes, as it were, the filling out and the complement of the Redeemer, while Christ in a sense attains through the Church a fullness in all things. (St. Thos., *Comm. in Ep. ad Eph.,* Cap. I, Lect. 8) Herein we find the reason why, according to the opinion of Augustine already referred to, the mystical Head, which is Christ, and the Church, which here below as another Christ shows forth His person, constitute one new man, in whom heaven and earth are joined together in perpetuating the saving work of the Cross: Christ, We mean, the Head and the Body, the whole Christ.[79]

Identified in this manner with the life of Christ the Head and animated by His love for mankind, the life of persons who consciously live as members of the Mystical Body will then be in conformity with the life of the historical individual, Jesus Christ. The earthly life of Jesus Christ was a life of love for both God and man, and therefore it was a life of intense and continual *toil* for the building up of His Mystical Body in order that this Body might offer to God "with and in Him" the fullest and most perfect glorification possible. In like manner, the life of the members of this Body which is animated by Christ becomes a life of *work* undertaken with the same spirit and with the same intention; namely, for the ever-increasing development of the Body of Christ:

As the vastness of the charity with which Christ loved His Church is equalled by its constant activity, we all, with the same assidu-

ous and zealous charity, must love the Mystical Body of Christ.
Now from the moment of His Incarnation, when he laid the first
foundations of the Church, even to His last mortal breath, our
Redeemer never ceased for an instant, though He was the Son of
God, to labor unto weariness in order to establish and strengthen
the Church, whether by giving us the shining example of His holiness, or by preaching, or conversing, or gathering and instructing
disciples. And so We desire that all who claim the Church as their
mother, should seriously consider that not only the clergy and
those who have consecrated themselves to God in the religious
life, but the other members of the Mystical Body of Jesus Christ
as well have, each in his degree, the obligation of working hard
and constantly for the building up and increase of this Body.[80]

Similarly, just as the life of Christ the man was a life of
love for God and mankind, and therefore a life of *prayer*
for those who were and are called to become members of His
Body and to share in His intimate life, to the glory of God,
so too the life of those in whom He lives and who live by His
life must be one of assiduous and fervent *prayer* for the entire
Body—for each of its actual members and for those who are
called to become such but have not yet responded:

Our Redeemer showed His burning love for the Church especially
by praying for her to His heavenly Father. To recall but a few
examples: everyone knows, Venerable Brethren, that just before
the crucifixion He prayed repeatedly for Peter (Luke 22.32), for
the other Apostles (John 17.9–19), for all who, through the
preaching of the holy Gospel, would believe in Him. (John
17.20–23)

After the example of Christ we too should pray daily to the
Lord of the harvest to send laborers into His harvest. (Matt.
9.38; Luke 10.2) Our united prayer should rise daily to heaven
for all the members of the Mystical Body of Jesus Christ; first
for Bishops, who are responsible in a special way for their

respective dioceses; then for priests and religious, both men and women, who have been called to the service of God, and who, at home and in the foreign missions, are protecting, increasing, and advancing the Kingdom of the Divine Redeemer. No member of this venerated Body must be forgotten in this common prayer; and let there be a special remembrance of those who are weighed down with the sorrows and afflictions of this earthly exile, as also for the suffering souls in Purgatory. Neither must those be neglected who are being instructed in Christian doctrine, so that they may be able to receive baptism without delay.

Likewise, We most earnestly desire that this united prayer may embrace in the same ardent charity both those who, not yet enlightened by the truth of the Gospel, are still without the fold of the Church, and those who, on account of regrettable schism, are separated from Us, who though unworthy, represent the person of Jesus Christ on earth. Let us then re-echo that divine prayer of our Saviour to the heavenly Father: "That they all may be one, as thou Father in me, and I in thee, that they also may be one in us; that the world may believe that thou hast sent me." (John 17.21)[81]

If, however, we consider the fact that Christ the man consecrated His love for God and mankind by living a life not only of work and prayer, but also one of *pain and suffering*, that He redeemed the world and formed His Mystical Body at the price of His Precious Blood, we will then understand why those who belong to Christ—members who live by His life— follow the *"royal way of the Cross"* in order to fill up in their flesh what remains of the sufferings of Christ on behalf of His Body which is the Church.

Moreover, Christ proved His love for His spotless Bride not only at the cost of immense labor and constant prayer, but by His sorrows and His sufferings which He willingly and lovingly endured for her sake. "Having loved his own . . . he loved them unto the end." (John 13.1) Indeed it was only at the price of

His blood that He purchased the Church. (Acts 20.28) Let us then follow gladly in the blood-stained footsteps of our King, for this is necessary to ensure our salvation: "For if we have been planted together in the likeness of his death, we shall be also in the likeness of his resurrection" (Rom. 6.5), and "if we be dead with him, we shall live also with him." (II Tim. 2.11) Also our zealous love for the Church demands it, and our brotherly love for the souls she brings forth to Christ. For although our Saviour's cruel passion and death merited for His Church an infinite treasure of graces, God's inscrutable providence has decreed that these graces should not be granted to us all at once; but their greater or lesser abundance will depend in no small part on our good works, which draw down on the souls of men a rain of heavenly gifts freely bestowed by God. These heavenly gifts will surely flow more abundantly if we not only pray fervently to God, especially by participating every day if possible in the Eucharistic Sacrifice; if we not only try to relieve the distress of the needy and of the sick by works of Christian charity, but if we also set our hearts on the good things of eternity rather than on the passing things of this world; if we restrain this mortal body by voluntary mortification, denying it what is forbidden, and forcing it to do what is hard and distasteful; and finally, if we humbly accept as from God's hands the burdens and sorrows of this present life. Thus, according to the Apostle, "we shall fill up those things that are wanting of the sufferings of Christ in our flesh for his Body, which is the Church." (Col. 1.24)[82]

In order to cast into bolder relief the significance of all that we have said up to this point and thus make it easier to understand the reality of the incorporation of every member into the Body of Christ and the contribution each makes towards the building up of the total Christ, it will be useful to dwell briefly on a consideration of how Christ is said to suffer in His members and in what sense these complete His Passion. When we speak of a living member of the Mystical Body suffering, we are obviously referring to the suffering of a human person, as we have emphasized time and again. But at the same time the suffering under discussion is that of a person who does not live in an order of pure nature and who, moreover—even in an historical order—does not lead a life estranged from God. Rather we are speaking of the suffering of a person who is incorporated into Christ, a member of His Mystical Body, animated by the Spirit of Christ, sharing in His life. The Christian who sustains, as a human person, his suffering in so far as he is incorporated into Christ, gives to Christ Himself the possibility of living His Passion in a new form, namely, according to the peculiar modalities in which only this person can live it. His suffering, therefore, is also in a truly profound sense the suffering of Christ Himself, who sustains this suffering not in that individual human nature which was hypostatically assumed by the Person of the Word, but in a human person incorporated into His humanity and supernaturally animated by His grace. In this sense the Christian truly fulfills in his flesh "those things that are wanting of the sufferings of Christ."[83]

We have taken the famous passage from St. Paul's Epistle to the Colossians (1.24) as an occasion for considering how the suffering of a member of the Mystical Body is truly sustained by Christ and fulfills what is wanting of His sufferings. We have dwelt on this point at length because we feel that this clarification enables us to grasp more concretely the basic truth which serves as a foundation for our entire thesis. What we have said specifically of suffering is applicable to every aspect of the existence of those who are members of the Mystical Body. Consequently, one can appreciate how persons who allow themselves to be vivified in all their activities by Christ's Spirit both share in His life and complete His salvific work inasmuch as they make Him visible to other men in their own persons, in the concrete circumstances of the environment and world in which they live. Every person, in fact, who in the ambit of his limited but unique personal circumstances and qualities lives the life of Christ the Head enables Him to live His life within the range of the possibilities freely offered to Him by the person who has become His member. Every person who shares intimately the life and love of Christ radiates the warmth and splendor of Christ's life and love, and makes His lovableness visible in the circumstances in which this person happens to be. Every person who is intimately united to Christ attracts men to Him because they are first captivated and fascinated by his goodness and then rise to the Source whence this attractive quality ultimately derives. Thus does Christ, through the concrete living example of those who offer themselves to Him without reserve, continue revealing to men of all times and places new forms and genuine styles of Christian living, practical ways of realizing, in the ever-changing circumstances of life, the Christian ideal of union and conformity with Christ. He continues to enlighten every man with the knowledge of how, in the particular circumstances of his life, he can, and must, allow Christ to live in him, in order that everything genuinely human in himself can be elevated and sanctified by Christ for the greater glory of God; that is, so that all may become Christ's, as all that is Christ's belongs to the Father.

In so far, therefore, as each person vivified by grace and made a living member of the Mystical Body associates himself freely, consciously, and generously with the life of Christ the Head, to that extent does he mediate the salvific work of Christ to his fellow men, whether living members already incorporated into the Body or members yet to be incorporated. These men derive greater benefit from the redemptive work of Christ because He now has a way to communicate His grace and to apply the fruits of His life, Passion, and death through the co-operation of His members. The activities— work, prayer, suffering—whereby members co-operate in

Christ's effort to build up His Mystical Body deepen the already existing bonds, or establish new ones, between these members and those of us who benefit from their efforts. In this way new motives are provided for entering into direct contact with those persons who "through, with and in Christ" are our benefactors and for addressing ourselves to them in order to express not only admiration and praise, but also deep gratitude. Obviously, we who have been benefited should acknowledge what we have received through the collaboration with the work of Christ of those members who are actively united to Him. While we realize that their effectiveness derives fundamentally and radically from Christ Himself, it must nonetheless be attributed to the fact that they, as persons, have freely done their part; therefore, we should address ourselves directly to those who have worked so that Christ could communicate His grace to us through them.

All of this is applicable to every member, because every good work performed by anyone vitally united to Christ entails beneficial consequences for all other members of the Body. But, as we have emphasized, it is applicable in proportion to the intensity and generosity with which the member freely and consciously associated himself with the effective love of Christ. It is evident, then, that the Saints—those pre-eminent members of the Mystical Body who participate most intimately in the life and active love of Christ—are outstanding benefactors of the other members, and consequently must justly receive the gratitude that is their due from those who have been the recipients of their graciousness.

We have intentionally used the expressions "those who have been the recipients of their graciousness" and "gratitude that is their due," because we wish to stress a stipulation of God's providential plan. Men are called to collaborate with Christ, as members of His Mystical Body, so that the distribution of grace and the application of the merits of Christ depend, at least in part, on the contribution and collaboration of the members who, in accord with their personal dignity, freely offer or refuse co-operation:

For although our Saviour's cruel passion and death merited for His Church an infinite treasure of graces, God's inscrutable providence has decreed that these graces should not be granted to us all at once; but their greater or lesser abundance will depend in no small part on our good works, which draw down on the souls of men a rain of heavenly gifts freely bestowed by God.[84]

Our reception of certain graces is to be attributed to the fact that this or that pre-eminent member has or is co-operating effectively with Christ for our benefit. Without his co-operation, without his personal contribution of work, prayer, and suffering, we would not have been accorded what we have in fact received. The expression of our gratitude, therefore, should be directed immediately to this benefactor of ours; nor will such an honor detract from what is due to Christ, but rather glorify Him all the more because, though we address ourselves directly to a created person, it is precisely as a member of Christ that we honor him, and thus indirectly we honor Christ who has granted us the grace in and through His member.

This consideration of the benefits deriving from collaboration with Christ the Head on the part of pre-eminent members (that is, of what the Saints contribute to the other members) enables us to realize that our prayers directed to them should not be limited to acts of admiration and praise, but should include acts of thanksgiving and the correlative of these, namely, acts of invocation. In fact, recognition of what they have done in and with Christ for the benefit of the Mystical Body, collectively and in each of its members, gives rise to the conviction that members intimately united to Christ have the power, through their merits, to effect a richer application of

Christ's infinite merits to mankind. This conviction naturally is projected into the future and serves as the basis for that form of recourse to other members—and especially to the Saints—which we call invocation; for this is simply a request for additional benefits from God through their intercession.[85]

Now if we take this aspect of recourse to the Saints and relate it to the doctrine of the Mystical Body, we will appreciate how their effective collaboration with Christ enables Him to realize His intention of uniting men to Himself more fully, to the greater glory of God. When we see that the co-operation of the Saints brings about an increase and a development in the supernatural life of the other members, we can easily understand that recourse to them and our petitions for their assistance must be inspired and dictated by a single motive, namely, the desire to receive that help which will lead us to live more intensely as members of the Mystical Body so that we, in turn, may more capably acquit ourselves of our function in that Body, to the greater glory of Christ and of God.

We have emphasized repeatedly the principle that every member can and must contribute to the total Christ something which he alone as a unique person can give. Concretely, this implies that God, who confers upon us every grace in Christ, makes the application of the infinite merits of the Head dependent, at least in part, on the merits and co-operation of the members. We may easily understand, then, how prejudicial to our fuller progress in Christ would be a refusal to invoke those who, according to the divine plan, can associate themselves—especially if invoked by us[86]—with the intercessory prayer of Christ and, in virtue of the merits which they acquired on earth, enable us to receive all that God has determined to grant us in dependence on their merits and intercession. In fact, if the grace merited by Christ the Head is granted to us, at least in part, in consequence of our invocation, so too the conferring of those graces that depend on the co-operation of the pre-eminent members will be linked to our invocation of those members.

What we said about recourse to the Saints when we were speaking of our full and perfect union with Christ and of our full and perfect glorification of the Father "through, with, and in Him" obtains as well for our ascending movement towards Christ and the Father, in so far as this is constituted by our full and perfect recognition of His salvific work in the building up of His Mystical Body. In fact, if we accept the truth that Christ wished to enrich and complete His work by associating with Himself persons whom He had animated and formed into His Mystical Body in order that they, by their personal contribution, might collaborate with Him in developing it further, then we must admit that it would be quite arbitrary and unjustifiable if we took it on ourselves to separate such members from Him and to refuse them—worthy and capable though they might be of receiving it—a manifestation of our admiration, praise, gratitude, and supplication in return for what they have done and are doing as persons to bring about the perfection of Christ's work.

Faith assures us of the vital reality of the Mystical Body and sheds light on the beneficent activity which vitally active members exercise for the good of the entire Mystical Christ and of each individual member.[87] We should recognize, therefore, that manifestations of admiration and esteem, thanksgiving and supplication, and all our direct personal contacts with these co-workers of Christ are desired by Christ Himself. Far from detracting from our relationship with Him, they complete it, because they enable us to honor, praise, thank, and invoke Him, seeing that He Himself has wished to assist us through these persons who opened themselves generously to His grace, lived by His life, and worked in union with Him, so that He might live and work in them and thus perfect His work.[88]

III. THE CULT OF THE SAINTS AND THE PERFECTION OF OUR PROGRESS TOWARDS CHRIST AND THE FATHER

In the preceding pages we already provided ample justification for the cult of the Saints by analyzing those aspects of our incorporation into Christ which have often been neglected, and demonstrating, on the basis of solid theological criteria, how this cult is compatible with theocentric religion and christocentric worship. But these considerations on the dignity and function of the Saints in the framework of the total Christ did not say all that could be said about the relations between Christ and the Saints. Further reflection will not only demonstrate the liceity and necessity of recourse to the Saints but also provide us with new motives for fostering a solid devotion which can deepen and intensify our communion with Christ and the Father.

Let us summarize what we have seen up to this point. Proceeding from the truth that the Saints are persons who, by giving free rein to the Spirit of Christ, live His life intensely and therefore are pre-eminent members of His Mystical Body, we saw that, as members, they retain their distinct personalities and yet complement the Head by placing at His disposal their unique personal qualities. They offer Christ the possibility of living in them, His mystical members, those human possibilities which He could not live in the human nature that was hypostatically His, since it was necessarily single and individual and therefore limited. Though we emphasized that they are persons and stressed that it is precisely in this capacity that they can freely place at the disposal of Christ personal qualities and talents not possessed by Christ's personal human nature, our attention was focused on the fact that they complement the Head *as members* and enable Him to build up the total Christ.

Up to this point we have not considered the corresponding reactions evoked in Christ's personal human nature by the generous response of the Saints. We will now concentrate on this aspect. How do the saintly members of the Mystical Body, by responding as persons to the personal love of Christ, complete Christ under another aspect in as much as by actuating intimate personal bonds of friendship they give Christ the opportunity of developing in His individual human nature, possibilities of perfection that He could not develop without them? In the preceding section we dwelt upon the consequences of the fact that the Saints as persons are *members*. Now we wish to investigate their role precisely as *persons* who are animated by the Spirit of Christ and His grace and give themselves to Him without reserve, enabling Him to live with them those mutual exchanges of friendship that complete our personal human life and consequently permit us to glorify God in a fuller and more perfect manner.

Naturally these two aspects (persons as *members* and members as *persons*) since they are simply two aspects of the same reality, cannot be separated in the actual order. In the reflections which follow we must always bear in mind that the

mutual relations, the exchanges and direct contacts of friendship between Christ and the Saints are at the same time mutual
relations and interchanges between Christ the Head and His
mystical members. There is no question of attempting to separate what is inseparable; we wish simply to consider distinctly
two aspects of a single reality which is so rich that our human
intelligence cannot encompass it in a single sweep or describe
it with sufficient clarity in a single set of concepts. Nevertheless, even when we subdivide the material and consider the
two aspects under distinct formalities, we must never forget
that the reality of the Mystical Body—which is neither a physical nor merely a moral body but one which combines certain
qualities of both—is a reality not only transcending our immediate experience and the scope of our simple concepts but
supernatural in the strict sense of that term and, therefore,
full of mystery.

A. IN VIRTUE OF THE CONTRIBUTION
WHICH ASSOCIATION WITH MEN MAKES
TO THE PERFECTION OF THE HUMAN
KNOWLEDGE AND LOVE OF JESUS CHRIST
FOR THE FATHER

When we were discussing the reason why we can speak of
a complement to the human nature of Christ we said that it
was due to the metaphysical constitution of man: a spiritual-
material, personal-individual being. Such a constitution makes
it impossible for any individual to realize in himself all the
possible means of human perfection. This very same constitution of man makes it impossible for any individual to develop
and actuate all the human perfection of which he himself is
capable as a person if he remains in isolation, that is, deprived
of the assistance of other men of whom he has need, as a social

being, and devoid of those mutual relationships and exchanges which constitute the richest source of human perfection. That even in Christ Jesus there should exist this possibility of being enriched and perfected by other men in His own personal cognitive and affective life (and, consequently, of being enriched and perfected by them in the very actuation of his human relations with the Father), is simply a consequence of the Word's desire to become like unto us in all things, becoming truly man in His Incarnation. He wished to live and experience what we men can live and experience through our social contacts, with the obvious exception of sin and its many ramifications in our lives. Over and above this important restriction, it must be emphasized that no comparison of strict equality can be established between the psychic life of the man Jesus Christ and that of any purely human person, especially a person still immersed in his time of earthly trial; for Christ, because of His hypostatic union, had from the first instant of His human existence, even as man, the clearest consciousness of His divinity, and enjoyed a face-to-face vision of the Father. This difference, this essentially superior manner of knowing and loving the Father which is proper to Christ, does not contradict the proposition we have set forth above. In order to clarify our position and confirm it with data from the Sacred Scriptures, we will concentrate on that type of human knowledge and love which the man Christ Jesus surely possessed here on earth and which bears the strongest resemblance to the mode of knowledge and love that is ours as wayfarers; namely, His knowledge and love that are called technically experiential or acquired.

Considering the acquired knowledge and love of the man Jesus Christ, we can state with assurance that in the various stages of His human development and in the progressive phases of His life and activity, the man Jesus Christ experienced the same human interchanges that we experience. Just as these human interchanges are destined, in our case, to promote and enrich our knowledge and love of the Father— which indeed they do—so too in the case of Christ human relationships promoted and enriched His knowledge and love of the Father. It is certain that every contact Jesus had with men evoked in His exquisitely sensitive human nature an enriching experimental knowledge and a new actuation of His affective life, manifested in accordance with the concrete type of contacts experienced: at times commiseration and mercy, at other times indignation and disappointment; occasionally sorrow and grief, but more often joy and gratitude, tenderness and happiness. It is equally certain that these contacts which Christ had with other men and the subsequent reactions registered in His humanity constituted for Him a continual occasion for spiritual elevation and prayer; and therefore, on this level of His knowledge and love, exerted a constant influence on the concrete actuation of His relations with the Father, evoking acts of homage and praise, thanksgiving and supplication.

This love which Christ had for men induced Him to seek to enter into contact even with those who were distant from God—the indifferent, the hostile. Even the experience of man's indifference and hatred contributed to the enrichment of His acquired knowledge and love, inasmuch as it offered Him new possibilities of living His union of love with the Father. We may say without hesitation, however, that no contact of Christ with men contributed more profoundly and more fully to the enrichment of His acquired knowledge and love of God than the contacts He had with human persons who opened their hearts to His grace and received Him, surrendering themselves unconditionally and totally to Him in loving faith.

We do not wish to minimize the transcendental function

—whether it be for our redemption, or for our Redeemer's human life—of the sorrow Christ experienced owing to the coldness of men and their rejection of His love; we must acknowledge that contacts of this sort contributed to the development of His acquired knowledge and love of the Father. But it must also be noted that in such contacts men made no positive contribution to Christ's human enrichment. Any such enrichment that occurred is to be attributed solely to the perfection of the man Jesus Christ Himself.

On the other hand there were other encounters between Christ and those who opened their hearts under the influence of His grace and gave themselves to Him. In those contacts, which developed in conformity with Christ's desires and achieved the ultimate goal of the Incarnation, men made a positive contribution to the enrichment of Christ's acquired knowledge and love precisely in so far as they gave Him the means of communicating Himself to them in the intimacy of supernatural friendship and of receiving in exchange their response of love.

In becoming Incarnate *propter nos homines et propter nostram salutem* (for us men and for our salvation), the Divine Word in His divine and human, spiritual and sensible love, desired nothing other than to enter into a relationship of supernatural friendship with men. His sole desire was that he should be able to communicate Himself to us, so that we, by receiving Him, might reciprocate His love and thus glorify the Father together with Him.[89] In the light of this we can easily understand how moving and enriching for the man Jesus Christ must be the human experience of being able to give Himself entirely to a person who opens his heart to His gracious invitation. How enriching must be the experience of receiving in return all that is this person's most intimate and precious possession—namely himself, with all that he is and

has as a human person—in order that such a one may be
His, so that He can live and work in him as in a member of
His Mystical Body. We can understand, moreover, that such
an experience of supernatural friendship with men, for which
the man Jesus Christ depends on the free co-operation of men
and which is distinguished both by the unique quality of each
person and by the various phases of each one's development,
constitutes for His acquired knowledge and love of the Father
an authentic enrichment and deepening. In fact, the experience of seeing the beauty of a person who without reserve
opens his heart to Truth and Love; of feeling understood and
loved; of observing the fruitfulness of one's labor, prayer,
and suffering; of having found among one's friends faithful
and willing collaborators for the carrying on of one's work;
of having secured for one's friends peace of soul and eternal
beatitude—all these experiences naturally constitute for Christ
added motives for praising, thanking and invoking the Father.
Moreover, we must always bear in mind that the totality of
this experience has an even deeper value: it fosters the fundamental human experience of the man Jesus Christ, which is
that of recognizing with joy that one has effectively corresponded with the salvific will of the Father and fulfilled His
intention of uniting, to His greater glory, all mankind in
Christ.

This observation brings us to a final and most valuable consideration of the enrichment given to the individual human
perfection of the man Jesus by those who have become His
members and exercise a relationship of supernatural friendship
with Him. The experience and realization that He, Head of
the Mystical Body, has in seeing men united to Him can not
but influence the modalities of the adoration He, in His individual humanity, offers to the Father. The intensity of His
adoration is increased by the very fact that it is effected by

Him in union with His members. It is true also of the man Jesus Christ that the knowledge that one is united to friends in a common enterprise and in the unfolding of a joint activity, the vital consciousness that they are acting together with us, not only re-enforces mutual love but also confers on the action itself an élan, a new vigor characteristic of those who are striving towards a goal together, in firm and affectionate social union.

It would not be difficult to confirm the foregoing remarks about the enrichment and perfection of Jesus Christ's acquired knowledge and love from the many passages in the Sacred Scriptures that clearly reveal the influences exerted on Him by His contacts with those persons who, opening their hearts to His grace, gave themselves to Him and became His friends and co-workers. The abundance of material available and the clarity of the idea in itself were the principal reasons why we took the acquired knowledge and love of the man Jesus Christ as our point of departure for these considerations.

If we may be dispensed from the need of adducing texts to prove our point, we would prefer to emphasize the fact that all we have said with reference to the acquired knowledge and love of the man Jesus Christ should be extended to the knowledge and love which He has had since the beginning of His human existence and still possesses, in virtue of the Beatific Vision. In fact, even though this mode of Christ's knowledge and love is essentially superior to that of His acquired knowledge and love, we must bear in mind nonetheless that He knows and loves in this manner as true man, and therefore as an individual and social human being. Now in the Beatific Vision the man Jesus Christ knows not only God as He is in Himself, but also, in Him, all creation, all mankind, all of His Mystical Body and the individual persons who constitute its membership. And so even in this superior form of knowledge,

the man Jesus Christ sees—in fact He sees therein with utmost
clarity—in what a profound sense He possesses those persons
who, in every age and in every generation, have opened their
hearts to the communication of His Spirit and of His grace,
surrendered themselves to Him, and become living members
of His Mystical Body. In this form of knowledge, Christ per-
ceives in what a marvelously rich and productive manner these
persons living with His life complete His humanity and thus
contribute to the realization of the salvific plan of God within
the "total Christ." Seeing how much the individual human
persons of all times, animated by His grace, bring to the total
Christ, He finds a fresh motive not only for honoring, praising,
thanking, and invoking God, but also for loving these very
persons and communicating Himself to them, so that He may
establish with them that friendship which enriches the intensity
of His worship of the Father. For, in virtue of this friendship,
He can offer worship as Head of redeemed humanity and
therefore in union with all those who, as members of His
Mystical Body, sing their paean of praise to the Father in a
union of love with Him.

We have intentionally dwelt at some length on this consideration, which certainly is not entirely new, but unfortunately
is often neglected and almost never systematically exploited
in relation to our argument. We have done so because, in our
opinion, an appreciation of how Jesus Christ is enriched in
His own life and human experience by contacts with men in
general and with Saints in particular and of how this increases
His human love and worship of the Father, constitutes (together with the reflections noted above) one of the fundamental premises for an adequate theological understanding of
the nature and importance of the cult of the Saints. If, in fact,
one understands in what a profound sense the living members
of the Mystical Body—and above all the pre-eminent mem-

bers—are the friends of Christ; if one can appreciate the significance of this friendship not only for them but for the very perfection of the man Jesus Christ; if one takes into account the truth that the Saints are loved and honored by Christ Himself and that His friendship with them and the manner in which it is manifested by direct personal contacts, far from detracting from or obscuring the worship that Christ offers to the Father, really enriches and completes it;—if one takes all this into consideration, there can be no difficulty in understanding how our direct contacts with the Saints (kept always within the limits proper to creatures) and our bonds of friendship with them can only quicken our movement towards Christ and "through, with, and in Him," towards the Trinity. It will be clear, then, that a genuine cult of the Saints, based upon the doctrine of the Mystical Body, can be inserted harmoniously into that healthy and fruitful lifestream of modern theology and spirituality which, drawing upon the same doctrine of the Mystical Body, insists on the social and communal element of a life of genuine Christian piety. The faithful of our own times are keenly interested in the psychic life of the man Jesus Christ, and even more keenly aware of the value and necessity of their union with others. It is simple, then, to take the attractive dogma of the Mystical Body and explain to the faithful how the cult of the Saints is precisely one of the ways in which we can and must realize most productively our social relationships in all their aspects, both natural and supernatural. From this it will be seen that cult of the Saints is a manifestation of that life which constitutes an integral part of christocentric and theocentric worship.

B. IN VIRTUE OF THE CONTRIBUTION WHICH ASSOCIATION WITH OTHERS MAKES TO THE PERFECTION OF OUR PROGRESS TOWARDS CHRIST AND TOWARDS THE FATHER

If we take as our point of departure the ideas just expressed and recall the principle that accounts for the enrichment which Christ Himself derived for His individual life by contacts with other men, we can see how this principle is applied to each of them and enjoys an even greater importance by reason of these truths elaborated above. Within the framework of the life of the Mystical Body, it is not difficult to make Christians understand the profound significance of the fact that each of them is a social being, a member of a supernatural organism, and as such must move towards Christ and, in Him, towards the Father. It is in fact easy to demonstrate to any Christian that he is a finite being, limited, open to numerous possibilities of ontologico-psychological enrichment by means of his contacts with other persons, and especially with the members of the same supernatural community of the Mystical Body. As a consequence, he must live and actuate his relations with others in order to give God the fullest glory. God, who made man a social creature, wants him both to receive and to give, so that in this exchange with others he will be enriched and perfected. If a Christian realizes that such relations are intended by God for his perfection, he will strive consciously to establish these vital contacts with others; and in the measure that he develops and lives them in the way intended by the Creator, so much the more will he be internally enriched, enabling his movement towards Christ and, in Him, towards the Father to acquire a new nobility, a greater fullness and a more profound efficacy. In fact, enriched by this network of vital experiences, he will not only glorify Christ and the Most Holy Trinity more completely by reason of the fact that he will thus objectively realize the divine plan, but he will also be endowed with a maturity of affective, intellectual, and personal life that will enable him to enter into a more lively and intimate relationship with Christ and the Father, because he will love Him more explicitly and glorify Him with greater intensity and richness.[90] It is of course evident that such relations and vital contacts among persons find their fullest expression in mutual communication: that is, in the exchange of goods, thoughts, affections and sentiments; in the mutual manifestation of what is most beautiful in the human personality; in the person-to-person expression of what one has in heart and mind; or, to put it quite simply, in an intimate personal "dialogue" in which one gives and receives, speaks and makes known one's wish for help.

The result of all this will be a deeper appreciation and a consequent practice of what constitutes the cult of the Saints. It goes without saying that these interchanges, though beneficial for all, are particularly fruitful when established with persons superior to us, persons whom we admire for their superior gifts and for their pre-eminent intellectual and moral qualities. It is a common experience that association with the noble and the good produces similar qualities in us. Even the slightest contact with the persons endowed with outstanding human qualities serves as a powerful incentive and invitation to scale the heights; one feels duty-bound to strive to reach their level, leaving behind what is base and ignoble.

If we are privileged to enter into more direct contact with such persons, so that we can actually express our admiration and esteem, we will derive from their affectionate and engaging response precious assistance in the form of enlightenment and strength, encouragement and support. If a sense of in-

feriority and need induces us to open our hearts and invoke
their help, we will not be deluded in our hopes and expecta-
tions, but will soon experience the efficacy of their interven-
tion. How often, in fact, do we encounter persons who impress
us by an almost transparent quality that thinly veils the presence of God within them. Their very presence benefits us,
leading us closer to Christ and the Father. What could be
more natural, in such a case, than to express our feelings by
turning to them reverently and respectfully, and asking them
to associate themselves with us in our prayers for our needs?
How often does it happen that an awareness of our pathetic
insufficiencies leads us to enlist the prayers of our friends, in
the hope that God will extend His protecting and sustaining
hand over us? And when a favor is granted, do we not express
gratitude and recognition for their gracious concern and invite
them to join us in thanking God for His gifts?

We know, moreover, from experience that such rewarding
associations occasionally spin a thread of intimacy which then
is slowly woven into a bond of friendship—one of the noblest
expressions of life and a most powerful means for effecting
our perfection.[91] The birth of a friendship is indeed an integral
part of God's providential plan. Because of the extraordinary
diversity among members of the human race, the differences
of temperament and education, the variety of inclinations and
ideals, the limitations inherent in man (especially as a wayfarer here on earth), it is impossible that an intimate personal
exchange should be realized with all other men. For this reason men in general, and Christians in particular, experience
the need and desire of forming associations with certain con-
genial persons. It is God Himself who arranges circumstances
so that the paths of certain individuals who will fulfill needs
in one another will cross. In our opinion, no judicious person
can fail to appreciate the contribution which these direct per-

sonal contacts among men make to human life and to our
progress towards Christ and, in Him, towards God. Far from
impeding our ascent to the Father, friendship makes the
journey more pleasant and more rewarding.

In making these basic observations on our relations with
members of the Mystical Body living on earth, we have indicated the usefulness and necessity of such relations if one
wishes, in accordance with the divine plan, to attain that fullness and maturity of experience which will enable one to
glorify God in the highest degree possible. It should be quite
obvious that these relations not only can but must be extended
to the members of the Mystical Body already in their glory,
namely, the Saints,[92] from the moment that the faith and practice of the Church assures us that such personal contacts with
them are possible. In the light of the foregoing exposition, it
is obvious that the greater the spiritual riches of these persons
and the greater our certainty of their holiness[93] and of their
ability and willingness to assist us,[94] so much the greater is
the need for an association with them, in order to realize and
exploit most effectively the potential riches latent in direct
contacts with them, for the greater glory of Christ and the
Father.

Even with regard to the Saints, then, the fullest realization
of our relations will be effected by our entering into a direct
personal dialogue with them. It should be evident that, in
dealing with the Saints, the very placing of oneself in their
presence will have an elevating and beneficent influence.
Their dignity necessarily evokes a reaction in the hearts of
their admirers. Their exemplary lives serve as a challenge for
us to fulfill our common obligation to live the Christian life
ever more perfectly. Their nobility represents an invitation to
scale the heights and leave behind all that could hinder us;
the knowledge of being united to them in our ascent to Christ

and, in Him, to the Father, comforts us, gives us new spirit and enthusiasm, and induces us to dedicate ourselves ever more generously to a life of loving service of God and neighbor. When we finally enter into a more direct contact, one more personal and candid, in which we pour out our needs as well as our reverent admiration, the bond established is profound and fruitful. On the part of the Saints, the personal interest they take in us will certainly communicate new strength and encouragement. In our associations with them we will recognize our own shortcomings and understand more clearly our imperfections and deficiencies; knowing that we are associated with holy persons whose entire lives were spent in doing good, we can be sure that we will meet with perfect understanding on the part of those whose goodness leads them to alleviate the misery of all in need. Consequently, when we invoke their help we will never fail to receive all that is necessary for our improvement.

This network of relationships and acts constitutes the authentic cult of the Saints, and when we view it in this light, we understand its spirit and beauty: a spirit of understanding, love, and confident appeal, in which the dominant note is the desire to intensify, by means of this contact, our ascent to Christ and to the Father.

But in saying that the cult of the Saints consists in establishing a personal contact or direct relationship with them, we have implied that the Saints are aware of the acts directed to them,[95] and react in their turn by directing their benevolent and efficacious attention towards those who invoke their aid.[96] If this were not so, the practice which the Church encourages of praying to the heavenly community both individually and collectively, not only occasionally but for every conceivable intention, would in the last analysis be a senseless and ineffectual practice. What would be the meaning of veneration and supplication if the person to whom these acts were directed remained totally unaware of them and powerless to respond? "Who indeed would invoke someone who can lend no assistance in return?"[97] (On the entire question consult the Appendices.)

It is evident, then, that the authentic cult of the Saints presupposes an equally personal reaction on the part of the Saints, that is, a solicitous and affectionate interest, a special bond of efficacious spiritual friendship with those on earth who turn to them.[98] The persons in question, of course, are persons who live in Christ with a life that is divine; everything they perceive is perceived in the light of that divine life. Since there is no possibility of a natural direct communication between us and the persons in heaven, the acts whereby we address ourselves to the Saints are made known to them by means of a supernatural communication imparted by God Himself.[99] They perceive our desires and expressions of esteem as God sees them; that is, they know whether they will promote God's glory and our eternal welfare. And since the will of the Saints is totally united with the divine will, so much the more efficacious can their concern and intercession be, inasmuch as they can perceive the correspondence between God's will and the intentions formulated in the prayers of the faithful.[100]

This is even clearer when we recall that the function of the Saints in the Church, whose pre-eminent members they are, is precisely to bring it about that we, by following their example, shall strive to live ever more faithfully as children of God, in Christ. Their benevolent concern will be all the more affectionate and active if they perceive in God that our intentions and requests are actually ordered towards God, and if they recognize their power to intercede and obtain for us the grace to live a more Christ-like life. But we must keep in mind that in every case their intercessory prayers will always petition those favors that will benefit us most. When we have accepted and utilized these graces, we will draw much closer to them, because our resemblance to Christ, and therefore to them, will become much more profound. Subsequent relations with them will become ever more productive.

From all this it should be evident that the reactions of the Saints to our expressions of cult will be marked also by the characteristic traits of a personal association. By exercising an efficacious concern, assisting those who invoke their aid, and protecting those who trust in their special care, the Saints too experience the joy that every good person feels when he is able to help others in their ascent to Christ and the Father. They delight in the power to continue their apostolic activity and enjoy to the fullest extent their sublime function as pre-eminent members of the Mystical Body, that is, of being united in a particularly vital manner to the unique mediator, Christ, so that He can employ them as co-workers in His salvific work.[101] In other words, they rejoice in having realized and in actually effecting the design willed and intended by God, and in casting into bold relief the redemptive work of Christ. We must not forget that the Father, who grants us every grace through Christ, is the one who raises up and extolls the Saints, not indeed to set them up in opposition to Christ, the unique Mediator, nor to set them on a level with Him; rather, it is that the power of Christ may shine forth in them and that He may lead all the faithful through the Saints to Christ, and in Christ, to Himself.

In contemplating the execution of this divine plan, which they can assist because they participate in the efficacious good-ness of God and have been associated with His activity in the Church, the Saints experience an increase in their joy and find a special motive for expressing glorious gratitude to God.

We have dwelt at length on the part we play in our relations with the Saints and then emphasized the complementary aspect of this mutual relationship, namely, the way in which the Saints react when we turn to them. Now we are in a position to appreciate the ensemble of our relations with the Saints and of their cult in its noblest and richest form; for we understand how we can establish even with the Saints a relationship of real spiritual friendship. When speaking of truly Christian friendship among persons living on earth, we explained how a Christian can have a loving esteem for all[102] and yet experience a special attraction and sympathy towards some. The same is true with respect to our associations with the Saints. The motives that will suggest and determine the choice of friends among Christians here on earth—supernatural motives that often presuppose an affinity of temperament, interests, and experience—will also guide our preference in establishing a particular relationship with this rather than with that Saint. Subjective factors of temperament and ideals, objective data such as common race, nationality, and country, identity of occupation, profession, or state in life, can have and actually often do have an influence on the origin of those particular relationships which unite certain Christians and certain groups to a Saint who shared the conditions of their life while on earth. Thus it can be easily understood, for example, why mothers prefer to pray to a Saint who fulfilled heroically the role of a Christian mother; why adolescents turn to an exemplary young Christian; why priests and religious prefer a particular Saint because he was a model priest, the founder, or an outstanding member, of their religious family.

These motives for preference and subsequent choice are also suggested and confirmed by the very action of the Church, which, in proposing Saints, often not only points them out

as examples for a specific category of Christians, but also
declares them patrons of that particular class and entrusts the
class to their special care.[103] The conscious realization of the
special bond that can be established between a Christian and
a Saint finds beautiful expression in the choice of a baptismal
name when this choice is not based solely on circumstantial
family considerations, but is dictated primarily by considerations of a spiritual nature, such as the desire to imitate a
particular Saint or to procure his protection[104]—practices
highly recommended by the Church.[105] This is obviously more
evident in cases involving an adult who, on the occasion of
his baptism or in other circumstances, selects the name of a
Saint.[106] The name represents for him an ideal incarnated in
the perfect life of its bearer. His type of holiness provides an
inspiring program particularly appropriate for the life and
circumstances in which the person happens to be who has
chosen the Saint as his model. In view of all this, that Saint
is particularly recommended to be the friend, the protector,
the heavenly patron of this Christian; to be, in brief, the one
who will help him in his ascent towards God.

Our exposition of the various elements and reasons for
honoring the Saints has indicated the wholesome spirit which
ideally animates the practice. We can conclude that the cult
of the Saints, conceived and practiced within the framework
proposed, is not only perfectly legitimate but also eminently
useful because it assists us effectively to live in full measure
a theocentric and christocentric cult. The spiritual advantages
of an authentic cult of the Saints are so great that we might
ask whether this practice should be considered a necessary
element of Christian worship. In approaching this question,
we will try to indicate the main lines to be followed in seeking
a solution. In so doing, we will also determine more clearly
the value of this practice as well as its limits.

IV. THE NECESSITY OF THE CULT OF THE SAINTS

Any scholar who turns to available theological writings in search of a definitive answer to the question whether and in what sense the cult of the Saints is a necessary element of Christian worship will soon discover that up to the present time this problem has never been treated systematically, nor has any exhaustive systematic study been devoted to its various complex aspects, which would involve the introduction of numerous distinctions and qualifications.[107] Since this is the present state of the question, we cannot pretend to offer in these few pages a complete treatise on the subject. We will be content simply to indicate the principal implications and then propose those principles which must govern any solution to the question of the necessity and limits of the cult of the Saints.

The key to the solution lies in the theological data already elaborated above. By bearing in mind that the authentic cult of the Saints is by its very nature totally subordinate to and a function of theocentrism and christocentrism, and that it is legitimate and fruitful only if conceived and practiced as a particular form and expression of basic Christian worship, we can reduce the question of the necessity of the cult of the Saints to a more basic query: is this practice so intimately connected with the theocentrism and christocentrism of Catholic worship that its contribution can be said to be indispensable?

Even after formulating the question so precisely, no simple reply of "yes" or "no" can be given, because we must distinguish between the two forms of Catholic worship: the public cult of the Church precisely as a community and private prayer. To treat the problem adequately, therefore, we must divide the question and ask: first, whether and in what sense the cult of the Saints is an indispensable element in the public cult of the Church as a community; and secondly whether and in what sense the cult of the Saints is an indispensable element in the worship of individual believers, either in their active participation in the public cult or in their private worship.

Having subdivided the problem in this way, we shall find it easier to formulate separate replies by drawing once again upon what seems to be the key to the entire problem; namely, the fact that the Church Militant:

is ontologically united to the Church Triumphant;

must possess and promote a precise consciousness of this union; and

must act in accordance with this consciousness.

Let us linger for a moment on this line of argument and recall what has already been amply developed in the preceding part, so that we may bring out the fundamental ideas essential to an adequate reply.

That the Church Militant is in Christ its Head, by its essential constitution, ontologically united to the Church Triumphant is so evident and so well-established dogmatically and theologically that further exposition of this point would be superfluous. It is equally evident that the Church Militant must cultivate a conscious awareness of itself in its essential constitution. Hence, it must possess and promote this consciousness of its ontological union with the Church Triumphant.

But possession of such self-awareness does not suffice. On the basis of the principles explained in the preceding part when we treated this argument, we can say that the Church necessarily acts in conformity with its state of being; that is, it must foster in a conscious, deliberate, reflective manner this ontological union with the Church Triumphant. In other words, it must act in such a way that all the possibilities inherent in its ontological relations are lived and developed in full measure, so that Christ and the Father may be given the greatest possible glory.

Now this total, conscious, deliberate actuation of all possible relations with the Church Triumphant necessarily implies that the Church Militant must establish direct contacts with the members of the Church Triumphant and pray to them. Such contact, as we have seen, constitutes cult in the proper sense of the word; namely, the manifestation of praise, admiration and love, the request for help from these glorious members of Christ's Mystical Body, so eminently united to Him that the Father has singled them out and destined them to help the Church Militant in its life and activity, and to enrich and complete the cult it offers to Christ and "through, with, and in Him" to the Most Holy Trinity.

It does not suffice, then, that the Church as such should teach and propose to the faithful the cult of the Saints; the Church itself must publicly practice this cult. In fact, in order to make its public cult as perfect as possible, the Church must actively promote all that can by its nature make this cult more efficacious. This is the theological reason why the Church as such frequently prays directly to the Saints; for example, the litany of the Saints and its use in various solemn liturgical

functions and the hymns in honor of the Saints which the
Church sings in the Divine Office. Even in the supreme act
of worship, the Eucharistic Sacrifice, the Church honors the
Saints with an explicit commemoration or prays to them at
least implicitly,[108] well aware that in this act more than in any
other it is vitally united to the Church Triumphant.

We know that the veneration of the saints in the Church developed out of the veneration of the martyrs, and that originally the
cult of a martyr was closely bound up with his tomb and with
the anniversary of his martyrdom. This annual and local veneration consisted essentially in the celebration of the Eucharist. St.
Cyprian, speaking of three martyrs of Carthage, tells his people,
"You know that we offer the sacrifice in their memory every year
when we commemorate the day of their passion." And it was
while he was celebrating the vigil that would terminate with the
Mass for the anniversary of St. Polycarp in 250, at Smyrna, that
the priest Pionius was arrested. When the veneration of the
Blessed Virgin and the confessors began their anniversaries were
celebrated in the same way.

The sense of these rites is that we remain in communion with
the saints, and that this communion is realized pre-eminently in
the liturgical action, particularly in the celebration of the sacrifice.
The Mass is the meeting place *par excellence* of the Church on
earth and the Church in heaven.

By reason of this conviction, the commemoration of the departed in all the anaphoras, beginning with the fifth century, is
prolonged into a commemoration of the saints, regarded as the
most illustrious of the Christians, the ones whose communion
with us is particularly important and worthy of note. And to make
a memorial of the saints means to offer them the homage of our
veneration, and at the same time to ask them to intercede on our
behalf that God, by reason of their merits and their prayers, may
grant us His protection: a twofold movement, which occurs especially in the Mass. "Then we make a memorial also of the de-

parted," says St. Cyril of Jerusalem, "first of all, of the patriarchs, the prophets, the Apostles, the martyrs, that by reason of their prayer and their intercession God may accept our entreaty."

Thus the liturgy considers the saints as our intercessors; and this is obvious, for example, from the collects or the litany of the Roman rite. To this idea is added the idea that the feasts of the saints are occasions for us to praise God for the marvels He has wrought in them. Finally, we venerate and honor the saints themselves for the perfection to which they have attained with the help of God's grace, and we propose them to ourselves as examples, with the hope of joining them one day in heaven. Such are the different aspects of our communion with the saints of paradise, that communion which the liturgy expresses in so many ways.[109]

That this cult of the Church militant must be extended beyond the members of the Church Triumphant in general to be focused on certain individual members derives primarily from the fact that God Himself in His providential design points out by means of signs (i.e., miracles)[110] certain members of the heavenly Church whom He intends to be related to the Church Militant in a special way. Recognizing this design, the Church not only presents the Saints to the faithful through the process of canonization as models and intercessors, but she herself directs to the Saints particular cultic acts —for example, Masses in honor of the Saints—and enables the faithful who participate in her cult to live and develop those special relationships which cannot be enjoyed with all the Saints together but which, if consciously exercised, constitute an efficacious aid in living our religious life more fully.

It should then be evident why and in what sense the cult of the Saints, understood and practiced according to the spirit we have described, is a necessary and indispensable element of the Church's theocentric and christocentric cult in so far as it has its origin in the Church's essential constitution.[111] It should be equally evident that those who suggest that the Church Militant can renounce this element and dispense with the teaching, promotion, and practice of the cult of the Saints are guilty of a gross error. Such a suggestion is based—at least implicitly—on the error that this vital association between the Church Militant and Triumphant is nothing but an accidental, marginal, dispensable element.

Now that the necessity of this practice has been established, we must re-emphasize the precise limits of our argument and therefore of the conclusion deduced therefrom. We have demonstrated simply the need for the Church Militant to teach, promote, and practice publicly the cult of the Saints in general and of certain Saints in particular.[112] We have said nothing of the extension which should be accorded this practice, of the intensity with which it should be exercised, of the forms in which it should be ultimately actuated. These further specifications do not depend exclusively on the principles we have explained up to this point, but involve many other circumstantial factors of opportunity and convenience. We must bear in mind that as long as we live on earth we are subject to the laws proper to our present material existence, and, as a consequence, we cannot live and actuate at one and the same time all the aspects which our existence as a part of the total Christ involves, nor can we express in a single act the various elements which, taken together, constitute the complete perfection of the Christian cult. For this reason the cult of the Saints must be practiced by us in distinct acts whose frequency, intensity, and modality are to be regulated by the basic principles explained above and which incorporate the cult of the Saints into our cult of Christ and the Father.

Anyone with a realistic sense of the limitations placed upon the Christian ideal here on earth will not be scandalized by the fact that there are individuals who fail—perhaps because of a lack of instruction—to practice the cult of the Saints according to the ideal we have delineated. Nor will anyone with balanced judgment criticize the Supreme Teaching Authority of the Church, whose prerogative it is to determine the various concrete modalities of public cult, when it refuses to deprive the faithful of an integral element of their religion simply because a practice involves the danger of exaggeration, especially inasmuch as the Church maintains due regard for the concrete circumstances which vary according to times and particular social conditions.

To carry out this delicate task, the Church, guided and assisted by the Holy Spirit who makes evident God's design, continues by means of canonizations to propose for public veneration some Saints in particular and inserts their feasts in the calendar of the universal Church (this entails the celebration of the Holy Sacrifice and the recitation of the Divine Office in their honor). According to various needs and circumstances moreover, the Church favors, promotes, and practices, with a pecular emphasis, the cult of different Saints at different times, because the life and example of these, corresponding in a particular way to specific situations, are considered suitable for establishing intimate rapport between the faithful and the Saints, with a consequent enrichment and spontaneity in the practice of their cult. It is evident that the religious spirit of the faithful will be nourished and sustained through association with persons who lived an heroic and inspiring life in circumstances similar to their own.[113]

In her efforts to promote and practice the cult of certain Saints, however, the Church is always guided by the principle that such a cult must be exercised in so far as it is compatible with and favorable to the basic Christian cult which, as we have already insisted, is totally christocentric and theocentric. From this one can understand why the Church, perceiving that the liturgical cycle representing the temporal sequence of God's saving acts might be overwhelmed and obscured by the multiplication of Saints' feasts, reorganizes the calendar to maintain an equilibrium between the temporal and the sanctoral cycle.[114] One can also understand why, proceeding as always from the principle of the practicality of the cult of the Saints and without in the least detracting from that principle, the Church, according to specific occasions and circumstances, prudently and gradually introduces among the faithful a cult which is directed to certain specific Saints. Thus, for example, in mission lands where the basic foundations of the Christian faith and cult are still being laid, the Church determines in what proportion and with what insistence it is prudent to inculcate and practice the cult of the Saints, and she continues to do so until the formation of the neophytes makes them capable of accepting and incorporating into their Christian cult this further dimension in all its fullness.[115]

Obviously, these considerations which we have proposed with respect to the public cult directed by the Church to the Saints are also applicable to all the other forms, which do not coincide with it but are legitimately practiced as integral parts of it. It is understandable, consequently, that competent ecclesiastical authority, in certain circumstances and places, insists more or less on these other forms of cult and restricts their extension and intensity if it seems opportune to do so.

Having established the need for the Church to practice the cult of the Saints, together with the consequent liberty she enjoys in determining the specific forms this cult may assume, we might observe that the concrete decision made by the Church with respect to actual practice is regulated by the principle of *tantum quantum*.

We have completed our exposition of the first question:

whether and in what measure the cult of the Saints is an indispensable element of the Church's cult, precisely as a liturgical community. Now we may direct our attention to a consideration of the correlative question regarding the cult which individual Christians must direct to the Saints.

The answer we must give is twofold because there are two distinct possibilities open to the Christian as an individual: he can honor the Saints either by participating in the public cult of the Church or in exercises of private piety. In the first instance, it is evident that if a Christian is a minister of the Church, he is obliged in virtue of his priestly function to participate in the cult which the Church, as such, directs both to all the Saints in general and to certain ones in particular, by celebrating the Eucharistic Sacrifice in honor of the Saint whose feast occurs and by reciting the corresponding Divine Office. On the other hand, of a simple Christian we can say that he is obliged to practice the cult of the Saints to the extent that he is obliged to participate actively in the public cult of the Church in all its forms and aspects. Consequently, if a Christian participated in the Church's cultic acts but systematically and deliberately refused to join in those acts directed to the Saints because he considered them superfluous or useless, he would be lacking in a conscious appreciation of the Church's mind, and he would be giving an indication of being under the influence of theologically erroneous ideas.[116]

As for the second question, that of individual personal piety, we cannot assert that private cult of the Saints is necessary for salvation. But we can and must insist that if a Christian who is sufficiently instructed should systematically and deliberately avoid every act towards the Church Triumphant, he would not only be lacking in reverence, courtesy, and charity towards his glorified brethren, but at the same time he would be depriving himself of a precious help and would not be utilizing all the God-given opportunities offered him for mounting up towards God ever more rapidly. He could not, therefore, be considered as exercising the full Christian cult, or earnestly aspiring to perfection.[117]

PART THREE

Reflections on the Extreme Tendencies Encountered in the Cult of the Saints

Our exposition up to this point has presented the theological principles which serve as a foundation for the cult of the Saints and with the aid of these principles explained its nature and the spirit that should inspire it. We are now in a position to reconsider what it was that initially gave rise to our study, namely, the presence of two extreme tendencies: one, minimalistic, that would eliminate entirely, or at least curtail drastically, the cult of the Saints; the other, maximalistic, which is in reality an exaggerated practice of the cult of the Saints. The validity of our initial assertion should be evident by this time: both of these tendencies, though diametrically opposed, stem from a common root, namely, a defective understanding of the genuine spirit of the cult of the Saints. A few additional observations regarding each of these tendencies will give us an opportunity to amplify the foregoing reflections and also enable us to indicate the groundlessness of the arguments advanced against the cult of the Saints.[118]

It might be more appropriate to call these arguments camouflaged attacks, because they are generally advanced "in the name of the liturgy" or "to promote a reunion among Christians." The objections advanced in this indirect and veiled manner are not proposed by qualified promoters or competent advocates of either the liturgical or the ecumenical movement, but by persons whose incompetence is manifested by either their selective use or their distorted application of the data provided by specialists. Such persons, intent on finding support for their cause, fail to appreciate the wisdom and balance of the specialists who present their considered opinions as the fruit of solid and serious studies, and who disapprove of any misinterpretation or extreme exaggeration that fails to take into account all the other elements that enter into and constitute the organic teaching, doctrine, and practice of the Church. We trust that no one will misconstrue our observations as criticism of the proponents of either the liturgical or the ecumenical movement, much less as an attack upon these movements themselves. On the contrary, it is precisely our profound esteem and affection for these two movements that lead us to align ourselves with their authentic proponents, giving whatever assistance we can by combating those attitudes and positions which are assumed "in their name" and serve only to discredit and diminish the serious efforts of those engaged in these enterprises.

In speaking of these attitudes that fall short of the ideal, we will do our utmost to present our position clearly and forcefully and to indicate the faulty bases of these deviations and the fallacies in their argumentation, but our primary intention is not to refute or condemn. This lies beyond our scope and competence. We wish simply to present our reflections as a modest contribution which might eventually enable praiseworthy (though immoderate) enthusiasms to attain their goal more effectively.

I. MINIMALISTIC TENDENCIES

As we begin our consideration of the tendencies opposed to the cult of the Saints, we are well aware that opposition to the devotion is to be attributed, at least in part, to the sad decrease in religious spirit and religious practice in general. We are convinced, however, that this is not the sole cause for the depreciation of the cult of the Saints. As a matter of fact, even among those inspired with a deep sense of religion, there is often discernible a trace of aversion and repugnance for this form of religious practice. Generally speaking, this aversion—rather indefinite and vague—stems from an inadequate appreciation of the nature of the cult of the Saints and, in the final analysis, an ignorance of its close connection with the rich veins from which modern spirituality is drawing its inspiration. We see no reason for delaying further on these attitudes, since we have already demonstrated how such prejudices and aversions are utterly devoid of foundation, when we explained how a spirituality founded on the doctrine of grace and incorporation in Christ becomes more fully integrated and enriched in its christocentric and theocentric movement, to the extent that we realize the relationships existing between ourselves and the pre-eminent members of the Mystical Body.

In other cases, however, the aversion and repugnance seem to find support in certain arguments. Reasons are advanced— not so much in written works as in conversation, and not as an articulated position, but usually in somewhat veiled terms —which allegedly give a kind of respectability to certain attitudes opposed to the cult of the Saints. These arguments are surely alien to the spirit of the Church and in sharp contrast to her teaching and practice. With such reasoned opposition in mind, we consider it useful to dwell briefly on the arguments advanced in order to cast some light on the apparent motives alleged when we are urged to diminish or reject the cult of the Saints.

(*a*) The liturgy and liturgical prayer are invoked by some as arguments against the cult of the Saints. The assertion is made that according to the spirit of the liturgy, one should address oneself to the Father "through Christ, in the Spirit"; consequently, there is no place for the Saints. The liturgy counteracts the evils of individualism and devotionalism, the argument continues; the cult of the Saints nurtures these human weaknesses. Finally, the argument draws additional force from the invitation to "return to the spirit of the primitive Church"; here we are treated to a rather unrestrained attack on the sanctoral cycle and are told that our attention should be focused almost exclusively on the temporal cycle, since this is entirely dedicated to the liturgical celebration of the great mysteries of our faith, and directly related to the person and work of our Saviour.

We have already indicated that such arguments are utterly groundless. It is true that Christ must be the center of our prayer and cult so that we go to the Father "through, with, and in Him." But it is equally true that, if we wish to realize fully the relationship existing between Christ and ourselves by reason of our incorporation into His Mystical Body, we must realize our relationship with the other members of this Body, especially its pre-eminent members. If, under the pretext of defending the truth that our religious movement must be "to Christ" and in Him "to the Father," we seek to reject and abolish relationships with other members of the Mystical Body of Christ, we will succeed only in rendering a disservice to the very movement we wish to promote. If we bear in mind what we have elaborated above, it should be evident that the cult of the Saints, practiced according to the true spirit advocated by the Church, not only does not impede christocentrism and theocentricism, but actually enriches and amplifies it.

In view of this, we see how pointless is the objection that would eliminate the cult of the Saints as an expression of particularism and individualism. From what we have already stated, it is evident that when one recognizes who the Saints are and the bonds that join us to them, entering into relationship with them does not foster individualism but rather a consciousness of the social bonds and solidarity existing among the members. This relationship with the Saints is precisely what brings us to an appreciation of the richness and beauty of our movement towards Christ and, in Him, to the Father, in union with the other members of the Mystical Body.

When we pass on to an appeal to the Christianity of the first centuries, which some make in order to promote a spirituality in which the Saints would no longer occupy a prominent position, we may reply to them simply by recalling the objective historical facts. It was precisely in the Primitive Church that the cult of the Saints began, and from the first days of the nascent Church it was closely associated with the Eucharistic Sacrifice.

All the elements that determine and constitute the cult of

the Saints—the motives that induce us to practice it, the very limitations deriving from its nature—are precisely those that inspired, animated, sustained and regulated the cult of the Saints by the Church from its very origin. A retrospective glance at the historical development of this religious manifestation will provide ample confirmation of this claim.

It was precisely the awareness, on the part of the Faithful, of the intimate union between Christ and the Martyrs that led Christians who were still suffering persecution to turn to the Martyrs and ask for their intercession to obtain from God the grace to imitate them in their integral and intrepid profession of the faith.

The cult of the Saints which originated and developed in the heart of the primitive Church was based on the conviction that the Saints could intercede for us. The foundation for this conviction was multiple: the certainty of the eternal life in Christ which the Martyrs had merited through the sufferings they had admirably sustained; the knowledge that they were holy and perfect because they had given the greatest proof of love by sacrificing their life through Christ;[119] recognition of the fact that they were friends of Christ, now closer to Him than when they walked the earth.[120] These principles provide us with an explanation of the celebrations held each year, not on the day of one's temporal birth in the manner of the pagan observance, but on the anniversary day of the martyrdom which was the date of a Christian's heavenly birth; for this reason the celebrations have the character of a feast and not of mourning.[121] They explain too the extensive introduction of their commemoration into the Eucharistic Sacrifice, the prayers and invocations addressed to the Martyrs, and, in brief, the various manifestations of authentic cult. This cult, we might note, was not only private but public as well because recognized, accepted and incorporated by the Church into her glorification of Christ and of the Father. As the cult of the Martyrs developed and expanded by being extended to include the "Confessors of the Faith" and afterwards those Saints who, though not martyrs, had borne witness to the teaching of Christ by the exemplary spiritual lives they had lived so heroically,[122] the Church confirmed the practice. On various occasions, confronted by the accusation that the faithful were guilty of idolatry or falsification of true religion, the Church emphasized the clear distinction between the worship due to God alone and the honor paid to the Martyrs and Saints in general. In the course of the passing centuries, confronted by deviations and distortions of genuine devotion that appeared here and there among the faithful, bishops and doctors who were trying to illuminate and clarify the practice admonished the faithful so that they might reduce the cult of the Saints to its proper proportions and practice it according to its true spirit.

It would not be difficult to substantiate this fact by amassing documentary testimony from Christian antiquity. What would become evident is that neither the possibility of danger nor the actual presence of errors and distortions ever occasioned in the mind of the Church the thought of suppressing the cult of the Saints or of reacting violently against this form of devotion. In fact, such dangers and distortions served only as an occasion for clear, calm exposition which endeavored to explain the difference between divine worship and cult of the Saints. In making this distinction, many doctors of the Church took the opportunity to include a fervent exhortation to the faithful to venerate the Saints and put forward clear explanations of both the licitness and the suitability of their cult. To cite a single but significant example of this attitude— one both theologically profound and pastorally balanced—we might point to the many sermons delivered by St. Augustine

on the occasion of the feasts of the Martyrs.[123] Occasionally
the holy doctor felt compelled to impress on his congregation
the limits of the cult directed to the Saints, as for example in
his sermon *"In Natali Martyrum Fructuosi episcopi, Augurii
et Eulogii diaconorum"* (On the Feast day of the Martyrs
Fructuosus, Bishop, and the Deacons, Augurius and Eulogius).[124] But this should not lead us to think—as some have
asserted[125]—that his teaching was limited to such negative
admonitions and limitations; for St. Augustine, in full harmony
with the teaching and practices of his time, was a fervent advocate of what we have come to call the cult of the Saints.
The celebrated Bollandist, H. Delehaye, writing on the invocation of the Martyrs in ancient times, calls our attention to this
aspect of St. Augustine's doctrine:

If additional proof is necessary, we might cite St. Augustine, a
staunch supporter of devotion to the Martyrs, both in his epis-
copal instructions and in his literary works. In these writings,
accounts of favors obtained through the intercession of the Saints,
as well as exhortations delivered on their feast days, occupy a
noteworthy position. The holy Doctor makes a clear distinction
between the Martyrs and the rest of the faithful: "The sanctification of the Martyrs is completed. In virtue of their sacrificial
deaths they have reached the summit of perfection. For this
reason, the Church does not offer prayers on their behalf. She
prays for the rest of the Faithful, but not for the Martyrs; for
they have departed from this world with such a high degree of
perfection that instead of being in need of our assistance, they
are actually in a position to assist us." (Sermon CCLXXXV, 5,
P.L. vol. 38, col. 1295)[126]

For St. Augustine it was evident that we must manifest our
admiration for those who have suffered martyrdom, express
our gratitude to those who pray for us, recommend our needs
to those who intercede for us:

We ourselves are the fruit of their labor. While we admire them, they have compassion on us; we rejoice with them and they in turn pray for us.[127]

Thus did the Saint express his thought quite simply. He then went on to develop it:

The Church does not pray for such as these. With good reason the Church prays for all other deceased members, but rather than pray for the Martyrs she commends herself to their prayers.[128]

To explain why it is that the honor which the faithful pay to the Martyrs does not detract from the honor paid to God, St. Augustine observed that we take nothing away from the praise due to God when we extoll the labors and struggles He has sustained in those who bear His insignia:

For we do not stop praising God when we praise His works and marvel at the struggles in which He engaged in the persons of His dedicated soldiers.[129]

In a beautiful text which we delight in citing because it provides an answer to much perplexity and to many of the objections advanced today, the great doctor draws upon the doctrine of the Mystical Body. While maintaining clearly that there is but one intercessor, Christ Jesus, he insists that the Martyrs, in virtue of their union with Him, are true intercessors without in the least obscuring the intercessory power of Christ, in much the same way that Christ's role as unique Pastor does not impede Peter and the Apostles from being true shepherds:

We pray for all the other faithful departed but not for the Martyrs; for they have departed from this world with such a high degree of perfection that instead of being in need of our assistance, they are in a position to assist us. Their role as our advocates, however, is not based on their own personal power, but on that Person to Whom they adhere as perfect members are joined to their head. He is in truth the unique advocate who intercedes for us (1 Jn. 2), seated at the right hand of the Father (Rom. 8.34); but He is the unique Advocate in the same sense that He is the unique Pastor. As He Himself said, "I must reunite those sheep who are not of this fold" (Jn. 10.16). If Christ is Shepherd, must we say that Peter is not a shepherd? Of course, Peter is a shepherd as the rest of them are—shepherds indeed. If he be not shepherd, how could Our Lord have directed to him the words "Feed my lambs" (Jn. 16.17)? Yet it is he who feeds the sheep who is the true shepherd. That is why Our Lord did not say to Peter "Feed *thy* sheep" but rather "*my* sheep." Peter is, then, not a shepherd in his own right or by his own power but only in so far as he is *in* the shepherd.[130]

With these clarifications in mind let us return to the alleged opposition existing between the temporal and the sanctoral cycles which we have referred to above.[131] We must admit that in certain periods, with the multiplication of feasts in honor of the Saints, their cycle tended to be superimposed on the temporal cycle, which, because of its singular importance, should always be preserved in full vigor. But if we may repeat our earlier observation, the Church alone has the authority to re-establish the former equilibrium between the two cycles by reorganizing the calendar of the liturgical celebrations. In fact, the Church has exercised this prerogative on various occasions, as evidenced by the recent revision. It is up to the Church, which is always solely guided by the realistic and total vision of the good of the faithful, to make opportune revisions; certainly the individual priest cannot take it upon himself to modify, in accord with his own judgment or pleasure, the order which the Church herself has prescribed for her official prayer. In the theoretical discussions revolving around this point, it would be advisable and even necessary to appraise at full value the contribution which a wholesome cult of the Saints makes to the Church's life, rather than, as sometimes happens, assume a hostile position of disdain towards those who practice this cult. It may well be that these latter are being guided by a profound practical penetration of the truths of the faith, and thus perceive something which is never perceived by those who—perhaps under the appearance of culture or owing to a dogmatic puritanism—labor under a serious ignorance of the basic implications of our faith.

We have been emphasizing the relationship between the cult of the Saints and the Church's liturgical prayer by indicating how the Church develops and encourages a social sense even in prayer. It might be well in this context to recall that liturgical prayer, though it is the highest and noblest expression of man's contact with God, does not constitute the totality of man's prayer. It does not exhaust the possibilities which the faithful have of entering into contact with the world beyond; for they may establish this relationship also by private prayer, which always retains its value and necessity.[132] Now it is certainly proper in this form of prayer for an individual person who is also moved and guided by the Spirit of Christ as an individual to make use of his personal liberty and follow those particular inclinations and inspirations of grace that lead him to develop a relationship of deep friendship with one Saint or another.

(*b*) A second group of opponents are those who have recourse to the legitimate principle that our spiritual life must be based on the word of God and therefore on Sacred Scripture. They press their point to an extreme, however, when they assert that the cult of the Saints must be reduced to minimal proportions if not totally rejected, inasmuch as nothing is said of this practice in the sacred writings. Naturally, we cannot deny the truth of the assertion that nothing is said explicitly in Sacred Scripture about the cult of the Saints as such; but, on the other hand, we cannot overlook the fact that it is precisely in the Bible that we find the foundation stones for this practice. Can anyone deny that the doctrine of the Mystical Body and of our incorporation in Christ, on which, as we have seen, a sound theological conception of the Saints and their cult is based, runs like a rich vein throughout the writings of both St. Paul and St. John? Moreover, the first Christians, nourishing their spiritual and cultural life on Sacred Scripture, understood and lived this doctrine of the union of the faithful with Christ and among themselves. Did not they, drawing the logical consequence of this doctrine, venerate and love the Saints as friends and co-workers of Christ, as intercessors and benefactors of those who still are engaged in their earthly struggle? These early Christians, basing their lives on the teachings of the Bible, experienced no difficulty in harmonizing the cult and veneration of the Saints with the teaching contained in the inspired writings. On the contrary, they found in the truths proposed by the Bible—belief in Christ, belief in the union existing among the faithful, belief in immortality—the principal foundations for a profound and sincere cult of the Saints. It seems somewhat strange, and yet apparently it is necessary, to recall that the principle "Scripture alone" cannot and must not be applied to this subject any more than to any other religious question. Tradition and the teaching of the Church, which interpret authoritatively the contents of Sacred Scripture, constitute a safe and infallible guide for action and prayer according to the Church's true spirit.

(*c*) A third source of difficulty and repugnance for some Catholics in discussing and defending the cult of the Saints is the fact that many non-Catholics do not accept this doctrine. The argument is advanced that insistence on this doctrine and practice, proper to the Catholic Church, presents an obstacle to achieving that unity among Christians which everyone so ardently desires.

Humanly speaking, it is quite understandable that in our contemporary atmosphere, in which the dominant note is that of doing everything that can draw separated brethren closer together, the desire should arise to avoid every abuse and exaggeration in devotion to the Saints which could constitute an occasion of scandal for our separated brothers—obviously a praiseworthy and desirable ideal; it is also understandable that some people should wish, for the sake of reunion, to reduce this cult to a minimum and not to insist on this aspect of Catholic piety. It is difficult, however, to understand how some Catholics can go beyond this present irenic ideal and excoriate (in unqualified terms) abuses in devotion to the Saints current at the time of the Protestant revolt and lingering on even afterwards. They portray the Reformers' opposition to this cult as if it were in every respect a healthy reaction dictated by authentic religious feeling, and consequently (with an agility that not only betrays superficiality but also reveals a lack of charity and a feeling of disdain) they refer to the cult of the Saints as a typical product of a shallow religiosity, characterized derisively as "southern," or "Latin."[133] What is more serious, in discussing this question of the cult of the Saints some feel constrained, when confronted by those who will not recognize the legitimacy of the practice, to apologize for the existence of such a manifestation within the life of the Church; to show themselves conciliatory and understanding, they stress solely the fact that the cult of the Saints is not necessary for salvation and present it as an accidental, marginal element of Christian piety which can, therefore, be dispensed with.

We acknowledge how, humanly speaking, such attitudes

as these can arise, and we recognize the zeal which dictates them as proceeding from the noble desire to promote union among Christians. We know, on the other hand, that our zeal must be guided by discretion and prudence, which are the sublime fruits of "truth in charity" and "charity in truth." We might ask, then, whether such a conciliatory frame of mind and mode of action do justice to the historical and dogmatic truth and whether they are inspired and sustained by that fullness of charity which must be the characteristic note of our love not only towards the Church but also towards our separated brethren?

Our reply to this question is, and unfortunatly must be, negative. To present a picture of Catholic spirituality at the time of the Protestant revolt painted solely in dark hues is an exaggeration and an injustice to objective historical reality. It is simply false to describe the complex situation of that period in terms of black and white. And it is especially erroneous to think that the opposition of the Reformers to the cult of the Saints (understood in its full integral sense, which includes invocation of the Saints as intercessors) had as its sole or primary reason the abuses which existed here and there.[134] It is patently evident from the writings of the Reformers themselves that their motive was much more deeply rooted. Abuses, to be sure, played a certain role, but they were used as an occasion to give currency to the basic principles of Protestantism, namely Scripture alone as the source of revelation and a novel interpretation of the dogma of Jesus Christ as sole Mediator.

A thorough historical and dogmatic analysis of the Reformers' attitude towards the cult of the Saints can never prescind from their teaching on justification and merit, their christological conceptions, and their ideas on the nature and function of the Church. Their notion of the Church in particular dif-

fered considerably from the Catholic conception, which recognizes in her a supernatural social and juridical organism, the
true Mystical Body of Christ. Their attitude towards the cult
of the Saints had its roots in the very interpretation they gave
to Christian revelation, and therefore it was much more than
a simple policy dictated by pastoral concern or a pure reaction
stemming from an authentic religious feeling, opposed to deviations and abuses prevalent in the way in which the Catholic
cult was practiced here and there.

Now, can we truthfully say that the difference which then
existed on basic points of doctrine and theological methodol-
ogy (namely, christology, redemption, internal justification,
merit, incorporation in Christ, structure of the Church, etc.)
have been removed, so that we now have a common acceptance of the same basic truths? Since, unfortunately, we know
that such profound doctrinal differences still exist, we may be
sure that corresponding differences also exist in the area pertaining to the Saints and their cult; for, as we have demonstrated, the doctrine and practice of the Catholic cult of the
Saints are not isolated elements standing by themselves, but
are immediate and logical consequences of the total composite
of Catholic dogma. It is evident, then, that the diversity of
opinion prevalent among non-Catholics respecting this tenet
of our faith and its subsequent rejection is not to be considered
simply the fruit of some vague feeling, but rather something
which involves and manifests the existence of a diversity of
dogmatic conceptions whose purport is much deeper and more
fundamental. Accordingly, one might say that the acceptance
on the part of a Protestant theologian of the Catholic teaching
and practice of the cult of the Saints would constitute a valuable and most significant indication that there has been a
genuine rapprochement in the area of the dogmatic truths
which serve as the foundation for the practice. In view, then,

of the general contemporary situation in the realm of doctrine, even though we note a revival of interest in the Saints among certain sections of the Protestant world, we should not be surprised when we learn somewhat sorrowfully that the acceptance of the truth of the intercessory function of the Saints and of the licitness and fittingness of petition directed to them is still far from the minds of even the best-disposed Protestants, so that the very mention of Saints and their cult usually evokes a negative reaction.

Now that we have made these clarifications necessary for a comprehensive and realistic view of the *de facto* situation, we are in a position to appraise more objectively the opportuneness of the course of action advocated by certain Catholics. Well-intentioned though they be, in our opinion they have failed to appreciate fully the facts we have noted above. From their limited perspective they would like to see the cult of the Saints reduced to truly minimal proportions and advocate a belittling of its importance to avoid offending the feelings of those who do not accept the doctrine. These Catholics fail to perceive that in so doing they would be rendering a disservice to the very cause of unity among Christians; for such unity can be attained only when it is based on a full acceptance of all the truths contained in our Lord's teaching. In treating the question of the necessity of the cult of the Saints, we demonstrated that the Church can never renounce this doctrine. We acknowledged that the modality, intensity, and proportions that should enter into the practice of the cult do not follow a fixed rule but must be left to the prudent judgment of the Church, which must determine the advisability of a greater or lesser emphasis. But we certainly did not mean to imply that such flexibility could be construed as an avenue for concessions so radical as those advocated by persons quite ready to relinquish (at least in the practical order) the cult of the

Saints. Would not such concessions and consequent restrictions in the exercise of this cult result in an impoverishment of the fullness of our worship of Christ and the Father corresponding to our integral faith? Could one really justify the sacrifice of this religious element? Would it really serve as an inducement for others to accept the full riches of our faith, or would it not rather be an arbitrary deprivation of something which God Himself intends to offer man and wants him to accept in order to achieve a fuller share of life in Christ? If we were to make the concessions advocated, adducing motives that seem to justify such a course, would we not be failing in the mission Christ entrusted to us to let the light shine forth—not just a few rays, but the full light in all its integrity? Our very sincerity, the very love and respect we have for our non-Catholic brethren, demand that we do not conceal or fear to bear witness to what we believe to be the teaching of Jesus Christ. In our opinion, it seems imperative that we emphasize that the decisive criterion in this matter must be the full and open confession of our integral faith, without the least trace of arrogance, certainly, but also without any shadow of fear or human respect that might induce us to conceal what must not be concealed. Our aim must be the greater good of the Church and the deeper realization of that glory which the Church can offer to Christ and, in Him, to the Father. It is our sincere conviction that the rich vitality of the Church and the full exercise of its activity will in the long run concretely, securely, and effectively prepare the way to union of all Christians in the acceptance of the total truth taught by Christ.[135]

In fact, the Church as a teacher, assisted and guided by the Holy Spirit, has always been conscious of her responsibility to defend and spread revealed truth, and thus procure the greatest spiritual good for her children. Throughout the centuries, she has always authoritatively and unequivocally taught the licitness and fittingness of paying honor to the Saints, and has refuted the error of those who denied or doubted this doctrine directly or indirectly. We do not wish to spend time in a lengthy consideration of the numerous liturgical texts which explicitly pronounce, implicitly contain, or merely pre-suppose the doctrine of the cult of the Saints. Let it suffice to recall that the Catholic teaching on the cult of the Saints —including the practice of directing our prayers to them— was already contained in the document promulgated on the occasion of the first canonization which can be attributed with certainty to papal authority.[136] To this could be added all the official documents emanating from the Supreme Teaching Authority on the occasion of numerous canonizations and beatifications over the years, as well as the official declarations whereby the Church rose *ex professo* to the defense of these truths when they were expressly attacked; (cf. the documents referring to images and relics of the Saints[137] and the propositions of Molinos).[138] Or we might refer simply to the most solemn explicit declaration relevant to our argument, that made at the Council of Trent,[139] namely, the decree "On the Invocation, Veneration, and Relics of the Saints and on Sacred Images":

The holy council orders all bishops and others who have official charge of teaching to instruct the faithful diligently, in accordance with the practice of the Catholic and apostolic Church from the early years of the Christian religion, and in accordance with the common teaching of the holy Fathers and the decrees of the sacred councils. First of all they should instruct the faithful carefully concerning the intercession and the invocation of the saints, the honor due to their relics, and the lawful use of images— teaching the faithful that the saints, reigning together with Christ, pray to God for men; it is a good and useful thing to invoke the saints humbly and to have recourse to their prayers and to their efficacious help to obtain favors from God through his Son Jesus Christ our Lord who alone is our redeemer and saviour. Moreover, they should teach the faithful that only men of irreligious mentality deny that the saints enjoying eternal happiness in heaven are to be invoked; or claim either that saints do not pray for men or else that calling upon them to pray for us even as individuals is idolatry or is opposed to the word of God and is prejudicial to the honor of the one Mediator of God and men, Jesus Christ (see I Tim. 2.5); or say that it is foolish to make supplication by word or by thought to those who are reigning in heaven.[140]

Since this is the clear and immutable teaching of the Church, any attempt to minimize it in the dialogues with our separated brethren would be illicit.[141] It would moreover be not only erroneous but also detrimental to pass over the doctrine in silence or diminish it to the point of saying that its practice is not necessary for salvation.[142] As long as the differences of opinion on doctrine remain, the only truly honest attitude, the only attitude inspired by an enlightened charity and therefore the only attitude positively conducive to unity, would be that which advocates a clear exposition of our doctrine. With all respect to our separated brothers, we must explain calmly how the Catholic interpretation of revelation according to the cult of the Saints is a direct consequence of our redemption and incorporation in Christ. In this way we will succeed in making them understand that the honor paid to the Saints, created persons though they be, is directed to them as mystical members of Christ, so that this cult is an integral element of our worship of Christ Himself and of the adoration offered to the Father "in Him, through Him, and with Him." We will present a clear dogmatic and theological exposition of the cult of the Saints, in reference to its ultimate foundations, only if we succeed in dispelling existing misunderstandings and prejudices. We must convey the idea that the

Church practices this cult precisely because it does not clash with the worship of Christ and of the Father, but rather renders that worship fuller and more integral; for, according to the Catholic conception, the Saints are not paragons of purely natural will-power—not heroes placed on a level with Christ—but persons who live in Him and by His life, so that in honoring them we honor Him.[143]

It would not be out of place, in the present context, to utilize the principles already developed in order to indicate how the acts by which we honor the Saints are differentiated from those whereby we worship God. Our intention is to give a concrete illustration of how one can render the necessary service we mentioned above of presenting the Catholic position integrally but irenically, thereby providing the light that dissipates clouds of misunderstanding and ignorance. When the question of honoring the Saints comes up, Catholics are frequently accused of practicing an illicit form of cult, of paying to the Saints what is due to God alone. In our opinion, however, any well-disposed person willing to dwell upon the significance of the comparison we are going to make will be able to appraise Catholic practices at their true value and realize that the acts directed to the Saints differ essentially from, and are subordinate to, those directed to God. Appreciation of this distinction will pave the way for an elimination of unfounded prejudice. Throughout the centuries, and especially since the sixteenth, this charge has been leveled at Catholics time and again, and this explains why so many doctors of the Church and Catholic theologians have treated the subject in their writings. They have bequeathed to us a vast legacy of commentaries, enabling us to adduce numerous citations and quotations from famous doctors and Catholic controversialists whose apologetic and expository treatises touched upon every aspect of the theological significance of honoring the Saints.[144]

COMPARISON BETWEEN THE ACTS OF
WORSHIP DIRECTED TO GOD AND THE
HONOR PAID TO THE SAINTS

The acts of worship directed to God

A Christian's religious attitude towards God is conditioned
by his knowledge of Him. This includes the recognition that
God is his Creator and Father in Christ and an awareness of
His transcendent majesty and excellence, crowned by a goodness that has no limits. The Christian realizes that God is in
fact the fullness of being, subsistent perfection, eternal and absolute value, self-sufficient life who receives nothing from anyone but gives everything to all that exists outside of Himself.
In the light of faith, moreover, the Christian knows that God
not only gives him life but has created him in order to communicate to him a new and far more marvelous life, to make
him a participant in His very own personal trinitarian life, as
a member of the Mystical Body of Christ, the Word Incarnate.

This recognition of the excellence of God's transcendent
majesty and of His paternal goodness serves as the foundation
for all the acts of worship paid to God.[145] We have said "serves
as the foundation" because it is evident that this recognition
is an interior summons, an invitation to that which such knowledge implicitly calls for and demands, but it does not in itself
constitute a response. Once a person is aware of God's greatness, he is still faced with the challenge of entering into a
personal relationship with Him in order to acknowledge His
infinite excellence and to accept the consequences which derive
therefrom. In the presence of God's transcendent majesty and
infinite goodness manifested in the mystery of the Incarnation,
man feels duty-bound to express his limitless admiration in a
spirit of faith, hope, and love; to praise, reverence, and thank

God by surrendering himself without reserve to His every wish, "through Christ, with Christ, and in Christ." But since man is aware also of his contingency and insufficiency, he is aware at the same time of a need to turn to God and beg for assistance, to implore "through, with, and in Christ," the grace to live as a true son of God.

This schematic exposition of our religious attitude towards God, Creator and Father in Christ Jesus, is sufficient to demonstrate how it differs from our religious attitude towards the Saints. We will follow the same line of development, casting into bolder relief the points of similarity and contrast.

The acts of cult paid to the Saints

Just as a recognition of God's excellence is the primary condition and foundation for the worship we pay Him, so too an awareness of the Saints' greatness is the basis for the honor rendered them;[146] for such an awareness is based on the appreciation we have of their excellence, which is radically of a religious character.[147] A Christian knows (or should know) that the excellence of the Saints consists in the degree of intensity and the depth of their incorporation into the humanity of Christ, which enables them to share as pre-eminent members in His theocentric life.[148] For this reason, the Christian is well aware that the excellence and perfection of the Saints is limited, participated, totally dependent from start to finish upon Him who freely offers and communicates His supernatural life. The Christian knows moreover that such greatness is the fruit of the gracious invitation and activity of God in Christ, joined to heroic correspondence on the Saints' part. He knows that it is the result of the work of God, who begins, continues and crowns it "through, with and in Christ," combined with the collaboration of those created persons who correspond with divine grace. In brief, when a Christian honors a Saint, he knows that he is in the presence of a created person whose greatness and excellence evoke an expression of admiration; but at the same time, he knows that the excellence in question is a supernatural and participated greatness, and therefore of itself mirrors back all honor and glory to its ultimate source, Christ and the Father.

These two aspects in the recognition of a Saint's excellence will necessarily also be present, because of their mutual and organic connection, in every authentic act consequent upon the recognition of such greatness. Even in those acts, therefore, in which our attention is focused on the persons of the Saints and on the heroism with which they responded to God's invitation, we turn to them as glorious *created* persons. We give expression to our reverent love, admiration, and gratitude for benefits conferred through their merits, and we recommend ourselves to their intercessory power so that we may realize our desire to follow in their footsteps; but we recognize always that they are creatures dependent upon God, the source of all good.

In these acts, therefore, we never pass over the supernatural element: it is God who has elevated the Saints to such a high level of excellence "through, with, and in Christ." In the Church's public expression of her cult of the Saints, which is subject to her closest scrutiny and direction, it is patently clear that direct recourse to the Saints is never indulged in as a manifestation of honor and admiration for an autonomous and independent excellence, on a par with that of God.[149] On the contrary, there is always question of recognizing an excellence which derives ultimately from God, whose ever-present grace, communicated through and in Christ, has lifted the Saints to a sublime union with God and made them His co-workers.

Similarly, when we turn to the Saints and implore their

assistance, an authentic cult does not conceive this relationship as if the Saints could help us through their own power and authority, even though we invoke their help so that they will obtain from God, through Christ, whatever is necessary or suitable.

Thus then we pray to God as the principal author of grace and glory, and of all the gifts that lead thereto, and as the first cause (and in a certain sense as the true and proper cause) of every good granted us in answer to our prayer, as we explained in the preceding chapter. We do not, however, pray to the Saints in this way; rather, we turn to them so that they may act as intercessors before God and pray for us. The Church has always observed and maintained this difference and wished to teach it to us in the very litany of the Saints: while she prays to the Divine Persons with the invocation *miserere nobis* (have mercy on us), she addresses Mary and the Saints with the words *ora pro nobis* (pray for us). In like manner, when in the Mass or during a public prayer she asks for something through the Saints, she addresses her request directly to God through the merits of the Saints. At times she asks of God Himself that some Saint may intercede for us; in the prayer on the feast of St. Luke, for example, the Church prays: *Interveniat pro nobis, quaesumus, Domine, Sanctus tuus Lucas Evangelista,* etc. (May St. Luke, your evangelist, intercede for us, we beg, Lord.)

Prayer addressed to the Saints with the spirit approved by the Church, does not contain anything resembling the *latria* (worship) due to God. This is evident because when we pray properly we do not subject ourselves to a Saint, as to our Creator or First Principle of everything; nor do we attribute to him anything that exceeds his dignity or power, because we do nothing more than request the help of his intercession, which is clearly within the scope of his power and proper to his condition. In fact, if we ourselves can pray for others, should we marvel at the fact that the Saints can do this more effectively? To indicate the difference in such prayers, it is customary to cite the words of Ps. 120: *Levavi oculos in montes, unde veniet auxilium mihi*—"I have lifted my eyes unto the hills (the Saints) whence cometh the help of the Lord," namely, through their intercession, because *auxilium meum a Domino, qui fecit coelum et terram*—"our help is from the Lord, who created heaven and earth." Thus does Augustine write in treating this passage, and in his first commentary on John, and still again in his book "On the Shepherds," chapter eight.[150]

It is certain, then, that the Catholic Church honors the Saints with acts of cult and that she praises, honors, thanks, and petitions both God and the Saints. But it is equally certain that in each instance her acts are motivated by a profoundly different spirit: we turn to God because of His transcendent, uncreated, infinite excellence; we address the Saints because of their participated, created, and limited excellence. Accordingly, though the same words of praise, honor, supplication and cult are used in each case, they are employed not in a univocal but in an analogous sense. In our encounters with God, our attitude is one of adoration, or the cult of *latria*[151]— one of total submission and absolute dependence; in our associations with the Saints, our attitude will be one of *dulia*[152] —of reverent supplication dynamically subordinated to the worship of God.[153]

An awareness of this substantial difference and of the total dependence of the Saints on God in Christ will assure that an act in which praise and honor for the Saints is manifested will never be confused or equated with the cult due to God; for every act will contain, at least implicitly, a reference to God and therefore recognition of His supreme excellence, which is cast into even bolder relief.[154] The consequence of such awareness will be that acts in which we express confidence that we shall receive assistance through the intercession of the Saints will not be opposed in any way to the prayers whereby we appeal to the merits of Christ; rather they will contain a reference to Him, the unique Mediator, and will make us even more conscious of the conviction that God gives us all things through Christ.[155]

The Saints are not our immediate intercessors before God; rather, everything that they ask of God on our behalf is asked through the power of Christ. In our prayer to God, three persons play a role: first, God Himself from whom we ask the blessing; secondly, Christ through whose merits we hope that the object of our desires will be granted; thirdly, the Saint who intercedes for us through Christ. As we have already demonstrated, a Saint cannot exercise either of the first two functions, but only the third. For this reason, when we invoke the Saints we do so with the intention that they will do what we ourselves can do as human persons. Why then do we bother to invoke them? Because their prayers are better and more effective than ours, better they and we together than ourselves alone.

We now come to the proof of the conclusion. Christ alone reconciled the world to God, Christ alone merited for us grace and glory and everything necessary for our salvation, as is evident from the Epistle to the Colossians 1: *Quia in ipso complacuit, omnem plenitudinem inhabitare, et per eum reconciliare omnia in ipsum, pacificans per sanguinem crucis eius, sive quae in terris, sive quae in caelis sunt.* (It was God's good pleasure to let all completeness dwell in him, and through him to win back all things, whether on earth or in heaven, into union with himself, making peace with them through his blood, shed on the cross), and the first Epistle of John: *Ipse est propitiatio pro peccatis nostris, non pro nostris autem tantum sed etiam pro totius mundi.* (He, in his own person, is the atonement made for our sins, and not only for ours, but for the sins of the whole world.) "For this reason Christ is called a *gateway* (Jn. 10) and a pathway (Jn. 14), because, as He Himself said, no one goes to the Father except through Him. He is called *mediator between God and man* (I Tim. 2) and in I Jn. 2, our *advocate in the presence of the Father*. Accordingly, we can ask of the Saints nothing more than that they intercede before God in order that the merits of Christ may be applied to us and that we may attain grace and glory through those merits of Christ.[156]

In other words, every act of cult offered to the Saints, though directed to them as persons, is in reality a new way to make explicit and conscious our conviction of God's greatness and Christ's universal mediation. Inasmuch as such a conviction will lead to acts acknowledging this greatness and mediation, it will increase the intensity of our theocentric cult in Christ.

This brief analysis and comparison will enable us to draw the conclusion that the authentic cult of the Saints not only does not detract or divert from a theocentric and christocentric orientation, but actually re-enforces and emphasizes this proper orientation of Christian cult:

If then we invoke the Saints in this way, such invocation not only does not obscure the glory of Christ our Lord and Saviour, but actually makes it more resplendent and extolls it ever more. The unique power and glory of Christ the Redeemer not only shines forth in Himself, but also is powerfully and marvellously manifested in His Saints, in so far as He Himself honors them and wants them to be honored on earth and in heaven. Through them and because of them God grants blessings and pardon to persons who have not merited such favors, as happened, for example, in the case of Abraham, Isaac, Jacob, David, and Jeremias of whom we read that—though they had departed this life—they were of assistance to the living. For this reason, when the Fathers speak of the Saints, they frequently refer to them as our patrons and supporting intercessors; and rightly so, because experience dem-

onstrates how precious is the help which the Saints give those
who invoke them humbly and devoutly in Christ.

In the Church of old, devotion to the Saints was as constant a
practice as it is today, because it is a doctrine transmitted to us
from hand to hand, praised by the sacred synods and the harmonious accord of the Fathers and confirmed by the example of
the faithful. Catholics adhere to this teaching even though it is
displeasing to the followers of Vigilantius, who already stand
condemned before the tribunal of history.[157]

(*d*) The final major difficulty which we must consider is
that deriving from the fact that the cult of the Saints consists
in a complex of religious acts directed to created human persons rather than to God. Many are acutely aware of this difficulty, which seems to be, at least in part, historically and
doctrinally linked to the rise and spread of Protestantism and
to the influence it exercised on Western religious thought. It
is particularly troublesome to those engaged in ecumenical
activities who are tending to minimize the cult of the Saints
as if it were a manifestation of a more primitive and less spiritual religious practice.

Confronted by this problem many good Catholics—in fact,
conscientious Catholics especially—experience a certain discomfort. The roots of this uneasiness are buried deep in their
religious training: they have been accustomed to think of God
as the Supreme Being, the Creator hermetically sealed and
separated from the world, and of creatures as contingent realities far removed from Him, vitiated by sin, lacking any value
in themselves, impediments rather than aids to our progress
towards God. Frequently even those who accept Catholic
teaching in its totality and live their faith with enthusiasm feel
somewhat at a loss because of this unconscious thought pattern. They are perplexed by the difficulty of reconciling the

cult of the Saints with the worship of God in such a way that in honoring the Saints they will not be taking anything away from God. Why, they ask themselves, must we seek the friendship and assistance of the Saints and give our love to those created human persons? Is it not enough to love God, cultivate His friendship, and invoke His help?

Some, in a rather superficial manner, would solve the problem through a practical expedient whereby we would no longer acknowledge any intrinsic value in the Saints, not even a created and dependent one, but would regard them instead as simple receptacles in whom God is present as in tabernacles or ciboria. In this view, the acts which, in terms of the authentic Catholic conception of the cult of the Saints, should be directed to them will be referred to God Himself present in them and worthy of adoration. Since then the cult of *dulia* would no longer have human, created persons, living and vital members of the Mystical Body of Christ, as its proper immediate term, it would quite simply be transformed into, and blended with, the *latreutic* cult of God present and working in His Saints. The consideration of the Saints as persons would then be reduced to a simple form of admiration manifested concretely in the desire to imitate their example.

In my opinion such a viewpoint and the course of action it proposes fails to correspond to the true Christian vision. Anyone who is living our faith in its fullness indeed recognizes the transcendent grandeur of God; but this does not prevent him from recognizing and appreciating the intrinsic value of the world and of creatures, because he is able to perceive and embrace God in the world, in His works, in man, and among men. He can find God in all things, especially in the Saints. We must be conscious of the dependence and frailty of creatures; we must believe in the reality of original sin and its dire consequences; we must be aware of the dangers of the "world" —a world alienated from God. But we must believe also that Christ has redeemed the world and humanity; that the consequences of His Redemption are already present in time; that His Mystical Body is a living reality already present here on earth, and that the grace of Christ has already triumphed magnificently in those of His members now in glory, the Saints. This is the reason why we have maintained that the genuine Catholic spirit refuses to undervalue—much less, disparage—that created reality which is willed, esteemed, and loved by God Himself, a reality redeemed by the blood of God-made-man. It is therefore wrong not to recognize in this created reality an authentic intrinsic religious value and hence to exclude it entirely from what constitutes our relationship with God. Karl Rahner's observation penetrates to the heart of the matter:

Today we are running the risk of venerating God (or at least of wishing to do so) while excluding the world from our religious practice because we consider it as practically devoid of God and estranged from Him. It would be more proper for Christians, on the contrary, to have a reverent attitude towards the world as something willed and loved by God, in a manner corresponding to the hierarchy of that very love of which it is the object on God's part. We should reverence the world, therefore, with a genuine religious spirit, especially that segment of the world which has already achieved the definitive state of its eternal value before God, that is, in the very first buds and in the finest flowering of its spiritual history—the Angels and Saints. One of the tasks of theology is to study more deeply and more vitally how, why, and with what dependence on the fundamental religious act addressed to God, that which is termed *dulia* (veneration)—in contradistinction from the act of *latria* (adoration)—is truly a religious act. It is the task of theology to make clear how each act can and must be practiced as a religious act without losing its own proper character, that is, without being conceived and practiced as an act of *latria* and practically absorbed by it.

Our relationship with God will be that of a mature Christian only if we have a vital appreciation of a series of truths which we can translate into religious practices. God must become for us, in an ever-increasing manner, truly God. He must become a consuming flame; He who is simply incomparable; He who has been led by His gracious love to leave the distant heights of His transcendent majesty and draw near to us, must be seen, in this very burning flame and in this dazzling light, as what gives reality to all that has been created and loved by Him, so that every creature possesses its own authentic value. We must understand that in this infinite sea of measureless flame everything else is not destroyed; on the contrary, only in this flame does all else become truly alive, not only in itself, but also for our benefit.

In view of the fact that such a mature attitude will fill us with joy and is also an obligatory step in our spiritual growth in God's grace (which always operates in a way other than we might think), we must strive to develop it. For us sinners, the first step towards finding God is to withdraw from creatures. But this is only the first step. A return to the world through apostolic service entrusted to us by God can be the second step. But there is still a third: to rediscover creatures in God. Creatures themselves, in their own proper reality and in their distinction from God—to rediscover them in the inexorability of the jealous flame of His being all-in-all; to rediscover these creatures in the very midst of this flame, the infinitesimal and the finite in the boundless and the infinite, the creature in the Creator. This alone constitutes the third and highest phase of our relationship with God.[158]

With the doctrine of the Mystical Body as a foundation, we can arrive at a full appreciation of the reality of the Saints and of their function in the Church. If we can grasp the profound significance and importance that their cult entails for a fuller development of the Christian and the Catholic spirit, we will be in a position to judge the error of those who see in the cult of the Saints only a deviation from the true spirit of Christian piety, a religious practice which is too human, or even sentimental and superstitious.[159]

II. MAXIMALISTIC TENDENCIES

Now that we have gained an appreciation of the spiritual riches latent in a well-ordered cult of the Saints, we are in a position to recognize how at times, unfortunately, its actual practice assumes forms that are not in accord with the authentic spirit which should inspire it. In such cases we are confronted with tendencies that err in the opposite extreme to those we have been considering. Though we took pains to demonstrate the falseness of the attitude which opposes the cult of the Saints on principle, we cannot deny that there are deviations in the actual practice of honoring the Saints. In certain centuries these deviations were very grave, and they linger, here and there, even to this day. Nor can we overlook the fact that these abuses present a distorted image of the Church to those who are not prepared to excuse them.

If we are convinced of the spiritual values which a genuine cult of the Saints can contribute to our lives, we will experience a feeling of regret and compassion when faced with its distortions; but instead of reacting with aversion or disdain for this Catholic practice, we will do our utmost to restore it to its proper forms and limits, always bearing in mind that the cause of such distortions lies not in the nature of the practice itself but in ignorance of what the true practice should be. And if we take into account the fact that every sphere of human life into which man's free activity enters is subject to the danger of aberrations, especially when there are no principles to guide that activity, we can easily understand how the precious relationship between man and the Saints can become clouded over with misunderstandings, and how secondary elements can assume proportions that effectively displace primary values. We can understand also how certain potential dangers in the exercise of this cult become a reality when a lack of proper instruction prevents the faithful from appreciating the true function of the Saints, so that they fail to discern what distinguishes the cult of the Saints from the primary and more basic cult of the Lord, and do not perceive that we should practice the cult of the Saints only in so far as it leads us to a more generous and unreserved self-surrender to God in Christ.

It has been established that deviations, misrepresentations, and exaggerations in the cult of the Saints have been most prevalent during those periods when religious instruction of the faithful was far from adequate. Ignorance of basic dogmatic truths caused Christians to have a defective knowledge, love, and appreciation of the Word Incarnate and of His redemptive work through the mediation of His humanity. In brief, aberrations follow upon a failure to preserve a truly christocentric religious spirit.[160]

This is the principal reason why at times among some groups in certain regions, during past centuries—and unfortunately even in our own day—the cult of the Saints developed beyond its proper limits and assumed exaggerated proportions, finding expression in erroneous and unhealthy forms which eventually threatened to encroach upon the cult owed to God.

Such exaggerated forms indicate that the cult of the Saints is not conceived and practiced according to its true spirit and with an awareness of its proper function. The exterior manifestations in which these forms are made visible—often mingled with profane elements—indicate that the religious spirit which animates them is unfortunately minimal. Often it is a case of traditions, originally rich in spiritual elements, which gradually allow the religious elements to be suffocated by externalism and folklore. Frequently we find that certain devotions once were understood and properly oriented towards God, but later degenerated into lifeless ritual which easily fell prey to superstitious corruptions.

What come most readily to mind are those popular feasts in honor of a patron Saint celebrated with an exterior pomp far more elaborate than that reserved for feasts of our Lord, which are actually the center of the liturgical cycle.[161] In these feasts so many foreign elements are intermingled that the religious spirit is no longer evident and their original sacred purpose is totally neglected.[162] Equally censurable are those aberrations which lead certain of the faithful to attach—at least in practice—more importance to certain forms of devotion to the Saints and to the recitation of formularies in their honor than to devout, active assistance at the Eucharistic Sacrifice in which they should consciously unite themselves to Christ who is offering Himself to the Father in a perfect act of worship.

At times we come across persons who carry out their daily practices of devotions to certain Saints with painstaking scrupulosity, while perhaps they never even turn their thoughts to the Lord, or if they do so, it is without intensity, confidence, and fervor. When these persons enter a church, they plant themselves in front of an image or a statue, without even adverting to the fact that there dwells in the tabernacle God Himself, the Giver of life and grace, the fount of holiness, before whom—in the company and with the help of the Saints—we should kneel in adoration.

If we proceed to analyze what is often the object of these devotional formularies, we will perceive how far certain practices have strayed from the genuine spirit of the cult of the Saints. Certain Catholics turn to the Saints solely to obtain favors of a material nature—assistance and success in certain enterprises which can even be at variance with the will of God and inimical to our spiritual progress.

In the light of these observations, a basic question must be raised: To what is the cult of the Saints reduced in such circumstances? Can there still be, perhaps, a minimal reference to service and love of God, and to that orientation of one's whole life towards God which constitutes, as we have emphasized, the very basis of authentic devotion to the Saints? How widespread among the faithful is an awareness that the reason we turn to the Saints is to arrive at a greater intensity of spiritual life, and not to negotiate with them for temporal blessings? Do they understand that in turning to the Saints they should be motivated by the desire to be able, with their help, to actuate more richly and more effectively their adoration of the Lord, recognized as the primary author of the holiness which the Saints possess, so that He may be praised and loved more fully? How many of them understand and appreciate the fact that the intercessory power of the Saints depends on their union with the unique mediator, Christ?

These questions and the answers which must be given to them lead us in many cases to but one conclusion: practices which have exceeded proper bounds must be reduced to well-defined limits; excesses must be subjected to the rein of moderation; real abuses must be eliminated. But how is this to be done?

To begin with, we must re-emphasize that it would be a serious error to reject the substance of a doctrine because of certain abuses and distortions in the practices consequent upon it. We must stress this simple principle because it is in reaction to the excesses of devotion that many are driven to the opposite extreme and attempt to eliminate what they scornfully and somewhat carelessly regard as accidentals. However deplorable the ignorance of those given up to an exaggerated cult of the Saints, more deplorable still, perhaps, is the error of those who, in the name of culture or theology, systematically attempt to deprive the Church and the faithful of a form of devotion clearly intended by God Himself, since, if practiced correctly, it greatly contributes to an intensification of our quest for Him. We must not be arbitrary in condemning out of hand and *ipso facto* every manifestation of popular piety simply because one or another of its phases has got out of control. Such a course would betray the superficial attitude which fails to recognize that certain forms of devotion, though distorted through exaggeration, nonetheless contain a solid nucleus of genuine spirituality.[163] It is narrow-minded to reject forms of piety motivated and animated by a truly sincere spirit of faith, untainted by superstition, merely because these forms do not appeal to everyone—and especially not to those who consider themselves above external manifestations of human feeling and who look down on certain exterior actions as childish and undignified.[164] The variety of expressions of piety and devotion should not be condemned outright; rather, we must endeavor to understand their motive and spirit so that we shall be able to distinguish their wholesome elements and eventually correct their distorted aspects. Most apposite in this connection is a passage of St. Jerome in which this great doctor of the Church, acknowledging that the devotions of the simple faithful are not always perfectly enlightened, nonetheless refuted those who disparaged the kind of Christian piety that finds spontaneous expression in external actions:

We do not light candles in broad daylight, as you accuse us of doing, to no avail; we do so in order to dispel the shadows of darkness and to remain awake to the light, rather than to sleep in dismal darkness as you do. If some persons—because of that ignorance and simplicity typical of uneducated men or pious old ladies, to whom the words of Scripture can be aptly applied: *They bear witness and have zeal for the Lord but without discretion* (Rom. 10.2)—light candles in honor of the Martyrs, what harm is done? The Apostles too once lamented the squandering of precious ointment, but they were reproached by the words of our Lord (Mt. 26 and Mk. 14). Christ had no need of the precious ointment, nor have the Martyrs need of the light of candles; but the woman in the Gospel performed this gesture in honor of Christ, and her soul's devout intention was most pleasing to Christ. In like manner, those who light candles receive a recompense corresponding to their faith, according to the words of the Apostle: Everyone is to follow his own conscience (Rom. 14.5). Do you call such persons idolatrous? I do not deny that all of us who believe in Christ have come forth from the darkness of idolatry, inasmuch as we were not born Christians but became such by the rebirth of baptism. Since we once erroneously paid homage to idols, perhaps we should refrain from paying similar homage to God out of fear of those who will accuse us of venerating God with an honor similar to that once paid to idols? Our former homage was directed to idols and must therefore be abominated; but our present homage is offered to the Martyrs and must therefore be accepted. Even though there are not relics of the Martyrs, nevertheless in all the Churches of the East candles are lit during the reading of the Gospel even when the sun is already far above the horizon. We do this not to dispel the darkness, but as a sign of our joy.[165]

If we wish to correct the excesses and deviations existing here and there in the cult of the Saints, it will not suffice to point the finger of scorn at errors and deformations, much less to condemn the entire practice outright.[166] It would be better to penetrate to the heart of the matter and lay bare the causes of these deviations, the wellsprings which nourish those excesses, so that we may eliminate the difficulty at its source. Then we will be in a position to educate the faithful more positively and thereby assure a wholesome practice of the true cult of the Saints.

As we have seen, the principal cause of aberrations in this sphere of religious life is the ignorance of the faithful, owing to deficient instruction about God and our relations with Him, about our Lord, His person and His works; for it is precisely the void created by this deficiency that the instinctive religious spirit of the faithful attempts to fill by recourse to the Saints. Obviously, then, our primary and maximum effort should consist in the diffusion of a more profound religious culture—a more vital, more direct and personal knowledge of God and of our Lord Jesus Christ, and of the legacy He has bequeathed to us in the form of the Church, the Sacraments, and the Liturgy. If we succeed in doing this, the piety of the faithful will inevitably be directed primarily to true worship of God, to an active participation in the Church's cult, and then to all other basic Christian devotions.[167]

Deviations from an authentic cult of the Saints, it is said, are often the result of certain pastoral attitudes which in turn stem from ignorance on the part of pastors of the basic principles governing the role of the Saints in our faith and religious practices. Such misguided pastoral concern can be rectified only by a more comprehensive theological and cultural formation of the clergy. This is the only way in which we can hope to eliminate the sad spectacle of numerous churches in which the meaning of God's dwelling place is obscured by the fact that the center of devotion is no longer the tabernacle but a statue or portrait of a Saint richly adorned—more or less in good taste—with flowers, and surrounded by tiers of burning candles which attract and focus attention upon themselves, as if such secondary shrines were the most important thing in the Church.[168] This is the only way in which we can prevent those stereotyped sermons on the Saints in which so many words are spoken to say so little—those panegyrics on local patron Saints in which the simple uneducated faithful are filled with greater admiration for them than for the Person of our Lord, of whom they hear so little and in such colorless sermons at that.

If we turn our attention to the enormous flood of hagiographical literature depicting the Saints in colors totally foreign to their real-life situation and insisting on extraordinary elements which then serve as the basis for legends and immoderate admiration that has no affinity with the genuine spirit of the cult of the Saints,[169] we shall realize how much must be done with regard to the formation of the clergy and of those entrusted with the education of the faithful. Here again, education is the key to eliminating errors and deviations, since religious guides, perhaps unconsciously, are the very ones who sometimes lead the flock astray.

Over and above the elimination of the basic causes for the rise and growth of deviations, there is need of a positive educational program which will provide the faithful with specific teaching on the genuine cult of the Saints. They must be made to understand its nature, spirit, and limits, so that they will fit it into its proper place in the framework of Catholic worship. Rather than placing it on the same plane as worship of God, they must be taught to use it as a means for enriching divine worship. With this in mind, Pius XII in his encyclical *Mediator Dei* discussed various aspects of Christian life, which at times seem to have no connection with one another, or even to be in opposition, and he insisted most earnestly on the necessity of uniting these aspects in harmonious equilibrium. E. Moureau, with special reference to those forms of religious practice most exposed to the danger of aberration, namely, the so-called popular devotions, made this astute observation:

The papal document establishes a clear hierarchy of values among the various acts (acts of religion which constitute formally the Church's cult; pious practices and popular devotions; and exercises of Christian ascesis), and it indicates how these can and must co-exist and constitute—for every individual Christian as well as for the community of the faithful as a whole—an harmonious equilibrium rich in spiritual benefits. The most important, according to our Holy Father, are obviously liturgical acts: the Mass, the Sacraments, and the Divine Office; for they have an objective value of the first order, which can not be found in any others. The Eucharistic Sacrifice and the Sacraments are the very actions of Christ, and their *ex opere operato* efficacy is infallibly assured by God's own word; we have but to participate in these actions if we wish to receive and make our own the riches which they contain. The Mass, the Sacraments, and the Divine Office—or, for that matter, any official act of the Church—have an additional value and efficacy *ex opere operantis Ecclesiae* in virtue of the holiness of Christ's Spouse who is intimately united to her divine Head. Finally, each person's active participation in these communal acts calls for personal effort and depends upon the dispositions *ex opere operantis individui* which the faithful bring to the task of assimilating themselves vitally to what is being offered to them.

Enriched by this treefold efficacy, liturgical acts are at the very center of every devotion, individual or communal. They occupy the top grade in the scale of values and must be esteemed accordingly.

Next in line are certain popular devotions which have been introduced into the religious life of the faithful during the course of time. These were accorded a favorable welcome by the Church; they "deserve our attention and respect," the Encyclical states quite explicitly. These devotions, which had their origin in the activity of the Holy Spirit ever living and working in the Church, are well-adapted to diverse mentalities and different cultural levels, and enjoy the added advantage of being able to use the vernacular which makes them easily assimilable. They serve, moreover, as a means to prepare the faithful for a more effective participation in the official acts (of worship), by nourishing those personal dispositions necessary if one is to derive true benefit from the official acts. If these personal dispositions are lacking, even the most important liturgical acts run the risk of becoming imbued with formalism on the part of both ministers and faithful, thereby losing a good part of their sanctifying value.

Undoubtedly, popular devotions present certain dangers: deviations, affectations, individualism. To preclude such dangers, the Encyclical recommends certain precautionary measures:

"When dealing with genuine and solid piety We stated that there could be no real opposition between the sacred Liturgy and other religious practices, provided they be kept within legitimate bounds and performed for a legitimate purpose. In fact, there are certain exercises of piety which the Church recommends very much to clergy and religious"; and it concludes: "If, on the contrary, they are an obstacle to the principles and norms of divine worship, or if they oppose or hinder them, one must surely conclude that they are not in keeping with prudence and enlightened zeal."[170]

In our study we have made a determined effort to examine carefully all that theology teaches us about the cult of the Saints. Our intention was to offer a modest contribution that might further the realization of those wise directives given by John XXIII, which exhort us to establish an harmonious blend and compenetration of the various elements which constitute and embellish Christian worship.[171]

We hope that it will be easier, in the light of our exposition, to understand how the Saints should be made known and how, in accord with such knowledge, their cult can and must be integrated into christocentric and theocentric worship, within the scope and limits envisaged by the principles of our faith.

Above all, we priests must analyze and deepen our appreciation of this aspect of the complex treasure of our religion so that we may incorporate this knowledge into our teaching, preaching, and writing, and thus propagate sound and fruitful ideas about the Saints. If we make the Saints known and loved as they should be, the faithful will recognize that their greatness depends on God, their lovableness derives from the fact that they are intimately united to Christ, their intercessory power is rooted in the fact that they are glorious and preeminent members of the Mystical Body and draw all their power from the Head. When these principles have been instilled, the cult directed to the Saints will certainly not rival or oppose a christocentric and theocentric cult; rather it will become a spontaneous, warm, and vital communion with our beloved brothers. They have gone before us and, precisely because they are God's friends and closely linked to us, they can and want to help us make our lives, like theirs, totally oriented towards God.

ON THE POSSIBILITY OF A COMMUNICATION BETWEEN WAYFARERS AND THE SAINTS

Our treatment of the cult of the Saints, in which we have tried to demonstrate how the very worship of God in Christ demands for its full realization a conscious actuation of the relations existing among the members of the Mystical Body, has had to touch upon some of the points which enter into the complex problem of the possibility of a mutual communication between the members of the Church Militant and those of the Church Triumphant.[172] We have intentionally avoided, however, a basic analysis of the entire question, particularly the question of how communication between wayfarers and the Saints in heaven can be established. This was not to ignore the problem entirely, but simply to avoid overburdening our exposition.

We feel that we have now established the dogmatic and theological foundations for the cult of the Saints and explained its nature and spirit. In the unified perspective of this rich Catholic teaching, we now wish to approach this problem of intercommunication, which in a sense stands apart and can therefore be consigned to an appendix. Once this problem has

150

been resolved, there should be no further difficulty in accepting completely the Catholic doctrine and practice of the cult of the Saints.

It is obvious that there do not exist between those on earth and those in heaven the same means of communication which are available among members of the Church Militant. How can wayfarers, then, address themselves to the Saints and unite themselves to them in such a way that they can consciously actuate the already existing ontological relationships? In other words, we must raise the question of whether it is possible that the bonds which join us to our brothers in heaven can be experienced as interpersonal contacts, in which a communicational dialogue can be established whereby initiative on the part of one will evoke a reaction in the other, arouse an interest, call for a response, in such a way that the petitioner can be aware of the interest he has evoked.

The answer to this question is obviously of fundamental importance for an adequate theological conception of our relationship with the Saints, and its solution can have a noteworthy effect on our practical life since it is often difficulties of the psychological order that impede the actual practice of the cult of the Saints. Despite this obvious practical bearing of the problem, no comprehensive treatment has ever been devoted to its solution[173]—an added reason why we should make an effort to face it on a theological level in the hope of filling this need, at least in a general way.

The principal difficulty or root of the problem, as we have indicated, lies in the fact that there do not exist between the members of the Church Militant and those of the Church Triumphant those natural means of communication available among wayfarers. On earth, personal contacts and mutual exchanges can be effected in virtue of our common corporeal nature: we simply have recourse to the spoken and the written word, or to other natural and conventional signs. There is no such "bridge" between those on earth and those in heaven. The Saints do not yet possess their glorified bodies, or if they do (as we know with the certainty of faith to be true of the Blessed Virgin Mary and with some theological probability of the Saints to whom Matthew refers in ch. 27, vv. 52–53),[174] the corporeity they enjoy does not follow the ontological and psychological laws of the bodies of wayfarers.

This is what gives rise to the question: is it possible for the Saints to receive our communications and in turn communicate with us? If so, how is this effected?

In approaching the question, we must state at the outset that no adequate solution to the problem will be forthcoming if we limit ourselves rigidly and exclusively to philosophical data and to the perspectives given us by our own earthly experiences, much less if we rely on the often fantastic reports of spiritism. The existence and nature of our relations with members of the Church Triumphant have been made known to us in the clear and certain light of faith (aided by theology which elaborates the data of faith). The basis for this relationship, as we have seen, is our common incorporation into the humanity of the Word Incarnate. We must look into this same light of faith (and to the science of theology) if we wish to obtain further clarification of the manner in which these relations can be consciously experienced and realized in direct, personal contact.[175]

The first stage of our exposition must consist, therefore, in a consideration of what theology teaches us about the way in which the Saints know and love our created terrestrial reality in general, and human persons still struggling through their period of trial in particular.

According to Catholic theology, the Saints' mode of knowing and loving is that of human persons who have attained the highest degree of their incorporation in Christ; that is, a mode of loving knowledge characteristic of those who—though remaining created persons—share in the highest degree possible, according to their personal capacity and in proportion to their merits, the intellectual and volitional life of the human nature hypostatically united to the glorious Word Incarnate. The Word Incarnate reveals to them—no longer in the light of faith but in the luminous clarity of the beatific vision—the mystery of His own life and that of the Most Blessed Trinity, whose infinitely rich life flows over into a salvific activity *ad extra*. This face-to-face vision of the glorious Word Incarnate includes a knowledge of salvation-history in general and of its realization in the person of the Saint who contemplates the Word.

Every Saint knows, therefore, in a perfect and exhaustive manner which is strictly supernatural, the kind, provident, merciful, and gracious love which the Incarnate Word has towards him. He realizes that he has been the constant object of this persistent love from the first instant of his earthly existence till his death and glorification in the beatific vision. Every Saint sees, therefore, the plan which Christ intended to realize and actually did realize through His sanctifying activity. He sees all the events and concrete circumstances of his existence, including his associations with other creatures and other persons. He recognizes how these circumstances and contacts, intended by divine disposition, were actually the means destined to effect his own more intimate union with Christ, as well as that of those with whom he associated. In this beatifying vision of the Word, in brief, the Saints perceive clearly how Christ wished to develop and perfect His salvific work and apostolate in and through their lives—a work which is not yet completely concluded because Christ wants His work completed through the efforts of those who constitute the members of His Mystical Body.

In virtue of these certain premises, we can understand how the Word Incarnate enables each Saint to know clearly all that can contribute to a more explicit and conscious association in His sanctifying work within the Church Militant in general, and especially within that portion which depends upon the collaboration and contribution which the Saint can and must provide. It is precisely with this end in view that the Saint gains an awareness of the persons whom he must help in a special way according to God's concrete salvific plan; for in order to do so he must know them more explicitly and consciously. Whether this awareness is communicated in the light of the beatific vision itself (which we think more probable) or through an infused supernatural knowledge which would be distinct from, though intimately linked with, the beatific vision, is a distinct question. The fact remains the same. The Saint comes to know the persons whom Christ moves and inspires to approach the specific Saint in question, invoke his aid, and enter into communion with him.

This, then, is the answer to the first part of the question we put to ourselves concerning the possibility of a personal communication between the Saints and ourselves: by means of a strictly supernatural communication which Christ Himself conveys to them, the Saints become aware of the acts made by those persons on earth who are invoking them.

There are two additional considerations which can clarify the significance of our solution and deepen our appreciation of its consequences. The first is a clarification of what we have said about the Saints' knowledge of salvation history. We stated above that Christ enables each Saint to see in a special manner those persons whom He Himself inspires to enter into association with the specific Saint in question. We might extend our inquiry to ask precisely how and for what reason each Saint has an explicit knowledge of certain members of the Church Militant and enters into close association with these particular persons.

A Saint's love is truly universal or catholic. Those who share in Christ's life and love in a pre-eminent degree exist in a glorious state wherein love is liberated from those limitations which flow from earthly existence and are proper to our condition as wayfarers.

It is equally true, however, that even in the glorious state of the beatific vision the Saints remain created persons and therefore limited. The beatifying knowledge they enjoy as a foundation of their love is not an omniscience: it is not a knowledge that gives them explicit and comprehensive awareness of everything that happens in the earthly existence of every single wayfarer. According to the doctrine common among theologians, each Saint knows with an actual explicit awareness only that which has direct reference to and intimate connection with him and his earthly life. To this is added anything which establishes a bond with him because of the apostolic work which he must continue to develop "through, with, and in Christ," as a glorious instrument working for the benefit of the members of the Church Militant. This last point, the apostolic work that the Saint must complete, explains why the Saint has a more explicit awareness of certain persons on earth and therefore enjoys more direct personal relations with them. It also introduces us to our second consideration, namely, that of a comprehensive view of the total design Divine Providence has for the life and work of a Saint, as well as the way in which He executes that design.

Christ's immediate aim is to make it easier for men incorporated into Him to realize more effectively the end for which

He created and elevated them, namely, their formal glorification. To do this God raises up in the heart of the Church Militant, "through, with, and in Christ," persons whose heroic exercise of charity and the Christian virtues enables them to share, even during their earthly existence, the life of Christ so profoundly that Christ shines forth resplendently in the circumstances and temporal conditions in which they live. Accordingly, their radiant example serves as an object lesson for all successive generations, teaching diverse classes of people how they can and must unite themselves to Christ in the changing circumstances and vicissitudes of life.[176] But in order that these pre-eminent members of the Mystical Body may be recognized as initiators of new styles of Christian living and as models of a Christian life lived in a manner adapted to a certain period or a specific class of wayfarers, Divine Providence points them out to men through the working of miracles. In this way God indicates that they are particularly pleasing to Him, because they are authentically perfect Christians, that is, *filii in Filio*—sons in the Son. God directs the attention of the ecclesiastical authority towards these holy persons, so that in its intent to follow God's plans, it will take an interest in their causes, study them attentively, evaluate accurately their lives, virtues, and miracles so that it may propose them to the faithful as true models and effective intercessors.

It is not only through these visible external means (namely, miracles and the Church's teaching authority) that God points out to men His dearly beloved sons. Often He awakens in the hearts of the faithful—especially those whom He intends to call to a particular form of life or spirituality—an inclination and devotion towards a particular Saint because his exemplary life will serve as a guiding inspiration. In this way, God's grace makes a particular Saint's life attractive to some of the faithful, and this internal fascination moves them to imitate him and induces them to express their admiration for the Saint and invoke his aid. In brief, God's grace operates within the hearts of the faithful and inspires them to honor the Saints.[177]

Divine Providence originally raised up the Saint in order to make Christ's presence in the world more palpable and utilized his voluntary collaboration while on earth as a means of communicating grace to other men more abundantly. It now continues making use of his heroic life and of the merits he acquired through, with, and in Christ, and enables the Saint to see, in the luminous clarity of the beatific vision, how he can heed the petitions of those whom God inspires to pray to him and thereby carry out that part of the apostolic task which God has entrusted to him for completion from his place in heaven.

When we take all these elements into consideration and keep in mind the total design which Divine Providence wishes to realize through the personality of the Saint, we can easily understand the validity of our earlier assertion to the effect that Christ enables a Saint to know certain persons on earth more explicitly; namely, those persons whom grace has inspired to approach the Saint in question because they have been attracted by his personality and style of Christian living and experience a profound desire to imitate him, so that they now are invoking him in the hope that he will help them progress along the path which he himself first trod.

So much for the Saints' awareness of persons on earth invoking their aid. Now we must turn to the second aspect of the problem: how can persons on earth have any assurance that their prayer has gained a sympathetic hearing and will be answered?

It will not be hard to deal with this difficulty since the key to the solution is found in the very same principles we have laid down above. (We might incidentally note in passing that

a similar problem exists with respect to the prayers we address
to God Himself, though the solution of that problem bears
only a remote analogous relationship to the one we will propose for our present problem.)

When we observed that it was divine grace which inspired
certain wayfarers to invoke a particular Saint whose exemplary
life had elicited thoughts of imitation and emulation, giving
as our reason the plan of Divine Providence which wishes to
utilize the Saint to further His design, we wished to emphasize
that when divine grace elicits such an attraction and desire,
what springs up in the heart of the faithful is not simply a
cold, rational, objective knowledge of the Saint's existence,
but a special type of knowledge which is vitally supernatural.
In this type of knowledge (which bears a certain similarity to
the vital supernatural knowledge of our act of faith in Christ
and is endowed with an intentionality all its own) the Saint
is not represented as a distant historical reality, but as a person
living here and now and able to communicate with anyone
who approaches him. Such vitally supernatural knowledge includes an interior inclination which is characterized by a warm
personal attachment. Through the operation of grace, the
Saint exercises an attraction and a fascination which influence
persons to approach him.

Through this supernatural knowledge the wayfarer gains
a vitally personal awareness of a fact already known and believed in faith: a particular Saint, though long since dead,
lives on. In fact, he lives on with greater intensity, so that we
can be united with him more intimately and more deeply than
with persons close to us in the body. The wayfarer is thoroughly convinced, with a knowledge all the deeper for its
being supernatural, that the prayers he directs to the Saints
gain a sympathetic hearing. He knows that the Saints, fired
with apostolic zeal, will not only welcome his request but

actually make it their own, presenting it enriched by their merits to Christ and to the Father.

It is natural that this vital knowledge of the intimate relationship existing between the Christian and the Saint should grow and deepen in keeping with the guiding inspiration of Divine Providence, which induces the wayfarer to model his life on that of his saintly friend. Gradually the Christian will realize, with a heart overflowing with gratitude, that all the prayers he has addressed to the Saint have been answered, everything he has requested has been granted with gracious liberality, and that his more intimate union with Christ and the Father has been effected by the graces obtained through the Saint's intercession.

This dialogue of love is the key to understanding how the relationship between the Saints and ourselves can continue to grow in depth and vigor; as the wayfarer becomes increasingly convinced of the gracious and beneficent assistance given him by the Saint, he will feel a corresponding need to approach the Saint for help in his progress towards God in Christ. The Saint, in virtue of his knowledge of these earnest efforts to progress, will reciprocate with an apostolic love that will never fail.

APPENDIX II

THE SAINTS IN THE CHURCH ACCORDING TO THE RECENT DOGMATIC CONSTITUTION "LUMEN GENTIUM" OF THE SECOND VATICAN COUNCIL

THE HISTORY OF CHAPTER VII

This conciliar document owes its origin to Pope John XXIII and is bound up with the theological and pastoral aim of the Second Vatican Council which set out to offer modern man a live and attractive vision of the Church and to invite him to a life more wholly dedicated to the following of Christ within the ambit of the Church He founded.

Understandably, then, this very aim of the Council led a number of the Fathers to realize how they could best stimulate the longing for God which is deep in every human heart. This could be done by setting in a clear light the wonderful example of Christian living which has been left us by those whom the Church has, from time immemorial, honored with the highly significant title of "Saints." More than any theoretical exposition—however profoundly and beautifully expressed—it is living example which gives courage and shows the way to our eternal home: *exempla trahunt.*

Yet a simple or merely a passing reference to that reality would not have sufficed. Even less satisfactory would have been a short exhortation of an ascetical nature. To remain true to the intention of giving a really theological description of the Church, her nature and end, her structure in whole and in part, it was essential to give a general exposition of the Church in heaven. To this Church all those belong who, having died in Christ, now live in the most intimate union possible with the risen Christ, and are by the same fact more than ever associated with His salvific work for the benefit of the whole human race. The teaching of the Council on the reality of the Church and on our life as Christians would have been seriously inadequate and incomplete if there had not been a coherent treatment of our union with the Church in heaven.

To these considerations of primary importance there was added yet another motive equally theological and also practical and pastoral in the highest degree. It is well known how the cult of the Saints was an authentic and a most dear expression of our Christian and Catholic faith for His Holiness John XXIII; it is known how he himself in a deeply human and virile manner loved the Saints and turned to them in the various vicissitudes of his daily life, whether in private or in public. As Supreme Pontiff he had shown in practice how he who lives by faith ought logically to make this communion with his brethren in the other world an integral part of his spiritual life. He therefore wanted it to flourish wisely and well.

However, just because of this wish he had every reason to know that in the Church of today there are two extreme tendencies with regard to the cult of the Saints; tendencies which are diametrically opposed to each other, yet both deriving from an inadequate understanding of the true nature and of the real spirit of this aspect of Christian cult: the minimalism of those who by appealing to the theocentric and christocentric nature of our worship think, and affirm, that the cult of the Saints keeps men from turning to the Blessed Trinity; the maximalism in practice of those who in their veneration of the Saints sometimes seem either to ignore or to forget the subordinate function of this cult which in its authentic exercise ought to be completely animated by the love of Christ and lead to a more intimate and fruitful union with Him. Although different in their origins and consequences both these exaggerations are contrary to faith and to Catholic theology. Both are an affront to the good sense of the Church, and they prevent a pastoral activity which is both balanced and mature.

Some time before the opening of the Council, Pope John XXIII had accordingly requested special studies to be made concerning the complex problem of the cult of the Saints: in particular, its spirit, nature and limits, its indispensability within Catholic worship and its authentic forms. Nor is it astonishing that already in the preparatory phase of the Council he had felt it necessary to provide for the Schema of the conciliar Constitution on the Church to be rounded off and integrated by a text which would explicitly deal with this matter.

The carrying out of this project was entrusted by the Supreme Pontiff to His Eminence Cardinal Larraona, Prefect of the Sacred Congregation of Rites, who with a small Commission of *Periti* chosen by himself should draft an appropriate text; initially it was intended that this text should form a special Constitution just as in the case of the conciliar text that would deal with the Blessed Virgin. However, when in the course of the Second Session of the Council it was decided that the text on Our Lady should be incorporated into the Dogmatic Constitution on the Church, it was only logical that the text dealing with our relationship to the Church in heaven, would likewise be transferred to the same Constitution.

In the meantime many Council Fathers had pointed out in their interventions that it would be necessary to treat *ex professo* of the Saints. As Cardinal Frings rightly said: "The Saints belong essentially to the Church." Pope Paul VI duly informed after his election of all the preparations made by his predecessor, approved of his project and sent the Theological Commission the text which had previously been drafted and then revised and perfected.

Consequently, a special Subcommission was instituted within the Theological Commission with Their Eminences Cardinals Rufino J. Santos and Franziskus König, and Archbishop Gabriel Garrone as members, and some theologians as *Periti*. Thanks to the rich theological substance of the text prepared under the direction of His Eminence Cardinal Larraona, the new Subcommission could fulfill its task without any particular difficulty. In fact it was decided to leave the whole doctrinal part of this text in its original form and to insert it in such a way into the Constitution on the Church that it would follow on the chapters dealing with the Church on earth and precede the chapter dedicated to the Mother of God. This decision implied that the beginning and the end of the text on the Triumphant Church had to be adapted with a view to its organic and logical insertion into the whole context of the Constitution "Lumen Gentium." A special section was therefore written which was to precede the new chapter and introduce it by explaining at some length the eschatological nature of the Pilgrim Church; as to the new ending of this chapter, no additions were required; in fact it was felt that it would be sufficient to omit a paragraph of the original text which had been intended to announce the major reforms in juridical procedure in the processes of beatification and canonization.

In this new form the text was then printed, and, together

with the other chapters of the Constitution on the Church, sent to the Fathers for the first time during the summer of 1964.

The discussion in the Council Hall, which took place on September 15, 16, 17, 1964, and in which 17 Fathers intervened orally while 32 others sent in their written observations, made it clear from the outset not only that the Assembly would approve of the insertion of this text into the Constitution "Lumen Gentium" but also that very few changes would be necessary.

After these few amendments had been effected by the Sub-commission, and discussed and voted on in the plenary meeting of the Theological Commission, the text was presented anew to the Fathers by His Eminence Cardinal Santos, who in his oral Relation justified the acceptance of some amendments and the rejection of others. The Council then proceeded to cast its first vote on Chapter VII.

According to the customary procedure of the Council these first votings which took place on October 19, 1964, concerned the four paragraphs into which the new chapter was divided; as is usual for this type of voting, the Fathers could only vote *Placet* or *Non-Placet*. The results of these votings gave a truly extraordinary, and even unique, success to the chapter. Out of a total number of more than two thousand Fathers who cast a vote, the *Placets* amounted to 99,05 for n.48; 99,62 for n.49; 99,62 for n.50; and 99,61 for n.51.

On the following day (October 20, 1964) the whole text was voted on, and on this occasion the Fathers could also give a qualified or conditional approval by voting *Placet-iuxta-modum*. This time out of 2183 Fathers who gave a valid vote, 1921 voted *Placet,* 29 *Non-Placet* and only 233 *Placet-iuxta-modum*.

In this way the text had been fully approved in all its parts and nothing remained to be done except to examine the *modi*, that is, the last proposals for the emendation of the chapter. However, since an overwhelming majority had approved of the text as it stood, no emendations could have been effected which would have changed the text substantially. Only 15 amendments were therefore accepted, mainly concerning stylistic improvements and a few points of minor importance.

Submitted to a final vote, Chapter VII obtained again a record approval: out of 2131 votes cast no less than 2127 were *Placets* and only 4 *Non-Placets*. The outcome of this vote reflects the general opinion of the Council that Chapter VII not only has most successfully filled a serious gap in the conciliar teaching on the Church but also has at the same time judiciously solved the difficult problem of organically joining the chapter on Our Lady to the other chapters of the Constitution "Lumen Gentium."

A BRIEF ANALYSIS OF THE CONCILIAR
TEACHING ON OUR UNION WITH THE
CHURCH IN HEAVEN*

If we now turn to consider more in detail the reasons which prompted both Pope John XXIII and Pope Paul VI as well as so many Council Fathers to insist so forcefully on the necessity of including in the Constitution on the Church a special chapter on our relationship to the Church in heaven, we must begin by pointing out that without such a chapter one of the principal objections of the Council could not have been accomplished adequately. Having defined this Church as the People of God and the Mystical Body of Christ, and having

---

* The texts of the Dogmatic Constitution "Lumen Gentium" are quoted from the American translation prepared by Fr. Gregory Baum, O.S.A., *De Ecclesia: the Constitution on the Church of Vatican Council II* (Glen Rock, N.Y.: Study Club Editions, Deus Books, Paulist Press, 1965).

insisted so strongly on its social and eschatological character, the Council could not have kept silence with regard to those countless Christians who, at the end of their earthly pilgrimage, have been initiated through death into the Church of God's Saints in heaven. It would have been incongruous, even inconceivable. Death marks the end of their being part of the Church on earth, but this does not mean, of course, that they are cut off from communion with Christ and all those who belong to Him. On the contrary, precisely in death the Christian who has lived in accordance with his calling, is incorporated indefectibly into the Mystical Body of his Risen Lord, shares therefore in a much deeper way in His eternal life and is thereby united in a new manner to all his brethren in the Lord:

Until the Lord shall come in his majesty, and all the angels with him (Mt. 25, 31) and death being destroyed, all things are subject to him (1 Cor. 15, 26–27), some of his disciples are exiles on earth, some having died are being purified, and others are in glory beholding "clearly God himself triune and one, as he is," but all in various ways and degrees are in communion in the same charity of God and neighbor and all sing the same hymn of glory to our God. For all who are in Christ, having his Spirit, form one Church and cleave together in him (Eph. 4, 16). Therefore the union of the wayfarers with the brethren who have gone to sleep in the peace of Christ is not in the least interrupted, but on the contrary, according to the perennial faith of the Church, is strengthened by a communication of spiritual goods. (Chapter VII, n. 49)

In fact, if union with Christ means union with all the members of His Mystical Body, and if this union by its very nature, implies an intercommunion and a vital exchange of mutual goods, then it is obvious that the members of the Church in heaven, precisely because they are more intimately united to

Christ, contribute in an outstanding manner to the life of the Pilgrim Church: likewise this latter cannot be described properly unless its relationship to the Saints in heaven is duly taken into account.

By way of anticipation, the concluding sentences of n. 49 mention in this context three essential functions which the members of the Church in heaven fulfill with regard to the Mystical Body in general and its wayfaring members in particular: on account of their deeper union with Christ they strengthen and consolidate the whole Church in sanctity; their worship of God ennobles the divine cult of the Church on earth; they contribute in manifold ways to its further edification:

For because those in heaven are more closely united with Christ, they establish the whole Church more firmly in holiness, lend nobility to the worship that the Church offers to God here on earth and in many ways contribute to its greater edification (cf. 1 Cor. 12, 12–27). For after they have been received into their heavenly home and are present to the Lord (2 Cor. 5, 8), through him and with him and in him they do not cease to intercede with the Father for us, showing forth the merits they won on earth through the one mediator between God and man (1 Tim. 2, 5), serving God in all things and filling up in their flesh those things that are lacking of the sufferings of Christ for his body which is the Church (Col. 1, 24). Thus by their brotherly interest our weakness is greatly strengthened. (Chapter VII, n. 49)

The underlying principle of this teaching is, of course, that "all who are in Christ, having his Spirit, form one Church and cleave together in him" (Eph. 4.16), which in its turn is further explained by the fact that all those who are in Christ and have His Spirit, truly live by His life to such an extent that He Himself is living, suffering, working and praying in them. Particularly worth noticing is the fact that in this context the Constitution has recourse to the famous words of St. Paul according to which Christians complete and fill up in their flesh what is lacking of the sufferings of Christ for His body which is the Church. The Constitution refers to this passage in its most literal sense, when it speaks of the sufferings which the blessed ones in heaven had to undergo during their earthly life and which are now the meritorious titles of their interceding prayers. But it is obvious from many subsequent sentences of the Constitution that the idea of Christ continuing and extending His life in those who correspond to His gracious calling is indeed the inspiring principle of all that is said about the excellence of the Saints and their loving care for us.

(a) This christocentric perspective is immediately obvious in the first specific explanation by which the Council illustrates the essential importance of our relationship to the heavenly Church and in particular to canonized Saints "whom the outstanding practice of the Christian virtues and the divine charisms recommend to the pious devotion and imitation of the faithful" (n. 50):

When we look at the lives of those who have faithfully followed Christ, we are inspired with a new reason for seeking the city that is to come (cf. Heb. 13, 14; 11, 10), and at the same time we are shown a most safe path by which among the vicissitudes of this world, in keeping with the state in life and condition proper to each of us, we will be able to arrive at perfect union with Christ, that is, perfect holiness. In the lives of those who, sharing in our humanity, are, however, more perfectly transformed into the image of Christ (cf. 2 Cor. 3, 18) God vividly manifests his presence and his face to men. He speaks to us in them, and gives us a sign of his kingdom, to which we are strongly drawn, having so great a cloud of witnesses over us (cf. Heb. 12, 1) and such a witness to the truth of the Gospel. (Chapter VII, n. 50)

While remaining men like ourselves in all things, the Saints
have been transformed by grace to such a likeness of Christ
that God's presence in them becomes visible, and He Himself speaks to us through them. These words call spontaneously
to mind the famous sentence by which St. Paul expressed the
doctrine of the Mystical Body of Christ in another of his
strikingly vivid formulas: "It is no longer I that live, but
Christ lives in me" (Gal. 2.20).

The very fact, then, that it is Christ Himself who lives and
acts and reveals Himself in those who freely and unconditionally offer their whole personalities to Him, explains why the
members of the Church on earth must needs treasure these
authentic examples and prototypes of truly Christian ways
of living in the ever changing conditions of space and time.
It explains at the same time why the lives of the Saints constitute one of the most attractive and convincing signs of the
truthfulness of God's Good Tidings and of His presence on
earth in the Church of Christ.

(b) Yet there is still another and even more important
reason why the wayfaring members of the Church should seek
and favor an intimate contact with the Saints in heaven. If it
is true that even in our contacts with our fellow-Christians
here on earth we may have the privilege of encounter or friendship with a person who in an outstanding manner lives by the
life of Christ and, accordingly, lifts us up and draws us closer
to the heart of our Redeemer, then how much more this holds
good with regard to any intimate contact with those who in
eternal bliss reign with Christ as His most dearly beloved
friends, brethren and joint heirs:

Nor is it by the title of example only that we cherish the memory
of those in heaven, but still more in order that the union of the
whole Church may be strengthened in the Spirit by the practice
of fraternal charity (cf. Eph. 4, 1–6). For just as Christian com-

munion among wayfarers brings us closer to Christ, so our companionship with the Saints joins us to Christ, from whom as from its fountain and head issues every grace and the very life of the People of God. It is supremely fitting, therefore, that we love those friends and coheirs of Christ, who are also our brothers and extraordinary benefactors, that we render due thanks to God for them and "suppliantly invoke them and have recourse to their prayers, their power and help in obtaining benefits from God through his Son, Jesus Christ, who is our redeemer and Saviour." For every genuine testimony of love shown by us to those in heaven, by its very nature tends toward and terminates in Christ who is the "crown of all Saints," and through him, in God who is wonderful in his Saints and is magnified in them. (Chapter VII, n. 50)

(c) Also the third and strongest reason which the Constitution proposes, in order to underline the essential importance of our relations with the Church in heaven, is inspired by the christocentric conception according to which the Church is the recapitulation in Christ of all mankind and as such destined to offer to the blessed Trinity through Christ, and with Him and in Him, that one canticle of glorification that is the end of our creation and salvation. This most sublime communitarian worship of God does not exclude, but presupposes, a mutual communication among the individual persons who as such are the members of the People of God and of the Mystical Body of Christ. In fact it is just this mutual communication in the Spirit of God's love that binds the individual members together into the full ecclesial unity intended by God and, consequently, makes possible and brings about that worship of God by the Church which is in the fullest possible sense communitarian because it is at the same time the actuation of all man's deepest personal aspirations and potentialities of loving. If our relationship to the Church

in heaven is seen in this perspective, it is not difficult to understand why the Church on earth commemorates and lovingly
unites itself to the Church in heaven and why the intrinsic
union of the *Christus totus,* Christ the Head and the members,
is actuated in its most noble manner in the Liturgy and most
particularly in the Holy Sacrifice:

Our union with the Church in heaven is put into effect in its
noblest manner especially in the sacred liturgy, wherein the power
of the Holy Spirit acts upon us through sacramental signs. Then,
with combined rejoicing we celebrate together the praise of the
divine majesty; then all those from every tribe and tongue and
people and nation (cf. Apoc. 5, 9) who have been redeemed by
the blood of Christ and gathered together into one Church, with
one song of praise magnify the one and triune God. Celebrating
the eucharistic sacrifice therefore, we are most closely united to
the Church in heaven in communion with and venerating the
memory first of all of the glorious ever Virgin Mary, of Blessed
Joseph and the blessed apostles and martyrs and of all the saints.
(Chapter VII, n. 50)

Before we conclude this rapid survey of the doctrinal statements of the Council concerning our relationship to the
Church in heaven and the Saints in particular, we want to
underline that the Council was aware of and explicitly intended to affirm the continuity of its teachings with one of the
most ancient beliefs of our Christian faith:

The Church has always believed that the apostles and Christ's
martyrs, who have given the supreme witness of faith and charity
by the shedding of their blood, are closely joined with us in
Christ, and she has always venerated them with special devotion,
together with the Blessed Virgin Mary and the holy angels. The
Church has piously implored the aid of their intercession. To
those were soon added also those who have more closely imitated

Christ's virginity and poverty and finally others whom the outstanding practice of Christian virtues and the divine charisms
recommended to the pious devotion and imitation of the faithful.
(Chapter VII, n. 50)

In the same sense are also to be understood the following
words of the Council by which it accepts and proposes anew
what previous Ecumenical Councils had already taught concerning certain aspects of this question:

This Sacred Council accepts with great devotion this venerable
faith of our ancestors regarding this vital fellowship with our
brethren who are in heavenly glory or who having died are still
being purified; and it proposes anew the decrees of the Second
Council of Nicaea, the Council of Florence and the Council of
Trent. (Chapter VII, no. 51)

Yet it would be a grave mistake to surmise that the Second
Vatican Council did not make any original contribution to the
fuller understanding of this point of our faith or that its for-
mulations repeat simply what previous generations had already
stated in just as many words. It is, on the contrary, one of the
outstanding merits of this Council to have offered, for the
first time in the history of dogma, a full and organic exposition of our union with the Church in heaven and to have
placed it in its proper christological and ecclesiological setting.
One needs only to consider the current manuals of Catholic
theology and even the technical contemporary theological literature to see at a glance that the conciliar document surpasses
them by far in depth and synthetic power. As Fr. Gregory
Baum, O.S.A., has recently written: "Chapter VII is a master-
piece. . . . It is a magnificent attempt to find a new theological
context for certain Catholic doctrines that have often appeared
to others, and sometimes even to ourselves, as rather unrelated

to the central Christian mystery, namely, the role of the Saints and the state of the individual after death."

The Council shows an equal familiarity with the pastoral problems concerning the cult of the Saints which exist here and there in the Church today, and since it has the intention, in a special way, of promoting Catholic life and piety, it takes care to invite all those whom it may concern to remedy less desirable situations:

In conformity with our pastoral care, we urge all concerned, if any abuses, excesses or defects have crept in here or there, to do what is in their power to remove or correct them, and to restore all things to a fuller praise of Christ and of God. (Chapter VII, n. 51)

It will be noticed that the Council speaks explicitly of two types of abuses, namely of "excesses" and of "defects"; that is to say, of two diametrically opposed extreme positions which either exaggerate or belittle the cult of the Saints.

With regard to the first abuse the Council specifies its teaching in the following manner, which needs no further explanation:

Let them therefore teach the faithful that the authentic cult of the Saints consists not so much in multiplying external acts, but rather in the greater intensity of our active love, whereby, for our own greater good and that of the whole Church, we seek from the Saints "example in their way of life, fellowship in their communion, and aid by their intercession." (Chapter VII, n. 51)

Not less clear, on the other hand, is what the Council teaches with regard to those who feel that the cult of the Saints, such as the Church has practiced it throughout the ages, weakens or even goes counter to the christocentric and theocentric nature of our Christian cult, and who therefore do not practice it and dissuade others from doing so:

On the other hand, let them teach the faithful that our communion with those in heaven, provided that it is understood in the fuller light of faith, in no way weakens, but conversely, more thoroughly enriches the worship of adoration we give to God the Father, through Christ, in the Spirit. (Chapter VII, n. 51)

In this context it is particularly important to advert to the fact that precisely this Council which explicitly and most earnestly intends to promote in all possible ways the ecumenical spirit and dialogue, not only does not follow, but flatly contradicts the opinion of those who feel that for the sake of our separated brethren we should prefer not to practice, or even to speak of, the cult of the Saints. On the contrary, by dedicating a special Chapter of this Dogmatic Constitution to our union with the Church in heaven and thereby also to the Catholic cult of the Saints, the Council offers us an authoritative and eloquent testimony of what a truly Catholic attitude should be in this regard, precisely in our efforts to contribute to the ecumenical dialogue.

It should be noticed in this connection that the Council, in the sentences which follow immediately upon the words which we have just quoted, explains under yet another aspect why our relationship to the Church in heaven and to the Saints in particular is an indispensable element of our Christian life and worship; it states, in fact, that all members of the Church constitute one family, and that this postulates that mutual charity which by its very nature manifests itself both inwardly and outwardly. Precisely because the Church is the communion of love between God and men, and men amongst themselves, the actuation of our relationship with the Saints in heaven is a foretaste and an anticipation of the end of time, when in mutual love we shall adore the Blessed Trinity:

For all of us who are sons of God and constitute one family in Christ (Heb. 3, 6), as long as we remain in communion with another in mutual charity and in one praise of the most holy Trinity, are corresponding with the intimate vocation of the Church and partaking in foretaste the liturgy of consummate glory. For when Christ shall appear and the glorious resurrection of the dead will take place, the glory of God will light up the heavenly city and the lamb of God will be the lamp thereof (cf. Apoc. 21, 24). Then the whole Church of the saints in the supreme happiness of charity will adore God and "the lamb who was slain" (Apoc. 5, 12), proclaiming with one voice: "To him who sits upon the throne and to the lamb blessing, and honor, and glory, and dominion forever and ever" (Apoc. 5, 13, 14). (Chapter VII, n. 51)

NOTES

1. Various Catholic reviews have for years been publishing periodically lists and information on current Beatifications and Canonizations; for example, *Nouvelle Revue Théologique, Zeitschrift für Aszese und Mystik* (from the year 1947: *Geist und Leben*), *Documentation Catholique, Katholiek Archief*. Interesting statistics can easily be tabulated from these lists. Noteworthy in this respect is the study of K. Richstätter, S.J., "Die Heiligen des letzten Jahrtausends," *Stimmen der Zeit* 112 (1927) 81–94; as well as the article of L. von Hertling, S.J., "Statistisches zur Geschichte des Heiligentypus," *Z. f. Aszese u. Mystik* 3 (1928) 349–352, and that of C. Kempf, S.J., "Lehr- und Trostreiches aus dem neuen Katalog der Ritenkongregation," *Z. f. Aszese u. Mystik* 7 (1932) 165–171. A more extensive and comprehensive study has appeared recently: P. Delooz, S.J., "*Conditions sociologiques de la sainteté canonisée* (2 vols.), Université de Liège, Faculté de droit, Année Académique 1959–1960.

2. P. Delooz, S.J., "Canonisations récentes (24 juin 1951–12 juin 1960)," *NRT* 82 (1960), 716.

3. P. Delooz, S.J., "Béatifications récentes (18 février 1951–5 décembre 1954; 17 avril 1955–3 mai 1959)," *ibid.*, 852–860, 959–967, 852. From 1800 until the end of the pontificate of John XXIII, the Church has canonized 163 Saints on 56 different occasions, as follows:

Pontiff	Ceremonies of Canonization	Saints
Pius VII (1800–1823)	1	5
Leo XII (1823–1829)	–	–
Pius VIII (1829–1830)	–	–
Gregory XVI (1831–1846)	1	5
Pius IX (1846–1878)	2	52
Leo XIII (1878–1903)	4	18
Pius X (1903–1914)	2	4

176

Pontiff	Ceremonies of Canonization	Saints
Benedict XV (1914–1922)	2	3
Pius XI (1922–1939)	16	33
Pius XII (1939–1958)	21	33
John XXIII (1958–1963)	7	10

With the exception of the canonizations made by Pope John XXIII, these data were taken from: Monulphus Gemmeke, O. Carm., "Overzicht van de Diocesane en Apostolische Zaligverklarings-Processen van Nederlanders of in Nederland gevoerd," *Katholiek Archief* 15 (1960) n. 40 and 41, 30 Sept. and 7 Oct., 933–998, p. 948.

For the canonizations under Pius XI, cf. A. Carinci, *Acta Canonizationum a Pio Papa XI peractarum,* Insulae Liri, 1939. For those under Pius XII, cf. F. Baumann, S.J., *Pius XII erhob sie auf die Altäre, Die Heilig- und Seliggesprochenen seines Pontifikats,* Würzburg 1960. Id., *Die Welt braucht heilige Vorbilder. Heilig- und Seligsprechungen Johannes' XXIII,* Kevelaer, 1963. A close examination of the successive issues of the *Index ac Status Causarum Beatificationis Servorum Dei et Canonizationis Beatorum,* which the Sacred Congregation of Rites publishes regularly (most recent edition, Rome, 1962) can provide us with valuable data for following the growth and continual increase in the number of Causes presented and in the process of examination before the Sacred Congregation (*Index et Status Causarum* of 1890: 152; of 1895: 215; of 1901: 287; of 1909: 321; of 1921: 328; of 1931: 551; of 1941: 764; of 1953: 936; of 1962: 1133).

4. In addition to the official Acts reported in the *Acta Apostolicae Sedis* and in the *Osservatore Romano,* consult the Allocutions of Pius XII, collected together in: *Discorsi e Radiomessaggi di Sua Santità Pio XII,* Tipografia Poliglotta Vaticana. Società Vita e Pensiero, vols. 1–7, Milan, 1941–1946, Tipografia Poliglotta Vaticana, Città del Vaticano, vols. 8–20, 1947–1959. Also, those of Pius XI, *Inviti all'eroismo. Discorsi di S. S. Pio XI nell'occasione della lettura dei Brevi per le Canonizzationi e Beatificazioni, le proclamazioni dell'eroicità delle virtù dei Santi, Beati e Servi di Dio,* Rome, vol. I (1941); vol. II (1942); vol. III (1942).

5. There comes to mind the devotion of the faithful to particular canonized Saints during the past few decades; to cite but a few: St. John Mary Vianney; St. Theresa of Lisieux, St. Mary Michael of the Most Blessed Sacrament, St. Bernadette Soubirous, the North American Martyrs, St. John Bosco, St. Gemma Galgani, St. Anthony M. Claret, St. Maria Goretti, St. Pius X.

6. By way of example, we might indicate the exceptional devotion which has surrounded certain persons recently deceased: e.g. Michael Pro, S.J., martyr of the Mexican revolution, Maximilian Kolbe, O.F.M.Conv., who died in the concentration camp at Auschwitz after having volunteered to replace a condemned man who was married and the father of a family; Rupert Mayer, S.J., the Apostle of Munich, before whose tomb there flows a daily stream of thousands of pilgrims (July 11, 1950: 8,514; Oct. 3, 1959: 9,045; these dates, chosen at random, were characterized by no extraordi-

nary factor which might account for such a number of visitors); Antonio
Molle, a young member of Catholic Action, cruelly murdered during the
recent Spanish Civil War because he refused to deny Christ; Brother Francis
Garate, etc. Or we might turn to figures from the past whose memory and
example remain untarnished and have even been enhanced by the passage
of time; for example, the English Hierarchy has recently decided to dedicate, in all the parishes of England and Wales, one Sunday to the veneration of a group of Forty Blessed Martyrs composed of diocesan priests,
religious, and members of the laity.

7. Considering the vast amount of literature on this subject, we would
direct the reader to a single work: R. Aigrain, *L'Hagiographie. Ses Sources
—Ses Méthodes—Son Histoire*, Paris, 1953. In this work the author has
devoted a chapter to: "L'Hagiographie au XIXe et au XXe siècle" (pp.
370–388). A reading of this chapter will enable one to encompass this vast
field with a single glance and find therein references to the principal hagiographical and bibliographical sources. The chapter contains the following
subdivisions: Les recueils de Vies des Saints; Les dictionnaires hagiographiques; Les éditions de textes: l'hagiographie dans les collections générales;
Les publications spéciales de textes hagiographiques; Quelques metteurs en
oeuvre; Les Collections récentes d'hagiographie; Les persécutions, l'hagiographie et l'histoire littéraire; L'hagiographie orientale; L'hagiographie de
la France; L'hagiographie régionale; L'hagiographie celtique et britannique;
L'hagiographie belge, suisse et germanique; L'hagiographie d'Espagne et
d'Italie; L'hagiographie des Réguliers. The same conclusion that can be
drawn from this chapter imposes itself on anyone obliged to peruse the
Bulletin des Publications hagiographiques of the *Analecta Bollandiana*,
which contains literally thousands of book reviews and notes on recent
publications and bibliographical references which appear in specialized reviews of spirituality and history.

8. We will dispense with any attempt to substantiate our assertion by
references to spiritual theology, medicine, psychology, and history. (Anyone
in the least familiar with the vast amount of studies in this field will appreciate the obvious reason for this and can refer to the preceding note.) We
would like to emphasize instead the fact that in recent years iconography
and graphology have been assuming an increasing importance in the field
of hagiography.

9. *Iconography*: for the obvious purpose of bringing the Saint as close
as possible to the reader and enabling him to establish a more thorough
psychological contact with the Saint, the desirability and necessity of intro-
ducing iconographical representations into biography is becoming ever more
evident. It is considered that iconography can contribute to the pyscholog-
ical interpretation of the Saint's personality. Accurate historical investigation has obviously led to a search for more faithful reproductions closer
to the time of the Saint himself. In addition to the classical work of K.
Künstle, *Ikonographie der Heiligen*, Freiburg im Br., 1926, we draw particular attention to W. Schamoni, *Das wahre Gesicht der Heiligen*, Leipzig,

1938, frequently re-edited and translated into different languages (*The Face of the Saints*, tr. by Anne Fremantle, New York, Pantheon, 1947). We wish to cite also the well-known hagiographical works of L. von Matt, consisting of a series of photographs accompanied by brief texts. He has treated the following Saints: St. Dominic, St. Ignatius, St. Francis of Assisi, St. Pius X, St. Bernadette Soubirous, St. Vincent de Paul, St. Benedict. An indication of the importance iconography has assumed is the fact that the *Enciclopedia Cattolica*, in treating of many of the Saints, has devoted a special section to their iconography, replete with annotation. Moreover, the series *Bibliotheca Sanctorum,* now in the course of publication under the auspices of the John XXIII Institute at the Pontifical Lateran University (Vol. I, 1961), has illustrated each article, where possible, with a portrait of the Saint in question. We cannot pass over in silence the increasing production of devotional images, statues, etc. representing the Saints. Even though these are often devoid of artistic value and much can and must be done to elevate the level of taste, they still constitute a manifest sign of popular devotion and of the role which the Saints occupy in the religious life of the faithful: "It is through popular religious art that trends in Christian piety are manifested, much more than through isolated attempts, often disconcerting, of famous artists. Popular religious art is the true heir of the image-makers of former times. . . . They numbered in their ranks true artists, whereas our artisans can scarcely be called such . . . but this is a question of art criticism, not of iconography." (G. de Jerphanion, *La voix des monuments,* Paris, 1930, p. 30, note 3, cited by E. Lamalle, S.J., on p. 705 of his article, "La popularité des Saints. A propos du plus populaire d'entre eux," *NRT* 59 [1932] 694–706—an article rich in excellent considerations on this subject.)

10. As an introduction to graphology, it will suffice simply to note the wide diffusion of G. Moretti, O.F.M., *I Santi dalla Scrittura, Esami grafologici,* Padua, 1952 (9th ed.), translated into French, German, Dutch, and English (*The Handwriting of the Saints,* New York, Macmillan, 1964). Among the many reactions it provoked, we call the reader's attention especially to A. Rodewyk, S.J., "Die Handschrift der Heiligen," *Geist und Leben* 31 (1958) 217–226. For concrete applications of graphology to the psychological study of the Saints, see, for example: A. Koch, S.J., "Aloysius' Charakterbild aus seinen Briefen," *Geist und Leben* 3 (1928) 42–60, which includes on pages 52–58 the expert opinion of the Swiss graphologist, Dr. F. Buomberger; and J. Warszawski, S.J., *Inquisitiones super Autographum S. Stanislai Kostka,* Rome, 1959. Also noteworthy is Schamoni's study (cf. note 9), which includes, beginning with the third German edition, an appendix consisting of reproductions of the autographs of thirty-one Saints.

11. Among the writers of international reputation who have written about the Saints are: R. Bazin, R. Bacchelli, G. Bernanos, G. Cesbron, G. K. Chesterton, P. Claudel, P. Dörfler, T. S. Eliot, D. Fabri, H. Federer, G. von le Fort, H. Ghéon, I. Giordani, I. F. Görres (Coudenhove),

G. Goyau, E. von Handel-Mazzetti, A. von Krane, G. Manacorda, F. Mauriac, M. van der Meersch, G. Papini, H. Queffélec, V. Sackville-West, R. Schneider, F. Timmermans, E. Waugh, L. Weismantel, F. Werfel.

12. Saints whose lives have been made the subject of screen productions include: St. Francis of Assisi, St. Ignatius Loyola, St. Vincent de Paul, St. John Mary Vianney, St. Pius X, St. John Bosco, St. Joan of Arc, St. Catherine of Siena, St. Margaret of Cortona, St. Bernadette Soubirous, St. Theresa of Lisieux, St. Maria Goretti, the Blessed Carmelite Martyrs, the Jesuit Martyrs of China. On this subject, see the following works: C. Fernández Cuenca, *Historia del Cine,* 1948 ss.; P. Leprohon, "Doit-on porter à l'écran la vie des Saints?" *Revue Internationale du cinéma* (1949, n. 2) 21; Ch. Ford, "La vie des Saints telle qu'on la voit à l'écran," *ibid.* (1957, n. 26) 36; A. Bazin, "Un saint ne l'est qu'après . . ." *Cahiers du cinéma* (1951, n. 2) 46; Ch. Ford, *Le cinéma au service de la foi,* 1953, pp. 85ss.; A. Ayfre, *Problemi estetici del cinema religioso,* 1953, pp. 123 and passim. In addition, see the various current notices on the subject of religious films which appear in *Razón y Fé* (C. M. Staehlin), *Etudes* (H. Agel), *La Civiltà Cattolica* (E. Baragli), *America* (M. Walsh) and in specialized Catholic reviews. All this is true not only of the cinema, but also of the theatre. Here too we find dramatic representations dealing with the Saints—works varying in artistic excellence but ever indicative of interest. Some which come to mind as having achieved outstanding success during recent years are: J. M. Pemán, *El divino Impaciente*; T. S. Eliot, *Murder in the Cathedral*; D. Fabri; *Veglia d'armi*; J. Anouilh, *L'Alouette*; P. Claudel, *Jean d'Arc au bûcher.* (On these last few, cf. e.g. F. Aparício, S.J., "Nuevo Teatro Sobre Juan de Arco," Razón y Fé 149 [1954] 541–552). R. Bolt, *A Man for All Seasons.* By way of example, we may note the fact that in Rome alone, in addition to T. S. Eliot's famous *Murder in the Cathedral,* Italian theatre groups have recently presented major performances dealing with the persons of St. Catherine of Siena, St. Theresa of Lisieux, St. Monica, and St. Agnes (the first of which has already gone through 3,000 performances in various parts of the world).

13. However, in contrast to these trends, in the ranks of Protestantism can be found scholars interested in the question of the Saints, seeking to put them in their proper perspective and to assure them their due. We have in mind particularly the interest aroused by the work of W. Nigg, *Grosse Heilige,* Zürich, 1946. We must acknowledge this fact even though we cannot accept certain of this author's basic concepts and interpretations. On this point, cf. F. Wulf, S.J., "Ein protestantisches Buch über die Heiligen," *Geist und Leben* 20 (1947) 156–158, and F. Hillig, S.J., "Die angebliche Beschränktheit des Pfarrers von Ars," *ibid.* 32 (1959) 13–25. Among other indications of this phenomenon in Protestant circles, attention should be called to the scientific work of R. Lansemann, *Die Heiligentage besonders die Marien-, Apostel- und Engeltage in der Reformationszeit im Zusammenhange der reformatorischen Anschauungen von den Zeremonien, von den Festen, von den Heiligen und von den Engeln,* Göttingen,

1939. It is obvious from this work that the attitude of many Protestants today is very different from their original rigid concepts.

14. "For several decades, we have noted the rise of a movement which aims to remove as far as possible all images of Saints from our places of worship, and even curtail the veneration of the Saints. The churches which have been constructed and decorated in accord with this tendency are distinguishable by a 'cold iconoclasm' that renders them mute and devoid of beauty. How are we to judge this tendency in the light of Catholic tradition? It is true that the Church leaves to each person the liberty of determining how great or how small a role in his personal piety he wishes to grant the veneration of the Saints. Nevertheless, no one can deny, without betraying his Catholic faith, that those whom the Church has elevated to the honors of the altar are worthy of even public veneration. . . . There is at the root of this tendency something unwholesome which is reflected in the lives and customs of some Christians, to their detriment. If this tendency were to prevail, there would soon be discernible, especially among the common people, a noticeable drying up of that rich stream of spiritual advantages which flows from the dogma of the 'Communion of Saints,' of which the veneration of the Saints—speaking with and invoking them —is an essential element. Anyone who wishes to return in this matter to a 'purer and more spiritual' form, ought to recall the practices of the Christians of the first centuries with respect to the memory and mortal remains of the Martyrs, and the inspiring examples of fervent veneration which they bequeathed to future generations. The veneration of the Saints is a very precious legacy left to us by primitive Christianity." (From the *Osservatore Romano,* 9th April 1959.) This discourse on Benedict XIV was to have been delivered by His Holiness Pius XII on the occasion of the solemn commemoration projected for November 1958.

15. His Holiness John XXIII drew attention to this fact in his allocution to the clergy of Rome (cf. *L'Osservatore Romano,* 25th November 1960).

16. On this subject cf.: K. Rahner, S.J., "Die Kirche der Heiligen," in *Schriften zur Theologie,* Band 3: *Zur Theologie des Geistlichen Lebens,* Einsiedeln, Zurich, Cologne, 1957 (2e), pp. 111–126, especially pp. 111–112. This study was originally published in *Stimmen der Zeit* 157 (1955–56) 81–91.

17. One might ask how it could be possible that precisely this wealth of vitality and spontaneity could have remained, during recent centuries, in the background or even at times totally overlooked. In our opinion, much of the responsibility for this sad state of affairs must be laid at the door of a hagiography which has remained for too long predominantly schematic and conventional. Only in recent times has this type of hagiography begun to yield ground to works which are the fruit of more accurate studies of primary sources and their theological interpretation. But we do not intend to dwell on this point. In particular the eminent Bollandist, H. Delehaye, S.J., has vigorously drawn the attention of scholars to the all too negative

influence exercised on current ideas concerning the Saints by well-intentioned but incompetent hagiographers. Delehaye did his utmost to remedy this situation through his own scholarly writings: *Les Passions des Martyrs et les genres littéraires,* Brussels, 1921; *Les Légendes Hagiographiques,* Subsidia Hagiographica 18, Brussels, 1955 (4e). Useful information on this subject can be found in the article in the *Dictionnaire de Spiritualité,* I, 1624–1719, entitled "Biographies Spirituelles" (I. Antiquité: G. Bardy; II. Epoque Byzantine: I. Hausherr, S.J.; III. Moyen Age: F. Vernet; IV. Epoque moderne: P. Pourrat, M. Viller, S.J.; R. Daeschler, S.J.). Cf. also the work cited by Aigrain and the abundant documentation contained therein: *L'Hagiographie. Ses Sources—Ses méthodes—Son histoire*; above all: Première Partie, II: Les sources documentatives et narratives, pp. 107–192. See also the interesting study of L. von Hertling, S.J., "Der mittelalterliche Heiligentypus nach den Tugendkatalogen," *ZAM* 8 (1933) 260–268.

18. On the sources, content, and consequences of the theology of the Mystical Body of Christ, the reader is referred to the abundant literature which preceded and followed Pius XII's encyclical, *Mystici Corporis* (June 29, 1943), especially the works of: K. Adam, J. Anger, L. Cerfaux, Y. Congar, O.P., C. Feckes, Ch.-V. Héris, O.P., Ch. Journet, F. Jürgensmeier, E. Mersch, S.J., A. Mitterer, P. de Poulpiquet, O.P., K. Rahner, S.J., S. Salaverri, S.J., E. Sauras, O.P., O. Semmelroth, S.J., S. Tromp, S.J., T. Zapelena, S.J., to cite but a few of the most important.

As for the implications of this doctrine for spiritual theology, cf., above all, the article "Eglise" in the *Dictionnaire de Spiritualité,* IV, 370–479, passim, but especially: II. Figures et Images de l'Eglise, 4. Le Corps, columns 396–401 (R. Brunet, S.J.). This is an excellent résumé, though it contains a rather unfortunate observation with respect to the knowledge of Christ (col. 398).

19. The reader should recall to mind the fine and succinct text of the Council of Trent: "The holy council orders all bishops and others who have the official charge of teaching to instruct the faithful diligently, in accordance with the practice of the Catholic and apostolic Church from the early years of the Christian religion, and in accordance with the common teaching of the Holy Fathers and the decrees of the sacred councils. First of all, they should instruct the faithful carefully concerning the intercession and the invocation of the saints, the honor due to their relics, and the lawful use of images—teaching the faithful that the saints, reigning together with Christ, pray to God for men; it is a good and useful thing to invoke the saints humbly and to have recourse to their prayers and to their efficacious help to obtain favors from God through his Son Jesus Christ our Lord who alone is our redeemer and saviour. Moreover, they should teach the faithful that only men of irreligious mentality deny that the saints enjoying eternal happiness in heaven are to be invoked; or claim either that saints do not pray for men or else that calling upon them to pray for us even as individuals is idolatry or is opposed to the word of

God and is prejudicial to the honor of the one Mediator of God and men, Jesus Christ (see 1 Tim 2:5); or say that it is foolish to make supplication by word or by thought to those who are reigning in heaven." Session XXV, Denzinger #984 (translation: *The Church Teaches*, Herder, 1955). For a commentary, cf. H. Jedin, "Entstehung und Tragweite des Trienter Dekretes über die Bilderverehrung," *Tübinger Theologische Quartalschrift* 116 (1935) 143–188, 404–429. The principal official documents of the Church on the Saints have been collected (in addition to Denzinger's *Enchiridion* and Cavallera's *Thesaurus*) in the convenient volume of J. de Guibert, S.J., *Documenta Ecclesiastica christianae perfectionis studium spectantia*, Rome, 1931 (see Index under "Sancti"). The encyclicals *Mystici Corporis* and *Mediator Dei* appeared after the publication of de Guibert's collection, and provide additional magisterial teaching on the Saints. For a general treatment on the intercession of the Saints and its dogmatic basis, cf. the classic work of J. B. Walz, O.P., *Die Fürbitte der Heiligen. Eine dogmatische Studie*, Freiburg im Br., 1927. As regards the Decrees of the Ecumenical Councils, see: *Conciliorum Oecumenicorum Decreta*. Edidit Centro di Documentazione. Istituto per le Scienze Religiose, Bologna-Basilea etc., 1962 (see Index Personarum, Locorum, et Rerum, s.v. Sanctorum cultus).

20. S. Tyszkiewicz, S.J., "La sainteté de l'Eglise," *NRT* 63 (1936) 449–479, 457–458. In addition to this article, cf. the interesting book by the same author: *La sainteté de l'Eglise Christoconforme, Ebauche d'une ecclésiologie unioniste* (Pont. Inst. Orientalium Studiorum), Rome, 1945.

21. In this context, we might emphasize the tremendous influence exercised on the history of the Church—from the earliest centuries until the present day—by the holy founders of movements and new styles of Christian living within Orders and religious institutes. Readily to mind come St. Anthony, St. Pacomius, St. Basil, St. Benedict, St. Bernard, St. Dominic, St. Francis of Assisi, St. Ignatius, St. John of the Cross, St. Teresa of Avila, St. Philip Neri, St. Francis de Sales, St. Vincent de Paul, St. John Baptist de la Salle, St. Paul of the Cross, St. Alphonsus Liguori, St. Joseph Cottolengo, St. John Bosco, and many others.

22. K. Rahner, S.J., *op. cit.* (in note 16), p. 120–121.

23. *AAS* 35 (1943) 209–219 (NCWC translation, #43–48).

24. The considerations presented above are obviously those which provide a foundation for the common consent of theologians on the Church's infallibility in Canonizations as they are now processed by the Church. It is well known that in recent times there have been discussions on (a) the precise scope of the object of these infallible declarations, occasioned by the opinion advanced by H. Delehaye, S.J., in *Sanctus, Essai sur le culte des Saints dans l'Antiquité* (Subsidia Hagiographica, n. 17), Brussels, 1927, pp. 251ss.; and (b) on the question whether this is defined as an object of divine or of only ecclesiastical faith, in accordance with the opinion advanced by F. Spedalieri, S.J., *De Ecclesiae infallibilitate in canonizatione Sanctorum quaestiones selectae*, Rome, 1949.

25. It is well known that St. Ignatius in his famous Rules for Thinking with the Church recommends the cult of the Saints and the veneration of their relics (cf. Rule 6). Apropos of this *sentire cum ecclesia* as it applies to the cult of the Saints, cf. the article of P. Leturia, S.J., "Sentido verdadero en la Iglesia militante," *Manresa* 14 (1942) 26–35, 118–131, especially, 118–121.

26. The Liturgy, in a "Preface" granted by the Holy See to several dioceses, offers a marvelous compendium of what we have been discussing in this dogmatic section: "Vere dignum et iustum est, aequum et salutare, nos tibi semper et ubique gratias agere: Domine, sancte Pater, omnipotens aeterne Deus, qui glorificaris in concilio sanctorum et eorum coronando merita, coronas dona tua; qui nobis in eorum praebes, et *conversatione exemplum, et communione consortium, et intercessione subsidium*: ut tantam habentes nubem testium, per patientiam curramus ad propositum nobis certamen, et cum eis percipiamus immarcescibilem gloriae coronam, per Iesum Christum Dominum nostrum, cuius sanguine ministratur nobis introitus in regnum aeternum. Per quem maiestatem tuam . . ." (emphasis added).

27. Universitas Catholica Lovaniensis Dissertationes ad gradum Magistri in Facultate Theologica vel in Facultate Juris Canonici consequendam conscriptae, Series II, Tomus 30, Louvain, 1937.

28. G. Thils treats of the historical development of the "Argumentum ex notis Ecclesiae" in general in the first part of his dissertation, *op. cit.*, pp. 1–120; in the second part he treats each specific note, pp. 121–286 (see pages 121–153 for the note of sanctity). The third part is devoted to "Jugements portés sur la Via Notarum," pp. 287–349 (see pages 294, 323, 336, 339–342, 346 for the note of Sanctity). It is well known that Thils' work evoked considerable reactions; e.g. T. Zapelena, S.J., "De Via Notarum in recenti quodam opere," *Gregorianum* 19 (1938) 88–109, 445–468; E. Valentini, "De firmitate argumenti ex Via Notarum," *Salesianum* 1 (1939) 201–208; R. Garrigou-Lagrange, O.P., "La sainteté de l'Eglise," in M. Brillant and M. Nédoncelle, *Apologétique*, Paris, 1948 (2e), pp. 623–664.

29. On the origin and development of this trend, cf. G. Thils, *op. cit.*, pp. 150–153 and the respective notes.

30. For example, I. Salaverri, S.J., *De Ecclesia Christi*, in *Sacrae Theologiae Summa*, I (Biblioteca de Autores Christianos 61), Matriti, 1962 (5e). Liber 3, cap. 3, art. 3: Notae discernentes veram Ecclesiam, Thesis 30, n. 1228ss., pp. 933ss.

31. Cf. the significant tabulation compiled by K. Richstätter, S.J., "Die Heiligen des letzten Jahrtausends" (cf. above, note 1), pp. 82–84. For information up to the year 1959, cf, the statistical tables and corresponding notations offered by P. Delooz, S.J., in the work already cited: *Conditions sociologiques de la Sainteté canonisée*, vol. II, ch. V-XV, pp. 123–287. Among the various considerations suggested by a close examination of these tables, not the least is the fact that during precisely those

centuries facilely and superficially styled periods of decadence within the Church (15th, 16th, 19th), there was an amazing appearance of Saints. Cf. on this point, K. Kempf, S.J., *Die Heiligkeit der Kirche im 19. Jahrhundert. Ein Beitrag zur Apologie der Kirche.* Einsiedeln, 1921 (7e); *Die fortlebende Kraft der Kirche. Die Heiligen, Seligen, Ehrwürdigen und Diener Gottes des 19. und 20. Jahrhunderts.* Saarbrücken, 1939, also, the timely reflections of C. Martini, S.J., in the article, "I Santi del Giubileo," *Civiltà Cattolica* 102 (1951, vol. I), 593–604.

32. In limiting ourselves to an explicit consideration of the Saints canonized by the Roman Catholic Church in accordance with the procedure in force since the year 1634, we certainly do not intend to exclude from our argument those Saints canonized prior to 1634 by a procedure less refined and developed than that of our own times. (Rather, it is precisely the all-embracing consideration of these very Saints that confirms the argument by emphasizing the continuity with which the Church has proposed the Saints as her authentic sons and daughters.)

We have restricted our treatment specifically to Saints canonized in accord with the current procedure because an analysis of this very procedure will make quite evident the twofold foundation of a canonization: (1) holiness typically Catholic, lived in an extraordinary manner; and (2) miracles. In fact, by proposing on an apologetical level the Church's holiness as a *nota notior ipsa Ecclesia,* and as a visible property easily discernible even by those who are not Catholics, and by adapting this argument to the demands of our times, it seems more effective to insist chiefly on Saints canonized in recent centuries, proposing them as typical representatives of the Church in virtue of a procedure that is strict and clearly delineated, and hence more readily grasped and discerned by those to whom this argumentation is directed. In this context, we might direct attention to the fact that a consideration of the process either to establish the heroic virtue of the Saint or to examine the authenticity of alleged miracle, is of truly providential assistance in adapting the apologetic argument in question to the needs of modern times.

33. The basic text in this field, as is well known, is the work of Cardinal Prosper Lambertini (afterwards Benedict XIV), *De Servorum Dei Beatificatione et Beatorum Canonizatione* (5 vols.), Bologna, 1734–1738. E. de Azevedo, S.J., has provided an excellent summary of this in: *Sanctissimi Domini Benedicti Papae XIV doctrina de Servorum Dei Beatificatione et Beatorum Canonizatione in Synopsim redacta,* which was re-edited by R. Coppola (Naples, 1853–54). The Code of Canon Law has synthesized these teachings in Book IV, Part II: "De Causis Beatificationis Servorum Dei et Canonizationis Beatorum," can. 1999–2141. In addition to commentaries on the Code which obviously treat the subject, we would call attention to: S. Indelicato, *Le basi giuridiche del Processo di Beatificazione,* Rome, 1944; F. Gagna, *De Processu Canonizationis a primis Ecclesiae saeculis usque ad Codicem Iuris Canonici,* Dissertatio in Facultate Iuris Canonici Pontificiae Universitatis Gregorianae, Rome, 1940; D. J.

Blaher, O.F.M., *The Ordinary Processes in Causes of Beatification and Canonization. A Historical Synopsis and Commentary.* Washington, 1949; S. Indelicato, *Il Processo Apostolico di Beatificazione*, Rome, 1945; *Codex pro Postulatoribus Causarum Beatificationis et Canonizationis*, editio 4a ad novi Iuris Canonici normas exacta cura Postulationis Generalis Fratrum Minorum, Rome, 1929. An excellent summary can be found under the terms, "Canonizzazione" and "Beatificazione," written by C. Salotti and G. Löw, C.SS.R., in the *Enciclopedia Cattolica*, respectively in vol. III, 569–607, and vol. II, 1090–1100. Similarly, under the term "Canonisation," written by L. von Hertling, S.J., in *Dictionnaire de Spiritualité*, II, 77–85. See the same author's "Kanonisationsprozess und Vollkommenheit," *Geist und Leben* 5 (1930) 237–266. As an illustration of the procedure, cf. G. Della Cioppa, *Come si fanno i Santi* (Causa di S. Giovanni Bosco), Rome, 1934. See also: P. Molinari, S.J., *I Santi e le Cause di Beatificazione e Canonizzazione*, Rome, 1962. An historical study on the relationship between canonizations and authority in the Western Church worthy of being mentioned is that of E. W. Kemp, *Canonization and Authority in the Western Church*, London, 1948, even though some of the interpretations and conclusions advanced by the author can not be shared from a Catholic viewpoint. On the concept of heroic virtue, so basic in the process of beatification and canonization, cf. R. Hofmann, *Die heroische Tugend. Geschichte und Inhalt eines theologischen Begriffes* (Münchener Studien zur historischen Theologie) Munich, 1933; also the briefer summaries in the manuals of spiritual theology, e.g. A. Lanz, S.J., *Lineamenti di Ascetica e Mistica* (Biblioteca ascetica 29) Milan, 1958(2e) P. I cap. III, Insegnamenti della Chiesa, pp. 30–37, and P. II, cap. I, Virtù eroica secondo la Chiesa, pp. 41–49; L. von Hertling, S.J., *Theologiae Asceticae cursus brevior*, Rome, 1947 (3e), n. 27–50, pp. 12–23; n. 368–392, pp. 200–212.

34. In addition to the studies cited in the preceding note, we call attention to the article of J. A. Hardon, S.J., "The Concept of Miracle from St. Augustine to Modern Apologetics," *Theological Studies* 15 (1954) 229–257, in which the author explains the theological concept and the function of miracles according to the mind of Benedict XIV, presenting it in the context of previous conceptions and then examining the developments it has undergone in more recent apologetics.

35. With respect to the manner in which miracles are treated and examined in the course of a process of beatification and canonization, the reader is referred to the works cited in the preceding notes. See principally the excellent study of F[ranciscus] Antonelli, O.F.M., *De inquisitione medico-legali super miraculis in Causis Beatificationis et Canonizationis*, Studia Antoniana, 18, Rome, 1962. In addition to these, we would like to point out the excellent work of F. Leuret and H. Bon, *Les Guérisons miraculeuses modernes*, Paris, 1950. Though this treats primarily the miraculous events of Lourdes, it provides an ample discussion of the general question of miracles and, in this context, examines attentively the norms and criteria used in the process of beatification and canonization. The

Acts of the Processes on Miracles are printed in the *Positiones* which constitute the basis for the discussions of the Sacred Congregation of Rites. Then they pass into the possession of the Cardinals, Consultors, Advocates and Postulators, and finally end up in different libraries. Unfortunately, there do not exist as yet general studies in which the procedural acts on miracles are reported extensively and fully annotated. There are several publications, however, with brief notations: A. Seitz, "Neuzeitliche Wunder bei Heiligsprechungen," *Theologisch-praktische Quartalschrift* (1918) 77–92; F. Baumann, S.J., "Heilige und Wunder," *ibid.* (1956) 22–42; H. Bon, *Le miracle devant la science*, Paris, 1957. For the current practices of the Congregation of Rites, cf. *Regolamento della Consulta Medica presso la S.C. dei Riti*, Rome, 1959.

36. L. Monden, S.J., *Le miracle signe de salut* (Museum Lessianum, Section Théologique n. 54) Brussels, 1960, originally published in Dutch. We call attention in particular to the articles of E. Dhanis, S.J., to which Monden refers with special praise (Intro., p. 15), even though these two authors differ on the manner of conceiving the physical transcendence of miracles: "Le problème de l'acte de foi," *NRT* 68 (1946) 26–43; "Un chaînon de la preuve du miracle," in *Problemi scelti di Teologia contemporanea*, Rome, 1954, pp. 63–86; "Qu'est-ce qu'un miracle?" *Gregorianum* 40 (1959) 201–241. Among the publications which appeared at the same time as Monden's and are therefore not cited by him, we call attention to: J. C. Carter, S.J., "The Recognition of Miracles," *Theological Studies* 20 (1959) 175–197. See also: J. M. Riaza Morales, S.I., *Azar, Ley, Milagro. Introducción científica al estudio del milagro*, BAC, 236, Madrid, 1964.

37. On the use of this text in the historical development of the apologetical argument *ex Nota Sanctitatis Ecclesiae,* cf. G. Thils, *op. cit.,* pp. 7, 17, 18. See also pages 138–152, in which the author does not speak directly of the text in Mark 16:15ss., but treats the growing tendency to include miracles in the argument from the note of holiness, and in this context, he refers to numerous relevant studies.

38. Since we are speaking on a strictly apologetical level, we naturally prescind from any argumentation which presupposes the doctrinal authority of the Roman Catholic Church, as for example, the *Risposta della Commissione Biblica* (Reply of the Biblical Commission) of June 26, 1912, treating of the final pericope in the Gospel according to St. Mark (Denzinger #2156). We refer the reader instead to the well-documented works of V. Larrañaga, S.J., *La Ascensión del Señor en el Nuevo Testamento* (Consejo Superior de Investigaciones científicas) Madrid, 1943; vol. I. Part One: La crítica textual en el triple relato de la Ascensión, II. El texto del final de S. Marco, 16, 9, pp. 147ss.; and M. J. Lagrange, O.P., *Evangile selon Saint Marc* (Etudes Bibliques) Paris, 1947, Appendice: "La finale de Marc (XVI, 9–20)," pp. 456–468.

39. Naturally, we do not pretend that our entire argument is contained explicitly in the text cited from St. Mark; the basis for it, however, is contained therein. What is stated explicitly is that miracles (literally:

"signs") will accompany believers. It is equally clear that this promise is strictly connected with the promise to preach the good news to every creature; so that the signs are promised as a confirmation of the truth of the Christian faith proclaimed by the Apostles and those who bear authentic testimony to Jesus' doctrine by living it in its full integrity. In this sense we can say that the Church of Christ must possess signs which attest to its authenticity or, in other words, which constitute a distinctive sign, a "note" in the technical sense of that term. And this must be true for all time because no temporal limitation was indicated in the words of the Gospel. This conclusion is drawn by the great majority of Catholic exegetes; to give but a few examples: *La Sacra Bibbia*, vol. 8: *I Vangeli* (edited by the Pontifical Biblical Institute) Florence, 1958, p. 188; *A Catholic Commentary on Holy Scripture*, London, etc., 1953, St. Mark, 743f., p. 934 (J. A. O'Flynn); M. J. Lagrange, O.P., *op. cit.*, p. 454; J. Huby, S.J., *Evangile selon Saint Marc* (Verbum Salutis, 2) Paris, 1924, p. 406, translated by John J. Heenan, S.J., *The Word of Salvation*, Milwaukee: Bruce, 1957, pp. 915–923; and among the more ancient commentators: Cornelius a Lapide, Maldonatus, Knabenbauer, etc., *in locum* (with many references to other authors). This is sufficient as a premise for our apologetical argument; it is enough that exegesis should testify that in the true Church of Christ, wherein His genuine faith and doctrine is lived and preached, one must be able to find, as an authenticating sign for all times, miracles. Our argument proceeds from this premise: the Roman Catholic Church proposes an immense array of persons—the Saints—as typical examples and living preachers of its faith and doctrine. The Church demonstrates, moreover, that their holiness, nurtured by the faith and teaching of the Church, is distinguished and distinguishable by miracles. Therefore she is the true Church of Christ. (It is significant that several exegetes see the fulfillment of this promise of the Lord not only in the Apostles, but also in the Saints throughout the centuries; thus, e.g.: Cornelius a Lapide, Maldonatus, Knabenbauer, Huby.) On the connection between holiness and miracles in their scriptural foundation, cf. L. Monden, S.J., *op. cit.*, pp. 68ss.

40. Many facts and considerations which can serve as a basis for these reflections are in L. Monden, *op. cit.*, Première partie: Théologie du miracle, ch. II: Sens du miracle, 1. Miracle et surnaturel, 2. Miracle et Incarnation, 3. Miracle et Rédemption, pp. 29–39.

41. The extent to which canonizations in the Catholic Church differ from those in the Russian Orthodox Church can be deduced from several studies: P. Peeters, S.J., "La canonisation des Saints dans l'Eglise russe," *Analecta Bollandiana* 33 (1914) 380-420; and "La Canonisation des Saints dans l'Eglise russe. Note complémentaire," *ibid.* 38 (1920) 172–176. P. de Meester, O.S.B., "La Canonizzazione dei Santi nella Chiesa Russa Ortodossa," *Gregorianum* 30 (1949) 393–407. Many useful facts about the canonization process in the Russian Church are found also in the work of E. Behr-Sigel, *Prière et Sainteté dans l'Eglise Russe*, Paris, 1950. For

an evaluation of this work, the reader is referred to the review of J. H. Ledit, S.J., in *Theological Studies* 12 (1951) 270–271. With respect to the possibility of true miracles outside the Catholic Church, cf. L. Monden, *op. cit.*, Première partie, Théologie du miracle, ch. 7, Le miracle hors de l'Eglise et le pseudo-miracle démoniaque, pp. 119–150, and Seconde Partie, Apologétique du miracle, ch. 3, Absence du prodige majeur hors de l'Eglise Catholique, pp. 221–282.

42. Cf. M. Claeys Boùùaert, S.J., "Raisons personnelles de croire. Lettre à un Professeur d'Université," *NRT* 60 (1933) 117-140.

43. L. von Hertling, S.J., "Canonisation," in *DS* II, 84. One of the few theological attempts to study this material as a source of the Church's ascetical teaching is that of S. Racioppi, *Il vero umile nei processi di Beatificazione* (Excerpta ex dissertatione ad Lauream in Facultate Theologica Pontificiae Universitatis Gregorianae) Salerno, 1953. (This dissertation was directed by K. Truhlar, S.J.)

44. In this context, the reader is referred to a conference organized by the College of Postulators and conducted by the author on April 7, 1960, in the presence of several Cardinals, members of the Congregation of Rites, and other scholars (cf. *Osservatore Romano*, 9th April 1960). The text of this conference was published in the form of an article: "Il problema della agiografia: esigenze storiche e uso della psicologia," *Civiltà Cattolica* 113 (1962) t. 3, 15–26; "Il problema della agiografia: forma letteraria e principi teologici," *ibid.*, 221–231. We would like to call attention also to the brief article of B. Matteucci, "Lo stile dei Santi," *Studi Cattolici* 5 (1961) maggio-giugno, n. 24, 15–19. The author explains some excellent notions with respect to the manner in which we must conceive the appearance and personality of the Saints. In so doing, he suggests sound principles which ought to be applied in the field of hagiography.

45. As in the preceding pages (a reprinting of what appeared originally in *Gregorianum* 42 [1961] 63–96), we will refrain in the following part from any consideration of the privileged status of the Mother of God, and restrict ourselves to that of the Saints. Nevertheless, we wish to point out that even though her function in salvation history is altogether special and she consequently occupies a privileged position in the Church's cult, the problem of the cult directed towards her has many points in common with our present problem. Let it suffice simply to recall the central questions of the mediation and intercession of Mary and the Saints, and to emphasize the identity of the objections which have been raised throughout the course of history and are still being advanced against the cult of the Virgin and of the Saints. In writing the pages which follow we have naturally taken into consideration the mariological literature which treats of these problems. We have refrained, however, from referring to these writings to avoid overburdening our documentation and to preclude the need for continual distinctions between aspects common to both problems and those proper to the cult of Mary. Whereas mariology has been considerably occupied with the latter, it cannot be said that theology in gen-

eral has taken any deep interest in our problem of the cult of the Saints. It is precisely this difference and the consequent lacuna which justify an extensive treatment of this subject, in the course of which will occur only occasional allusions to mariological problems and to the solutions proposed thereto. (Cf. notes 146, 152, etc.)

46. For generic systematic notions, cf. G. di Napoli, "Culto," *Enciclopedia Filosofica.* Centro di studi filosofici di Gallarate, 1 (1957) 1368; "Culto," *Enciclopedia Cattolica* 4 (1950). I Nozioni generali. II Le varie specie di c. (L. Oldani) 1040–1044. III Origine e sviluppo del c. cristiano (P. Paschini) 1044–1945; A. Chollet, "Culte en général," *DTC* 3 (1908) 2404–2427; "Culto," *Dizionario di Teologia Morale,* diretto da F. Roberti, Rome, 1954, 366–367; E. Jombart, S.J., "Culte." *Dictionnaire de Droit Canonique* 4 (1949) 861–879. We refer the reader also to the basic treatment of St. Thomas, *Summa Theologica,* IIa-IIae, q. 81–100, and to the commentators thereon; to the work of F. Suárez, *Commentaria in Secundam Secundae D. Thomae, Opus de virtute et statu religionis,* tract. 1–4, Opera omnia, ed. Vivès, Parisiis, t. XIII and t. XIV, 4–437. See also, O. Lottin, O.S.B., *L'âme du culte. La vertu de religion d'après S. Thomas d'Aquin,* Louvain, 1920; I. Mennessier, O.P., "L'idée de 'sacré' et le culte d'après S. Thomas," *Revue des Sciences Philosophiques et Théologiques* 19 (1930) 63–82; J. Lécuyer, C.S.Sp., "Réflexions sur la théologie du culte selon saint Thomas," *Revue Thomiste* 55 (1955) 339–362; M. L. Guérard des Lauriers, O.P., "Tu adoreras le Seigneur ton Dieu," *La Vie Spirituelle* 83 (1950) 417–455; A. Stenzel, S.J., "Cultus publicus. Ein Beitrag zum Begriff und ekklesiologischen Ort der Liturgie," *Zeitschrift für Katholische Theologie* 75 (1955) 174–214; C. Vagaggini, O.S.B., *Il senso teologico della Liturgia. Saggio di liturgia teologica generale.* Edizioni Paoline, Theologica 17, Rome, 1958 (2a), tr. by Leonard J. Doyle, *Theological Dimensions of the Liturgy,* Collegeville, Liturgical Press, 1959 (abridged); J. Jungmann, S.J., *Der Gottesdienst der Kirche,* Innsbruck, etc., 1957 (2a), tr. by Clifford Howell, S.J., *Public Worship,* London, Challoner, 1957; H. A. P. Schmidt, S.J., *Introductio in liturgiam occidentalem,* Rome, etc. 1960. Abundant information about the cult of the Saints among contemporary Protestants can be found in G. Hoffmann, "Die liturgische Erneuerung im Protestantismus als Problem und Verheissung," *Trierer Theologische Zeitschrift* 66 (1957) 276–297; E. J. Lengeling, "Der gegenwärtige Stand der liturgischen Erneuerung im deutschen Protestantismus," *Münchener Theologische Zeitschrift* 10 (1959) 83–101; 200–225.

47. On the origin of the cult of the Saints, cf. note 120. Many important ancient witnesses have been recorded by the following: M. J. Rouët de Journel, S.J., *Enchiridion Patristicum,* Barcelona, 1946 (14a): Index Theologicus: Religio et cultus Sanctorum, nn. 283–284. Cf. also B. Altaner, *Patrologie. Leben, Lehre und Schriften der Kirchenväter,* Freiburg i. Br., 1955 (4a), s.v. Heiligenverehrung, tr. by Hilda Graef, *Patrology,* New York, Herder, 1960. J. Quasten, *Patrology,* Utrecht, etc., I 1950, II 1953, III 1960 (U.S. ed. Westminster, Md., Newman); M. Viller, S.J., *La*

spiritualité des premiers Chrétiens, Bibliothèque des sciences religieuses, Paris, 1930, especially pp. 178–181; M. Viller, S.J.-K. Rahner, S.J., *Aszese und Mystik in der Väterzeit. Ein Abriss.*, Freiburg i. Br., 1939, especially pp. 29–40. The teaching of the early scholastics is briefly synthesized by Peter Lombard, *Liber III sententiarum*, d. 9, c. unicum. Among the commentators on the Master of the Sentences, cf., above all, St. Bonaventure, *In IIIum Sententiarum*, d.9, a.l, q.5, and St. Thomas, *In IIIum Sent.*, d.9, q.1, a.2 and q.2, a.1–2; *In IVum Sent.*, d.15, q.4, a.5; d.45, q.3, a.1–3. Also consult St. Thomas' *Summa Theologica*, IIa-IIae, q.83, a.4; q.85, a.2; q.103, a.1–4; IIIa, q.25, a.5–6; *Supplementum*, q.72, a.2. and the Commentators on St. Thomas.

The first systematic essays on the cult of the Saints were composed after the attacks of the Reformers (cf. note 49). The best treatment of that period is the one offered by St. Robert Bellarmine in: *Disputationum Roberti Bellarmini Politiani S.I. De Controversiis christianae fidei adversus huius temporis haereticos: Quarta Controversia Generalis: De Ecclesia Triumphante, sive de gloria et cultu Sanctorum*, lib. 1, De beatitudine et canonizatione Sanctorum, esp. cc 11–20, Opera Omnia, Neapoli, t. II, 1857, pp. 439–462; *Apologia Roberti Bellarmini . . . pro responsione sua ad librum Iacobi Regis cuius titulus est "Triplici nodo triplex cuneus"* . . ., c. 8, Opera Omnia, ed. cit., t. IV, 1858, pp. 375ss.; *Dichiarazione più copiosa della Dottrina Cristiana composta in forma di dialogo, dichiarazione del Credo*, art. 9 and *dichiarazione del primo comandamento di Dio*, c. 6, Opera Omnia, ed. cit., t. VI, 1862, pp. 171, 180–181. Cf. also: J. de la Servière, S.J., *La théologie de Bellarmin*. Bibliothèque de Théologie Historique, Paris, 1909, ch. 7, L'Eglise triomphante—Les Saints, pp. 297–325. Among the authors of the second golden period of Scholasticism, cf. especially: F. Suárez, S.J., *Commentaria in Secundum Secundae D. Thomae, De virtute et statu religionis*, tract. 1, lib. 1, c. 5, Opera Omnia, ed. cit., t. XIII, 1859, pp. 53–61; tract. 3, c. 5, nn. 1–6, *ibid.*, pp. 456–457; c. 6, n. 19, *ibid.*, p. 465; lib. 3, c. 6, n.6, *ibid.*, pp. 616–617; tract 4., lib. 1, cc. 9–11, Opera Omnia, ed. cit., t. XIV, 1859, pp. 31–48; *Commentaria et Disputationes in Tertiam Partem D. Thomae, De Incarnatione*, In q. 25, a. 2, disp. 52, sect. 1–3, Opera Omnia, ed. cit., t. XVIII, 1866, pp. 563–572; comm. in q. 26, a. 1, *ibid.*, pp. 664–666; *Defensio Fidei catholicae et apostolicae adversus anglicanae sectae errores*, especially cc. 8–9, Opera Omnia, ed. cit., t. XXIV, 1859, pp. 156–168.

A classic summary is: Benedict XIV (Prosper Lambertini), *De Servorum Dei beatificatione et Beatorum canonizatione*, passim, especially, lib. 1, c. 1, Editio tertia auctior et castigatior. Opera Omnia, ed. Palearini, Romae, t. I, 1747, c. 1, pp. 1–10 and cc. 12–13, *ibid.*, pp. 91–109; cf. E. de Azevedo, S.J., *Sanctissimi Domini Benedicti Papae XIV doctrina de Servorum Dei beatificatione et Beatorum canonizatione in synopsim redacta*, P. I, cc. 1 and 12–13, ed. novissima, cura et studio R. Coppola, Neapoli, 1854, pp. 1–2 and 13–15. Among contemporary writings, the work which can give the most balanced theological appreciation of the foundations of the Catholic cult of the Saints is, in my opinion, that of S. Tromp, S.J., *Corpus Christi quod est Ecclesia*: I. *Introductio generalis*. Pontificia Universitas Gregoriana, Romae, 1946 (2a). II. *De Christo Capite Mystici Corporis*, ibid. 1960, III. *De Spiritu Christi Anima*, ibid., 1960. See also the fine synthetic essay of: A. Michel, "La Communion des Saints," *Doctor Communis* 9 (1956) 1–130, especially pp. 34–39; 59–60; 68–72; 76–77; 109–118 (cf. C. Boyer, S.J., "La Comunione dei Santi," *Civiltà Cattolica* 108 [1957, I] 620–622). A. Piolanti, *Il Mistero della Communione dei Santi nella Rivelazione e nella Teologia*, Teologia e Vita, I, Rome, etc. 1957, especially pp. 781–789 (cf. G. Quadrio, S.D.B., "La Comunione dei Santi," *Salesianum* 20 [1958] 129–135); also the excellent article of J. Pascher, "Die 'Communio Sanctorum' als Grundgefüge der Katholischen Heiligenverehrung," *Münchener Theologische Zeitschrift*, 1 (1950 n. 3) 1–11; J. Hild, O.S.B., "Le Mystère des Saints dans le Mystère chrétien," *La Maison Dieu*, n. 52 (1957) 5–18; A. Molien, *La Liturgie des Saints: leur culte en général*, Avignon, 1932; J. A. Jungmann, S.J., *Public Worship* (tr. by C. Howell, S.J.), London, Challoner, 1957, pp. 216–223; C. Vagaggini, O.S.B., *op cit.*, especially pp. 257–263; H.A.P. Schmidt, S.J., *op. cit.*, 519–527; A.G. Martimort, *L'Eglise en prière, Introduction à la liturgie*, Paris, 1961, especially pp. 766–785, written by P. Jounel.

Among works of a popular character are the following: J. Douillet, *Qu'est-ce qu'un Saint*, Coll. Je sais-Je crois. Quatrième Partie; La Vie en Dieu, Les Médiateurs, Paris, 1957, pp. 71–122; F. X. Weiser, S.J., *Handbook of Christian Feasts and Customs. The Year of the Lord in Liturgy and Folklore*, New York, Harcourt, 1958, pp. 275–343. Among general works on the cult of the Saints may be cited: P. Séjourné, O.S.B., "Saints (culte des)," *DTC* 14 (1939) 870–978; "Heiligenverehrung," *Lexikon für Theologie und Kirche* 5 (1960²), I. Dogmatisch (H. Vorgrimler) 104–106. II. Normen (J. Brosch) 106–107. III. Geschichte (id.) 107. IV. Die volkstümliche H. (H. Schauerte) 107–108; "Santi, culto dei," *Enciclopedia Cattolica* 10 (1953), I. Nozioni. II. Dottrina Cattolica e suo sviluppo (C. Vagaggini) 1851–1855. III. Conferma de culto (G. Löw, C.SS.R.) 1855–1856; "Santi," *Dizionario di Teologia Morale*, diretto da F. Roberti, Rome, 1954, 1201–1202; E. Jombart, S.J., "Culte, III. Culte des Saints," *Dictionnaire de Droit Canonique* 4 (1949) 879–883.

48. For the concept of "cult" in the strict sense of the term, cf. I. B. Umberg, S.J., "De religioso cultu relativo," *Periodica de re morali canonica liturgica* 30 (1941) 161–192. In this article, especially on pages 166–170, the author emphasizes with good reason: "distinguendum esse inter cultum sensu stricto (vel cultum sine addito), qui includat submissionem, et cultum sensu latiore (vel venerationem, honorem), qui careat nota submissionis" (p. 169). He then goes on to indicate the consequences which follow from the distinction for the proper interpretation both of ancient authors and of certain documents of the Magisterium.

49. For a clear summary of the teaching of the Reformers, cf. the well-documented article of P. Séjourné, O.S.B., "Saints (culte des), VI. Attaque

et défense de la doctrine au XVIe siècle, I. Les Adversaires," *DTC* 14 (1939) 962–965; and the historical study of R. Lansemann, *Die Heiligentage, besonders die Marien-, Apostel- und Engeltage in der Reformationszeit,* Göttingen, 1939; see also: L. E. Halkin, "Hagiographie protestante," *Analecta Bollandiana* 68 (1950) 453–463; A. Ebneter, "Der 'Heilige' im Protestantismus," *Orientierung* 25 (1961) 216–220; Id., "Fürsprache und Anrufung der Heiligen," in *Orientierung* 27 (1963) 222–226. Concerning the attitudes of the first Reformers, cf. also the useful bibliographical references provided in the work of E. G. Léonard, *Histoire Générale du Protestantisme,* vol. 1, "La Réformation," Paris, 1961, Bibliographies Générales, pp. 312–368; see especially under: liturgie, vie chrétienne et piété, culte et liturgie, etc.

As is well-known, it was precisely the attacks of the Reformers which occasioned the composition of the first systematic treatises—obviously of an apologetic character—on the part of Catholic theologians of the Counter-Reformation. For example: Jacobus Hoogstraeten, O.P., *Dialogus de veneratione et invocatione Sanctorum,* Coloniae, 1524; Joannes Eckius, *Enchiridion locorum communium adversus Lutherum et alios hostes ecclesiae,* XV, De Veneratione Sanctorum, Ingolstadii, 1549, pp. 98–107 [ed. la. Landshut, 1525]; Joannes Faber, *De intercessione Sanctorum,* in Opuscula quaedam Joannis Fabri Episcopi Viennensis, p. c. 3ss, Lipsiae, 1537; Joannes Cochlaeus, *De veneratione et invocatione Sanctorum,* Ingolstadii, 1544; Joannes Hessels, *De invocatione Sanctorum,* Lovanii, 1568; see also the works of St. Peter Canisius, S.J., especially: *Commentariorum de Verbi Dei corruptelis Tomi Duo. Prior de Venerando Christi Domini praecursore Joanne Baptista,* c. 14, Ingoldstadii, 1583, pp. 203–215; *Posterior de sacrosancta Virgine Maria Deipara,* lib. 5, cc. 13–15, *ibid.,* pp. 676–707; *Catechismus Maior seu Summa doctrinae christianae* [antetridentina], c. 3, 1, n. 44, ed. crit. F. Streicher, S.J.; *S. Petri Canisii Doctoris Ecclesiae Catechismi Latini et Germanici, Societatis Jesu Selecti Scriptores,* II. Pars Prima, Catechismi Latini, Romae-Monachii, 1933, pp. 15–16; Id. [posttridentina], c. 3, 8, n. 49, ed. cit. pp. 100–101; *Catechismus Minor seu Parvus Catechismus Catholicorum,* c. 3, n. 46, ed. cit., p. 247.

The positions taken up by contemporary Protestants on this point are rather varied and at times conflicting. Cf. E. J. Lengeling, "Der gegenwärtige Stand der liturgischen Erneuerung im deutschen Protestantismus," *Münchener Theologische Zeitschrift* 10 (1959) 83–101, 200–225, especially pp. 211–212 and note 125 (p. 212); cf. also M. Thurian, "Les grandes orientations actuelles de la spiritualité protestante," *Irenikon* 22 (1949) 388–389, and "Le mémorial des saints, Essai de compréhension évangélique d'un aspect de la piété catholique," *Verbum Caro* 13 (1959) 7–28. We might also refer to the report of the commission appointed by the Archbishop of Canterbury, London, 1957: *The Commemoration of Saints and Heroes of the Faith in the Anglican Communion.* As a current observation, cf. the notice reported in the *Ephemerides Theologicae Lovanienses* 33 (1957), Chronica: Angleterre, p. 677: "Le Right Rev. Leslie

Hunter, évêque anglican de Sheffield, prêchant à Sheffield regretta que son Eglise n'avait plus depuis le moyen âge procédé à de canonisations. Il voudrait que l'Anglicanisme proclame la sainteté de quelques éminents fidèles anglicans des temps modernes."

Despite these and other indications of a change in attitude on the part of some Protestants and Anglicans, it would be a serious error to think that this is true of Protestants and Anglicans in general, or to conclude immediately that sporadic signs of renewed devotion are a perfect counterpart of the cult of the Saints practiced in the Catholic Church. Such an opinion would fail to take into account, erroneously, the profound differences which still exist with respect to the basic dogmatic truths upon which the Catholic cult of the Saints is based.

50. Cf. "La figura e l'opera di Benedetto XIV in una sintesi storica del Pontefice Pio XII," *Osservatore Romano,* 9th April 1959. The text of this allocution which His Holiness Pius XII intended to deliver in November 1958, has been printed in: *Discorsi e Radiomessaggi,* ed. cit., vol. XX, p. 464ss. and in *La figura e l'opera di Benedetto XIV,* Bologna, 1959.

51. Unfortunately, it is precisely these deviations from genuine cult of the Saints which by their nature tend to be externalized and, when observed by both Catholics and non-Catholics, cause a certain uneasiness and even disdain for something which is good in itself. On this problem, cf. Part Three of this present study, especially Section II: Maximalistic Tendencies.

52. Cf. Denzinger-Schönmetzer, *Enchiridion Symbolorum,* Herder, 1963,[32] Index systematicus, K 2 dc. The teaching of the ordinary Magisterium of the Church concerning the cult of the Saints is clearly evident from the unanimous recommendation made in the catechisms. To cite but one of these, the *Catechismus ex decreto Concilii Tridentini ad parochos,* (Part III, cap. 2, nn. 10–24) which appeared at Rome in 1566, written by order of Pius IV, and then was re-edited and translated countless times. (For the dogmatic value and authority of the catechism of the Council of Trent, cf. J. B. de Tóth, *De auctoritate dogmatica Catechismi Romani,* Budapest, 1941.) Studies on the Council of Trent's teaching concerning the Saints are rather rare. In fact, aside from the Decree, hardly anything is found either in the proceedings of Massarelli or in the other conciliar sources. The explanation of this lies in the fact that, fearing the imminent death of the Pope, the Council endeavored to terminate its work rapidly, and therefore the last session was anticipated and no discussion was held. Cf. I. M. Hanssens, S.J., "De universa liturgica Concilii Tridentini opera," *Periodica* 35 (1946) 209–240. Even though the proceedings and the conciliar sources are brief, a valuable contribution to the study of the teaching of the Council of Trent on the Saints, and in particular on their sacred images, has been made in the work of H. Jedin, "Entstehung und Tragweite des Trienter Dekretes über die Bilderverehrung," *Tübinger Theologische Quartalschrift* 116 (1935) 143–188; 404–429. In this article, the author has collected the relevant pre-conciliar literature, both of the Reformers

and of Catholic apologists. By publishing the statement of the University of Paris of February 11, 1562 (pp. 181–186) he makes quite clear the influence which that document had in the drawing up of the Tridentine decree.

53. We would mention in particular Pius XII's encyclical *Mediator Dei et hominum* of November 20, 1947. In this document, which is the magna carta of the liturgy, the role of the Saints in Catholic worship is clearly explained. Cf. *AAS* 39 (1947) 581–583. In addition to the many commentaries on the encyclical the reader is referred to: A. Wissing, "O culto dos Santos segundo 'Mediator Dei,'" *Rev. Ecl. Brasileira* 11 (1951) 71–84.

The doctrine of the lawfulness and usefulness of the cult of the Saints is continually being confirmed anew in every canonization, in the documents issued on such occasions, and in the allocutions pronounced by the Supreme Pontiffs to honor the Saints canonized.

54. In the *Calendarium Breviarii et Missalis Romani,* after the most recent reform, 195 feasts of Saints are listed. Of these, five are of First Class (March 19: St. Joseph, Spouse of the B.V.M., Confessor and Patron of the Universal Church; May 1: St. Joseph the Worker; June 24: St. John the Baptist; June 29: Saints Peter and Paul, Apostles; Nov. 1: All Saints); Seventeen are of Second Class (twelve in honor of the Apostles and Evangelists, and the other five in honor of St. Anne, St. Joachim, St. Stephen, St. Lawrence, and the Holy Innocents); 173 are of the Third Class. In addition, there are 104 commemorations of Saints. Since this is the calendar of the universal Church, feasts proper to individual nations, dioceses, religious Orders, etc., are not listed. Cf. C. Braga, C.M., "In novum Codicem Rubricarum," *Ephemerides liturgicae* 74 (1960) 217–257.

55. Cf. *Enchiridion Indulgentiarum,* Città del Vaticano, 1952, Pars I, c. VII. Listed here are the invocations, offices, litanies, hymns, exercises of piety, novena prayers and other prayers directed to the Saints, and the indulgences attached thereunto. On the Catholic teaching concerning indulgences and a recent bibliography, cf. the article "Ablass," in *Lexikon für Theologie und Kirche,* I (1957²) 46–54.

56. For a correct understanding of the honor paid to relics and to sacred images, we refer the reader above all to the article already cited of I. B. Umberg, S.J., "De religioso cultu relativo," *Periodica* 30 (1941) 161–192. The author explains in seven propositions the type of honor due to relics and sacred images.

57. Cf. V. Grumel, "Images, culte des," *DTC* 7 (1922) 766–844. Concerning the teaching of the Council of Trent and its influence on art, cf. E. Mâle, *L'Art religieux après le Concile de Trente,* Paris, 1932.

58. The dogmatic teaching on the cult of the Saints is obviously the basis for the ecclesiastical legislation expressed in the Code of Canon Law, and for the Church's liturgical legislation. The general principle is formulated in canon 1255, 1–2; particular prescriptions are found in canons 1276–1289. Concerning liturgical regulations, cf. *Decreta authentica Con-*

gregationis Sacrorum Rituum ex Actis eiusdem collecta eiusque auctoritate promulgata, Rome, 1898–1927. The decrees after 1909 have also been published in the *AAS*.

59. For a thorough treatment of these concepts, see the well-documented work of Z. Alszeghy, S.J.–M. Flick, S.J., "Gloria Dei," *Gregorianum* 36 (1955) 361–390.

60. The Magisterium of the Church considered it necessary to criticize certain related errors; cf. *Mystici Corporis, AAS* 35 (1943) 236; and *Mediator Dei, AAS* 39 (1947) 528.

61. In fact, in the Church's official worship, the liturgy, this orientation was manifested in a marked manner from the earliest times. With reference to this, see the basic work of J. A. Jungmann, S.J., "Die Stellung Christi im liturgischen Gebet," *Liturgiegeschichtliche Forschungen*, Heft 7–8, Münster, 1925, passim, see Index: s. v. Anrede. As is emphasized by the author, the approach "ad patrem per Christum"—the standard practice of ancient liturgical prayer, which became less frequent only with the passage of time—in no way excluded the keen awareness of the divinity of Christ the Mediator; quite the contrary, it included such an awareness formally. History in fact teaches us that it was precisely this consciousness that led the faithful, from the earliest days of Christianity, to address their prayers directly to Christ as God in their private exercises of piety. The existence of such a practice was so deeply rooted and widespread that the formulas used served as an argument in the refutation of trinitarian heresies. Cf. J. Lebreton, S.J., *Histoire du dogme de la Trinité dès origines au Concile de Nicée*, Paris, 1928, vol. II, pp. 174–247 (tr. by Algar Thorold, *History of the Dogma of the Trinity*, London, 1939). On the influence which these trinitarian discussions and the reactions of the faithful against Arianism exercised on the redirection of liturgical prayer to Christ, cf. J. A. Jungmann, S.J., *The Early Liturgy to the Time of Gregory the Great*, Notre Dame, Indiana, 1959, ch. 15, "Christological disputes and their influence on the liturgy," pp. 188–198.

62. The encyclical *Mystici Corporis* does not treat our problem *ex professo*, but explains the doctrine of the Mystical Body with special emphasis on the Church Militant. One can appreciate, however, that such a document contains and presents an authoritative exposition of the dogmatic and theological foundations of our subject, and even explicit references to the relationships between the members of the Church Militant and those of the Church Triumphant, the Saints. In his commentary on the encyclical, S. Tromp, S.J., points out these relationships: Romae, Pont. Univ. Gregorianae, 1943, p. 69.

63. Cf. *Mystici Corporis*, Part I, section II: The Church is the Body of Christ, which is subdivided as follows (NCWC paragraph enumeration): *Christ was the Founder of the Body* (26–33): [a] By preaching the Gospel (27), [b] By suffering on the Cross (28–32), [c] By promulgating the Church on the Day of Pentecost (33). *Christ is Head of the Body* (34–51): [a] By reason of His pre-eminence

(36), [b] By reason of government (37–43), [c] By reason of mutual need (44–45), [d] By reason of similarity (46–47), [e] By reason of plenitude (48), [f] By reason of communication of grace and power (49–51).

Christ is the support of the Body (54–59): [a] By reason of her juridical mission (54), [b] By reason of the Spirit of Christ (55–56), [c] Who is the Soul of the Mystical Body (57–58).

Christ is the Saviour of the Body (59).

64. *Mystici Corporis AAS* 35 (1943) 215–216 [NCWC #48–49].

65. *Ibid.*, p. 200 [NCWC #15].

66. *Ibid.*, pp. 230–231 [NCWC #77].

67. *Ibid.*, p. 221 [NCWC #61].

68. Nothing, perhaps, can serve as a clearer illustration of this reality than the consideration of how a human person, even while living here on earth as a member of Christ's Mystical Body, uses in this very capacity what is his most sublime and distinguishing prerogative, namely, his personal liberty. In fact, the act specifically proper to a person incorporated into Christ and living on earth as such, the act which is supernaturally meritorious, is the product of the grace of Christ the Head and of the free co-operation of the person incorporated into Him. Without the grace of Christ the Head this act would not be a Christian, supernatural, meritorious act; and without the free personal human collaboration it would not be a human act, much less a personal one. If ever either of these two elements—grace and personal liberty—is lacking, there can be no meritorious supernatural act of a Christian person. Both must be present. They should not, however, be conceived as juxtaposed; as two autonomous and independent factors, two forces operating separately, with each producing independently part or all of the total effect. On the contrary, they must be viewed in their internal and dynamic synthesis, in their reciprocal and organic unity in which the grace of Christ the Head, far from excluding or suppressing the free collaboration of the human person, renders it fully active, efficient and meritorious. Catholic teaching, in fact, when insisting on the need for free human co-operation in a supernatural meritorious act, explains that this very co-operation is already the effect and fruit of the redemptive, liberating and sanctifying grace of Christ the Head. In other words, the Church emphasizes that the free human co-operation of a member is a co-operation subordinated to the operation of the grace of Christ the Head, who anticipates, accompanies, and makes that co-operation possible. Grace is conceived then as a vital and vivifying force which penetrates to the most intimate depths of the human personality, reaching and influencing from within the very roots of the will, healing it of any weakness, freeing its personal liberty in order to make it capable of corresponding effectively with the gracious and loving invitation of Christ. He wishes to live His life in the human person who has become His member, but He wishes to do so according to the manner proper to a human person.

69. "But if we compare a mystical body with a moral body, it is to be noted that the difference between them is not slight; rather it is very con-

siderable and very important. In the moral body the principle of union is
nothing else than the common end, and the common co-operation of all
under the authority of society for the attainment of that end; whereas in
the Mystical Body of which we are speaking, this collaboration is supple-
mented by another internal principle, which exists effectively in the whole
and in each of its parts, and whose excellence is such that of itself it is
vastly superior to whatever bonds of union may be found in a physical or
moral body. As we said above, this is something not of the natural but of
the supernatural order; rather it is something in itself infinite, uncreated:
the Spirit of God, who, as the Angelic Doctor says, 'numerically one and
the same, fills and unifies the Whole Church' (*De Veritate,* q. 29, a. 4 c.)"
Mystici Corporis, AAS, 35 (1943) 222 [NCWC #62].

70. It should be no cause for amazement that in describing the effect of
our incorporation we use a double formula, emphasizing that while Christ
lives His life in the human person who has become His member, it is also
true that the human person incorporated into Christ lives a new life deriving
from Christ. We have used this manner of expression to give a deeper
appreciation of the significance of this reality and a clearer understanding
of how one and the same life can be, from one aspect, the life of Jesus
Christ in His member, and from another the life of the person incorporated
as a member of the Mystical Body of Christ. We wish to preclude the
frequent misunderstanding whereby the expression "Christ lives in His
member" is interpreted as if we were dealing with a presence of Christ in
an individual who is no longer a person but merely a receptacle or even
an impersonal member of a physical body.

71. For the problem of how men complete the human perfection of
Christ, cf. the clarifications offered by F. Malmberg, S.J., in the third part
of his book, *Ein Leib—Ein Geist, Vom Mysterium der Kirche,* Freiburg,
etc., 1960, Dritter Teil: *Die Einheit, Die Inkarnation als Fundament der
Einheit*: A. *Die positiven Grundlagen,* pp. 223–243; B. *Die spekulativen
Erläuterungsversuche,* pp. 243–263; C. *Versuch einer spekulativen Synthese,*
pp. 263–273. After listing the major arguments and positive data relevant
to this problem and then subjecting to a critical examination the tentative
speculative essays of L. Malevez, S.J., Y. Congar, O.P., Th. Soiron, O.F.M.,
E. Mersch, S.J., and others, the author presents a profound and original
speculative solution for the problem of our "inclusion" in Christ. Much
of what he says contains valuable elements for the argument which we are
here presenting. Father Malmberg's book appeared originally in Dutch under
the title: *Eén Lichaam en één Geest. Nieuwe Gezichtspunten in de Ecclesi-
ologie.* Theologische Bibliotheek, Utrecht, etc., 1958. Prior to this, the
author had treated these questions in a series of articles also written in
Dutch: "Onze eenheid met den Godmensch in de Kerk [Our union with
the God-man in the Church]," *Bijdragen* 5 (1942) 168–204; 360–393;
6 (1943–45) 48–63, 246–267; 8 (1947) 223–255.

72. This means concretely that Christ is the male descendant of a specific
human mother, of a definite family and race; that He possesses a definite

biological heredity; that He has definite somatic qualities and character-istics, definite psychic, cognitive and affective dispositions, which are natu-rally reflected throughout his human life. Such specific properties of Christ, in fact, immune from the slightest shadow of imperfection because He was not subject to original sin, were not suppressed or eliminated by the hypo-static union, but rather elevated and ennobled. The fact that Christ was an individual man means, moreover, that He was born and lived during a fixed period of human history, in a specific religious and cultural atmos-phere, in a definite country, people, and social class. It means that the possibility of immediate and direct social contacts between Christ living on earth and other men was restricted to those which He was able to have in the concrete situations and circumstances in which He lived and with that limited number of persons who approached Him.

73. We shall treat of these different characteristics at greater length when we contrast the acts proper to the worship of God with those whereby we honor the Saints.

74. In the context, it might be well to recall the fact that the latreutic cult which we offer to Christ is a cult which is directed to Christ in His total reality; that is, as the Word *Incarnate*. Now it is precisely the fact that our adoration is directed to Jesus Christ, God-made-man, that leads us to an understanding of the profound sense in which other *created* realities can—because of and in proportion to the intensity of their union with the Word Incarnate—be worthy of love and veneration in themselves. The cult of the Saints is really one of the consequences of the Incarnation of the Word. Between the latreutic cult of the Incarnate Word and the cult of dulia of those persons who are indefectibly incorporated into His Mystical Body there exists not an opposition but rather a bond of intimate coherence. This explains why the denial and systematic rejection of the cult of the Saints usually occur in those very circles in which we find also the absence of a true cult of the humanity of Christ, of His Sacred Heart, of His Precious Blood—in brief, a christological conception which is far from the one proclaimed by the Council of Chalcedon. We know of no historical survey which elucidates fully the intrinsic bond which connects the positions taken up by various non-Catholic authors in their treatment of both Christ's humanity and the cult of the Saints. Much useful material, however, can already be found in the third volume of the classic work on the Council of Chalcedon. *Das Konzil von Chalkedon. Geschichte und Gegenwart*. Im Auftrag der Theologischen Fakultät, S.J., Sankt Georgen, Frankfurt/Main, herausgegeben von Aloys Grillmeier, S.J., und Heinrich Bacht, S.J., Band III. *Chalkedon heute*, Würzburg 1954, IX, *Chalkedon im Gespräch zwischen Konfessionen und Religionen*, spec. Y. M.-J. Congar, O.P., *Regards et réflections sur la christologie de Luther*, pp. 457–486; J. L. Witte, S.J., *Die Christologie Calvins*, pp. 487–529; J. Ternus, S.J., *Chalkedon und die Entwicklung der protestantischen Theologie. Ein Durch-blick von der Reformation bis zur Gegenwart*, pp. 531–611; H. Volk, *Die Christologie bei Karl Barth und Emil Brunner*, pp. 613–673; R. Schnacken-

burg, *Der Abstand der christologischen Aussagen des Neuen Testamentes vom chalkedonischen Bekenntnis nach der Deutung Rudolf Bultmanns*, pp. 675–693; B. Leeming, S.J., *Reflections on English Christology*, pp. 695–718. If we view our problem in this context, it seems superfluous to emphasize that this single fact should suffice as a warning that we should not view the difference which exists between the Catholic Church's teaching and the opinions of many Protestant theologians concerning the cult of the Saints as if it were a difference regarding merely accidental and marginal points occasioned largely by those devotional excesses found among Catholics at the time of the Reform and even afterwards. Consequently, we must also be cautious in entertaining hopes for a genuine agreement and we should not think that the last word has been said on this matter when we state that the Church does not teach the cult of the Saints as necessary for salvation.

75. We wish to emphasize the importance of having accepted death in a truly Christian manner, since this is a basic consideration by reason of which the Saints have been *ipso facto* elevated, in dignity and merit, above any member of the Mystical Body who is still a wayfarer. With good reason does contemporary theology emphasize that death, rather than being only a painful experience which each of us must undergo, really constitutes for the wayfarer the supreme proof of his submission to God and consequently the crowning of an entire existence lived in a loving spirit of dependence upon Him. Death offers the Christian who has lived in Christ the possibility of being conformed to Him—under the influence of grace—in the fullest and most definitive way possible, by associating himself with Christ's salvific death and thereby living fully his baptism and incorporation into Christ. On this topic cf. K. Rahner, S.J., *Zur Theologie des Todes*, Quaestiones Disputatae 2, herausgegeben von K. Rahner, S.J. und H. Schlier, Freiburg i. Br., 1958, esp. III. "Tod als Erscheinung des Mitlebens mit Christus," pp. 55–72 (published originally in *Zeitschrift für Katholische Theologie* 79 (1957) 1–44; tr. by Charles H. Henkey, *On the Theology of Death*, New York, Herder & Herder, 1961); cf. also "Zur Theologie des Todes," in *Synopsis. Studien aus Medizin und Naturwissenschaft*, Heft 3, Hamburg, 1949, 87–112; and the article "Martyrium, II. Theologisch," in *Lexikon für Theologie und Kirche* 7 (1962²) 136–138. H. Volk, *Der Tod in der Sicht des Christlichen Glaubens*, Münster, 1957; R. W. Gleason, S.J., "Toward a Theology of Death," *Thought* 32 (1957) 39–68, and *The World to Come*, New York, Sheed and Ward, 1958, especially c. 3, pp. 43–77. F. Wulf, S.J., "Das Lob des Todes," *Geist und Leben* 26 (1953), 321–324; *Christus*, Cahiers spirituels, n. 34: La Mort, 9 (1962). With some reservations, we note the following: R. Troisfontaines, S.J., "La mort, épreuve de l'amour," *Cahiers Laënnec* 4 (1946) 6–21; *Je ne meurs pas . . .*, Paris, 1960 (tr. by Francis E. Albert, *I Do Not Die*, New York, Desclée, 1963); Hans Urs von Balthasar, "Eschatologie," in *Fragen der Theologie heute*, hrsg. von J. Feiner, J. Trütsch, F. Böckle, Einsiedeln, 1957, 403–421; L. Boros, S.J., *Mysterium Mortis. Der Mensch in der letzten Ent-*

scheidung, Olten und Freiburg i. Br., 1962. As a confirmation of our position, it might be well to recall that the Church, in the very processes of beatification and canonization, conducts a thorough investigation into not only the life of the Servants of God but also all the circumstances of their death in an attempt to arrive at the highest possible degree of certitude that their death was a truly Christian one. The most perfect Christian death, obviously, is found in the case of martyrdom, and it is precisely for this reason that the sanctity of the Martyrs has come to be considered as sanctity par excellence, and explains why the cult of dulia was initially given exclusively to the Martyrs. It was only at a later date that honor was paid also to non-martyrs; but even then the reason was that, though they had not poured out their blood for Christ, they had lived a life so generously consecrated to love of Him that it could be considered the equivalent of martyrdom. (Appropriate bibliographical references may be found in note 119.) A penetrating analysis of martyrdom can be found in: "Ueber das Martyrium. Exkurs," in the book of K. Rahner, S.J., cited above, *Zur Theologie des Todes,* Freiburg, 1958, pp. 73–106 (published originally in *Stifter-Jahrbuch* V, hrsg. von H. Treidel, Gräfelfing bei München, 1957, pp. 251–263).

76. We wish to emphasize that it is precisely the indefectibility of the union of the glorious members with Christ (which implies a degree of incorporation so profound as to exclude the possibility of sin or moral defect) that confers on a person the plenitude of membership of Christ and, at the same time, makes him worthy of veneration. On this point, cf. F. Malmberg, *Ein Leib—ein Geist, op. cit.,* pp. 295ss.

77. These were the words we used above when we proposed a theological description of a saint. Cf. p. 14.

78. "Charity more than any other virtue binds us closely to Christ. How many children of the Church, on fire with this heavenly flame, have rejoiced to suffer insults for Him, and to face and overcome the hardest trials, even at the cost of their lives and the shedding of their blood. For this reason our Divine Saviour earnestly exhorts us in these words: 'Abide in my love.' And as charity, if it does not issue effectively in good works, is something altogether empty and unprofitable, He added immediately: 'If you keep my commandments you shall abide in my love; as I also have kept my Father's commandments and do abide in his love' (Jn. 15. 9–10). But, corresponding to this love of God and of Christ, there must be love of the neighbour. How can we claim to love the Divine Redeemer, if we hate those whom He has redeemed with His precious blood, so that He might make them members of His Mystical Body? For that reason the beloved disciple warns us: 'If any man say I love God, and hateth his brother, he is a liar. For he that loveth not his brother whom he seeth, how can he love God whom he seeth not? And this commandment we have from God, that he who loveth God love also his brother' (1 Jn. 4. 20–21). Rather, it should be said that the more we become 'members one of another' (Rom. 12. 5), 'mutually careful one for another' (1 Cor. 12. 25),

the closer we shall be united with God and with Christ; as, on the other hand, the more ardent the love that binds us to God and to our divine Head, the closer we shall be united to each other in the bonds of charity." *Mystici Corporis, AAS* 35 (1943) 228–229 [NCWC #73–74].

79. *Ibid.,* pp. 230–231 [NCWC #76–77].

80. *Ibid.,* p. 241 [NCWC #98].

81. *Ibid.,* pp. 241–242 [NCWC #100–102].

82. *Ibid.,* p. 245 [NCWC #106].

83. With respect to this text of St. Paul (Col. 1. 24), cf. J. Kremer, " 'Was an den Leiden Christi noch mangelt.' Eine interpretationsgeschichtliche und exegetische Untersuchung zu Kol. 1, 24b," *Bonner Biblische Beiträge.* 12, hrsg. von F. Nötscher und K. Th. Schäfer, Bonn, 1956; published also in part as an excerpt from a doctoral dissertation at the Theological Faculty of the Pontifical Gregorian University, Bonn, 1956, xx, 26pp.

84. *Mystici Corporis, AAS* 35 (1943) 245 [NCWC #106].

85. Acts of admiration, praise, and thanksgiving are therefore complemented by acts of invocation to other members, at least for the period in which we address ourselves to them in our capacity as wayfarers. It is obvious, however, that this aspect of our personal contacts with other members will cease at the end of time, whereas the manifestation of admiration, praise, and thanksgiving—or, in brief, of love—will remain forever since this is the conscious realization of the most profound and vital bond permanently joining together members of the Mystical Body.

86. The ecclesiastical documents that speak *ex professo* of the intercession of the Saints refer expressly to the intercession which they exercise in response to the invocation directed to them by wayfarers. The theologians likewise restrict their considerations almost exclusively to this case. Nevertheless, this does not exclude absolutely the possibility that the Saints, at least at times, intercede for us and for our special needs even if they have not been expressly invoked. Cf. the reply given by A. Michel to a query on this precise point: "Les saints et les anges prennent-ils au ciel l'initiative de prier pour nous?" *L'Ami du Clergé* 60, 6e serie (1950) 723–727.

87. This beneficent activity naturally redounds favorably upon those who, though not formal members of the Mystical Body, are called to become such or are already somehow linked to that Body. That such beneficial effects are possible and actually are communicated is due to the peculiar nature of the Mystical Body which is not that of a physical body.

88. Above (note 26) we cited a liturgical text in which the various aspects of the cult of the Saints are beautifully illustrated. We have refrained from advancing other texts drawn from the liturgy (e.g. the Collect, Secret, and Postcommunion prayers of Masses in honor of the Saints) in which the various acts that constitute the cult of the Saints are expressly contained, sometimes grouped together, at other times separately stated. A valuable collection of the numerous prayers contained in the Roman

Missal, equipped with a complete index and critical data, is that of Dom P. Bruylants, O.S.B., *Les oraisons du Missel Romain, Texte et Histoire*, vol. I: Tabulae synopticae fontium Missalis Romanis—Indices—vol. II: Orationum textus et usus juxta fontes, Collection Etudes Liturgiques, Louvain, 1952.

89. Cf. the marvelous summary that Pius XII gave of this doctrine in his encyclical on the Sacred Heart, *Haurietis aquas*, of May 15, 1956, *AAS* 38 (1956), esp. pp. 320–337.

90. It will be useful to develop this concept because one often meets with tendencies which, when applied to the spiritual life, depreciate certain aspects of the reality created by God and redeemed by Christ, or make them artificial, thereby depriving many generous souls of valid, or even necessary, assistance in their ascent towards God; for these helps, if correctly utilized, might lead these persons to richer knowledge and a livelier love of the Lord. No one should lose sight of the fact that because of our physical and psychic, our natural and supernatural, constitution, according to the ordinary design of Divine Providence, the Christian not only can, but also must, cultivate his relationships with other men who share together with him the vocation to realize the profound reality of the Communion of Saints even in this life. In living these relationships, man actuates the plan of God and loves Him living in all His creatures, but especially in the members of His Mystical Body. Thereby he enriches himself through knowledge and experience which make him capable of knowing God Himself more intimately and loving Him more intensely; for the more extensive and comprehensive one's knowledge and experience, so much the greater is his capacity to know and love God. This truth is so profoundly significant that even those who consecrate themselves to particular forms of life in which they withdraw from human commerce, renounce contact with persons and thereby sacrifice genuine opportunities for amassing spiritual values, can licitly dedicate themselves to this type of life only because they have been called to it by God and thereby are assured of receiving from Him graces peculiar to that state which give them the conviction that they can live—even along this extraordinary path—a life rich in values for their own sanctification and that of others. By stressing these principles we in no way intend to ignore or underestimate the fact that, in our order of "fallen nature" these social contacts can constitute—and *de facto* frequently do constitute—dangers and obstacles in man's ascent to God. We must emphasize accordingly the need for man not only to use great prudence and supernatural discretion to regulate his relations with others in accordance with God's will, but also to practice mortification.

91. On the spiritual value of Christian friendship and the role it can play in man's ascent to God, together with the caution that must be exercised, especially in the case of those who live in religious community, see J. de Guibert, S.J., *Leçons de Théologie spirituelle*. Bibliothèque de la Revue d'Ascétique et de Mystique, Seconde Série, Fascicule II, Tome I. éd. nouv., Toulouse, 1955, Trente-deuxième Leçon, "L'amitié spirituelle," pp. 381–393 (tr. by Paul Barrett, O.F.M.Cap., *The Theology of the Spir-*

itual Life, New York, Sheed and Ward, 1953, pp. 179–185). This treatment is based in large measure on the balanced and well-documented exposition of G. Vansteenberghe, "Amitié," *Dictionnaire de Spiritualité* I, 500–529. Another excellent article is that of C. Browning, C.P., "Friendship among Religious," *Review for Religious* 18 (1959) 257–264.

92. Cf. St. Jerome, *Liber contra Vigilantium,* 6, *PL* 23, 344; St. Thomas Aquinas, *In IVum Sententiarum,* d. 45, q. 3, a. 2; d. 15, q. 4, a. 6, qa. II. Also: St. Robert Bellarmine, *De Ecclesia Triumphante . . .,* lib. 1, c. 10, ed. cit., t. II, p. 439; F. Suárez, *De Virtute et statu Religionis,* tract. 4, lib. 1, c. 10, n. 17, ed. cit., t. XIV, p. 41; *De Incarnatione,* disp. 52, sect. 1, n. 2, ed. cit., t. XVIII, p. 565; *Defensio Fidei catholicae adversus anglicanae sectae errores,* lib. 2, c. 9, nn. 11–13, ed. cit., t. XXIV, p. 163; n. 15, p. 164.

93. In view of what we stated above in Part One, section one, it is clear that in canonizations the Church, by declaring that a person is a Saint, gives us infallible assurance that he is in heaven, i.e. "actu gaudet visione beatifica"—he is actually enjoying the Beatific Vision. It is precisely this assurance that makes us certain that we can direct our prayers to a particular Saint as an intercessor.

94. Cf. St. Thomas, *Summa Theologica,* IIa–IIae, q. 83, a. 11, c. and ad 1. Also: St. Bonaventure, *In IVum Sententiarum,* d. 45, a. 3, q. 2; St. Robert Bellarmine, *De Ecclesia Triumphante . . .,* lib. 1, c. 13, ed. cit., t. II, p. 445; c. 19, p. 452; c. 20, p. 456; F. Suárez, *De virtute et statu Religionis,* tract. 4, lib. 1, c. 10, n. 22, ed. cit., t. XIV, p. 43; St. Peter Canisius, *Commentariorum de Verbi Dei corruptelis Alter tomus, De Maria . . .* lib. 5, c. 13, ed. cit., p. 684.

95. Cf. Peter Lombard, *Liber IV Sententiarum,* d. 45, c. 6, n. 411, ed. cit., t. II, p. 1010; St. Thomas Aquinas, *In IVum Sententiarum,* d. 45, q. 3, a. 1, sol. and ad 4 and ad 5; *Summa Theologica,* IIa–IIae, q. 83, a. 4, ad 2. Also: St. Bonaventure, *In IVum Sententiarum,* d. 45, a. 3, q. 1 c.; ibid. q. 3, conclusion; St. Robert Bellarmine, *De Ecclesia Triumphante . . .,* lib. 1, c. 16, ed. cit., t. II, p. 447; F. Suárez, *Defensio Fidei Catholicae adversus anglicanae sectae errores,* lib. 2, c. 9, n. 3, ed. cit., t. XXIV, p. 160; n. 7, p. 162; n. 13, p. 163, n. 20, p. 166. The basic argument, obviously, remains the Church's doctrine and practice of invoking the Saints directly, since these are based on the certainty that the Saints know our prayers.

96. One of the most important bases for the Catholic teaching on our relationship with the Saints is the fact that the Saints not only are aware of the prayers that we direct to them but also, as a result of those prayers, intercede and plead for us before God. It will suffice to refer to the expositions of the following: Peter Lombard, *Libri IV Sententiarum,* lib. 4, d. 45, c. 6: Quomodo Sancti et glorificati et Angeli audiunt preces supplicantium et intercedunt pro eis, ed. cit., t. II, nn. 411–412, pp. 1009–1011. St. Thomas, *In IVum Sent.,* d. 45, q. 3, a. 1: Utrum Sancti orationes nostras cognoscant; a. 2: Utrum debeamus Sanctos orare ad interpellandum pro

nobis; a. 3: Utrum orationes Sanctorum pro nobis ad Deum fusae semper exaudiantur; *Summa Theologica*, IIa–IIae, q. 83, a. 11: Utrum Sancti qui sunt in patria orent pro nobis; Supplem., q. 72, a. 1: Utrum Sancti orationes nostras cognoscant; a. 2: Utrum debeamus sanctos interpellare ad orandum pro nobis; a. 3: Utrum orationes Sanctorum ad Deum pro nobis fusae semper exaudiantur. St. Bonaventure, *In IVum Sent.*, d. 45, a. 3, q. 1: An Sancti orent pro nobis; q. 2: An Sancti impetrent nobis aliqua suis orationibus; q. 3: An utile sit nobis rogare Sanctos. St. Robert Bellarmine, *De Ecclesia Triumphante* . . ., lib. 1, c. 15: Proponitur controversia de invocatione Sanctorum; c. 16: Deteguntur aliquot fraudes et mendacia haereticorum; c. 17: Quomodo Sancti invocandi non sint; c. 18: Sanctos pro nobis orare; c. 19: Sanctos esse invocandos; c. 20: Solvuntur argumenta adversariorum, ed. cit., t. II, pp. 446–462. F. Suárez, *De virtute et statu Religionis*, tract. 4, lib. 1, c. 10: Quomodo rationales creaturae possint a nobis orari, ed. cit., t. XIV, pp. 35–45; c. 11: Utrum omnes spiritus beati et justi orare possint, *ibid.*, pp. 45–51; *De Incarnatione*, disp. 52, sect. 1: Utrum Sancti et beati Angeli, vel homines, sint adorandi; sect. 2: Quae adoratio, et propter quam causam Sanctis tribuenda sit, ed. cit., t. XVIII, pp. 563–568; *Defensio Fidei catholicae adversus anglicanae sectae errores*, lib. 2, c. 8: De iis quae circa cultum Sanctorum in Regis Praefatione notantur; c. 9: De Sanctorum invocatione, ed. cit., t. XXIV, pp. 156–168. Benedict XIV, *De Servorum Dei beatificatione et Beatorum canonizatione*, lib. 1, especially c. 12: De potestate canonizandi; and c. 13: De Benefacto, ut aliquando Solemnia Canonizationis expleantur, ed. cit., t. I, pp. 91–109. Proof that the Saints respond effectively to our prayers is particularly evident in the cases in which the Church, as a prerequisite for Canonization (or Beatification) of a Saint, judges that a miracle was obtained through the intercession of that Beatus, or Servant of God, to whom the prayer was addressed. Cf. Benedict XIV, *op. cit.*, lib. 3, c. 5, n. 16, ed. cit., t. III, pp. 52, 53.

97. St. Robert Bellarmine, *De Ecclesia Triumphante* . . ., lib. 1, c. 16, ed. cit., t. II, p. 447; F. Suárez, *De virtute et statu Religionis*, tract. 4, lib. 1, c. 10, n. 19, ed. cit., t. XIV, p. 42.

98. It seems that precisely this truth is not expressed with proper clarity in the phrase in which H. Vorgrimler speaks of the "Fürbitte der Heiligen" [the intercession of the Saints]: "The intercession of the Saints is not to be understood as a new historical initiative, independent of their lives on earth, but is, in substance, simply the abiding value for the world of their lives in God's sight" (or: the continuance and completion of their love, Origen, *De Orat.* 11); H. Vorgrimler, "Heiligenverehrung," *Lexikon für Theologie und Kirche*, 5 (1960²) 106, and K. Rahner–H. Vorgrimler, *Kleines Theologisches Wörterbuch*, Herder-Bücherei, Band 108/109, Freiburg i. Br., 1961, art. "Heiligenverehrung," p. 160. Obviously, Vorgrimler wishes to underscore—and with good reason—that the earthly and the heavenly life of the Saints are not to be considered as two completely distinct realities unrelated to one another. On this point he seems to have been inspired

by these remarks of Rahner: "We are dealing here with the same kind of situation as we have in the intercession and supernatural mediation of the Saints in heaven for us. This latter too does not imply a new (historical) initiative of the Saints that would be independent of their genuinely historical lives on earth and be added on to it from without. It is, in substance, simply the abiding value of their lives, in God's sight, for the world in its oneness. This value God knew as a factor in the coherent universe of the spirit, of morality, and of faith, when He willed this one world, in which every part depends upon the whole, to be precisely 'this world.'" (K. Rahner, S.J., *Die Kirche der Heiligen, Schriften zur Theologie*, III, p. 121, note 2.) It seems that the formula used by Vorgrimler, however, tends to ignore the fact that the Saints in heaven know, through a supernatural communication from God, and respond to, the prayers directed to them by the faithful. Although this response to our prayers should not be conceived anthropomorphically but in a way perfectly proportioned to the ontological state of the Saints and to the type of intellectual and volitional activity proper to their state, this response is undoubtedly an actuation of their charity in a form which they neither had nor could have had during their earthly lives. In this sense then the heavenly intercession of the Saints constitutes a new fact which Vorgrimler seems to overlook, or at least explains in a manner so obscure as to lend itself to misunderstanding. The reference which the author makes to a passage of Origen leads us to think that he used an expression which was unfortunate but might be excused in view of the brevity of his article. Cf. Origen, *Peri Euchēs*, ed. P. Koetschau, p. 321 s., *PG* 11, 448s. (English translation by John J. O'Meara, *ACW* n. 19, London-Westminster, 1954, pp. 43–44): "It is not only the High Priest who prays with those who truly pray, but also the angels who have joy in heaven upon one sinner that doth penance, more than upon ninety-nine just who need not penance, and also the souls of the saints who have passed away. This is clear from the case of Raphael offering a rational sacrifice to God for Tobias and Sara. For the Scripture says that after they had prayed, the prayers of them both were heard in the sight of the glory of the great Raphael, and he was sent to heal them both. And Raphael himself, in revealing to them his mission to them both, enjoined upon him as an angel by God says: When thou didst pray now, thou and thy daughter-in-law Sara, I offered the memory of your prayer before the Holy One; and a little further on: I am Raphael, one of the seven angels who bear up [the prayers of the saints] and enter before the glory of the holy one. And so, according to the word of Raphael, prayer is good with fasting and alms and justice. And in the case of Jeremias, who appears in the Macchabees as admirable for age and glory so that an extraordinary dignity and greatness was about him, and who stretched forth his right hand and gave to Judas a sword of gold—to him another holy man who had died bore witness saying: This is he that prayeth much for the people and for all the holy city, Jeremias the prophet of God. And as knowledge is revealed to the saints now through a glass in a dark manner, but then face to face, so it would be unreasonable not to employ the analogy for all the other virtues also, which if prepared already in this life will be perfected in the next. Now the one great virtue according to the Word of God is love of one's neighbor. We must believe that the saints who have died have this love in a far greater degree towards them that are engaged in the combat of life, than those who are still subject to human weakness and are engaged in the combat along with their weaker brethren. The saying: If one member suffer any thing, all the members suffer with it, or if one member glory, all the members rejoice with it, does not apply only to those who here on earth love their brethren."

From this passage and from further development of these ideas in the same work, it is clear that Origen considers the activity of the Saints as a truly new actuation of their love; cf. E. G. Jay's note on the passage cited above: *Origen's Treatise on Prayer*, London, 1954, p. 111, note 1: "Origen held a strong doctrine of angelic ministration towards man and of the Communion of Saints. Cf. De Princ. III.ii.4; Comm. on Mt. XXVII.30; Comm. on John XIII.57; Hom. in Num. XXVI.6; Exhortation to Martyrdom XXX.38. See also VI.4 and XXXI.5 of this treatise."

99. Cf. Peter Lombard, *Liber IV Sententiarum*, d. 45, c. 6, ed. cit., t. II, nn. 411–412, pp. 1010–1011; St. Thomas, *In IVum Sent.*, d. 45, q. 3, a. 1 c.; *ibid.* ad 5; *Summa Theol.*, IIa–IIae; q. 83, a. 4, ad 2; *Suppl.*, q. 72, a. 1; F. Suárez, *De virtute et statu Religionis*, tract. 4, lib. 1, c. 10, n. 20, ed. cit., t. XIV, p. 42.

100. Cf. Peter Lombard, *Liber IV Sententiarum*, d. 45, c. 6, ed. cit., t. II, n. 412, p. 1011; St. Thomas, *In IVum Sent.*, d. 45, q. 3, a. 1, ad 3; *ibid.*, a. 2 ad 5; *ibid.* a. 3, sol. and ad 5; *Summa Theol.*, IIa–IIae, q. 83, a. 11, ad 2; IIIa, q. 72, a. 1, ad 3.

101. St. Thomas often supports this idea: "iste ordo est divinitus institutus in rebus secundum Dionysium, ut per media ultima reducantur in Deum. Unde cum sancti qui sunt in patria, sint Deo propinquissimi, hoc divinae legis ordo requirit, ut nos qui manentes in corpore peregrinamur a Domino, in eum per sanctos medios reducamur; quod quidem contingit, dum per eos divina bonitas suum effectum diffundit," *In IVum Sent.*, d. 45, q. 3, a. 2, sol.; cf. also *ibid.* ad 1; *Summa Theol.*, IIa–IIae, q. 83, a. 11, c. and ad 4; *Supplem.*, q. 72, a. 1, c.; a. 2, c. and ad 1. This co-operation with God, according to St. Thomas, is an element in the glory and blessedness of the Saints: "Hoc autem ad eorum gloriam pertinet quod auxilium indigentibus praebeant ad salutem: sic enim Dei cooperatores efficiuntur, quo nihil est divinius, ut Dionysius dicit III cap. eccles. Hierarc." *In IVum Sent.*, d. 45, q. 3, a. 1, sol.; cf. also *Supplem.*, q. 72, a. 1, c.; *ibid.* a. 2, c.; F. Suárez, *De virtute et statu Religionis*, tract. 4, lib. 1, c. 10, n. 20, ed. cit., t. XIV, p. 42. For a systematic treatment of this principle in the doctrine of St. Thomas, cf. J. H. Wright, S.J., *The Order of the Universe in the Theology of St. Thomas Aquinas*, Pont. Univ. Gregoriana, Rome, 1957. As for the direct application of the general doctrine to the specific case of the influence of the Saints' prayers on the order of the universe, cf.

p. 154. For further information and references to the classic authors, cf. A. Michel, "Intuitive (vision), V, 2º, 3, c." *DTC* VII, 2388; "Gloire, gloire des Elus, II. Gloire accidentelle, 2º," *DTC* VI, 1404ss; P. Bernard, "Communion des Saints (Aspect dogmatique et historique)," *DTC* III, 429–454, especially columns 436–447.

102. This truly Catholic or universal love, full of reverence, admiration, praise, and confidence, which is directed to all those who reign with Christ in heavenly glory—be they canonized or not—is admirably expressed in the liturgical feast of All Saints. For the history and significance, both theological and liturgical, of this feast, cf. M. Righetti, *Manuale di Storia Liturgica*, vol. II, Milan, 1955[2], n. 226, pp. 356–360; J. Löw, C.SS.R., "Ognissanti (festum omnium Sanctorum)," *Enciclopedia Cattolica*, IX, 86–90; H. Frank, "Allerheiligenfest," *Lexikon für Theologie und Kirche*, I, (1957[2]) 348; C. Vagaggini, O.S.B., *op. cit.*, pp. 262–263.

103. *CIC,* canon 1278. See also: *Decreta Authentica Congregationis Rituum*, ed. cit., vol. V, Index Generalis, s.v. Patronus, pp. 374–377. For the liturgical notion of "patron" cf. A. Bugnini, "Patrono (Liturgia)," *Enciclopedia Cattolica*, IX, 983–990, which contains useful information about the history, function, and choice of patrons; we join the author in lamenting the lack of any comprehensive treatment of this subject. See also: H. Leclercq, O.S.B., "Patron," *DACL* 13, 2513–2524; E. Jombart, S.J., "Culte, III. Culte des Saints," *Dictionnaire de Droit Canonique* 4, 882–883. A complete list of Patrons and Saints can be found in F.v.S. Doyé, *Heilige und Selige der römisch-katholischen Kirche, deren Erkennungszeichen und lebensgeschichtliche Bemerkungen*, Leipzig, 1929, Register der Patronate, vol. II, pp. 890–905. We would like to emphasize, however, that a large number of such patronages were never officially approved by the Church.

104. This practice, so rich in spiritual content, was particularly prominent, as we have noted, in the latter part of the Middle Ages—that is, when the idea of the patronage of the Saints was fully understood and lived: "Under the rubric 'the asking of the name' we need not raise the question of baptismal names. For one thing, such names exercised no influence on the composition of the ceremonial, and for another the very phrase 'baptismal name' is questionable from the viewpoint of tradition. W. Dürig (*Geburtstag und Namenstag*, Munich, 1954) has shown how slight the connection between name and baptism is. The name in question was the name given the child at birth and, at baptism, entered into the baptismal register; this name became the 'Christian' name only when the veneration of the Saints reached its peak in the late Middle Ages, i.e. when the choice of a patron determined the person's own name. The Church indeed has an interest in the person's name, and the emphatic recommendation of the Roman Ritual (title 2, ch. 1) is quite understandable. But the fact that the Church never demanded a special name for adults (as long as adult baptism was practiced) shows that she has seen no immediate connection between baptism and the person's name. Cf. W. Deinhardt, 'Namen,'

LThK VII 432f; E. Nied, *Heiligenverehrung und Namengebung.* Freiburg, 1924." A. Stenzel, S.J., *Tie Taufe. Eine genetische Erklärung der Tauflitur-gie.* Forschungen zur Geschichte der Theologie und des innerkirchlichen Lebens, Heft VII-VIII, Innsbruck, 1958, p. 291.

105. Such is in fact the spirit of ecclesiastical legislation on this point. Cf. *Rituale Romanum,* Tit. II, c. I, n. 30; *CIC,* can. 761. The motives are more explicitly indicated in the Rituale, *ibid.,* n. 70, where it is stated: "Et quoniam iis qui baptizantur, tamquam Dei filiis in Christo regenerandis, et in eius militiam adscribendis, nomen imponitur, curet ne obscoena, fabu-losa, aut ridicula, vel inanium deorum, vel impiorum ethnicorum hominum nomina imponantur, sed potius, ut iam supra num. 30 dictum est, Sanc-torum, quorum exemplis fideles ad pie vivendum excitentur, et patrociniis protegantur." We must point out then that anyone who speaks of the practice of giving a Christian name at Baptism as simply a "noble custom" of Christian families (cf. J. F. Bonduelle, O.P., "A la recherche d'un saint Patron," *La Vie Spirituelle* 94 (1956) 495–511, esp. p. 495) fails to do full justice to the texts cited above. This article elicited such reactions that the author was obliged to take up the topic a second time: "Obligation d'un nom chrétien," *ibid.* 95 (1956) 160–171. As an example of a useful publication for selecting the name of a Saint, cf. *Is It a Saint's Name?* compiled by Wm. P. Dunne, Chicago (pamphlet), n.d.

106. Consider the practice prevalent among many Religious Orders and Congregations of taking a new name; or of the choice made by the Popes at the beginning of their pontificates. In this context, recall the moving words with which John XXIII indicated the reasons for the choice he made on the day of his election. Cf. *AAS* 50 (1958) 878–879.

107. The authors of theology manuals and encyclopedia articles ordinarily restrict themselves to the statement that the veneration of the Saints does not fall under a positive precept and is not necessary for salvation. The manual by J. Pohle-J. Gummersbach, S.J., *Lehrbuch der Dogmatik,* Wis-senschaftliche Handbibliothek, eine Sammlung theologischer Lehrbücher, vol. II, Paderborn, 1956[10], which is outstanding among modern manuals for its extensive, solid, and richly documented treatment of our subject, goes no further than this simple negative statement; cf. p. 466.

108. In note 109, the reader will find a list of the prayers in which the Saints are mentioned in the Mass celebrated according to the Roman rite. The same note also contains references to the classic work of J. Jungmann, S.J., which explains the origin and significance of such prayers. As is evi-dent from the way in which the prayers are formulated and the author's commentaries on each, the nature of these references to the Saints varies. Although in the "Confiteor" we turn to them as well as to God and con-fess our sins and then make a direct petition to them to pray for us "ad Dominum Deum nostrum," the usual formula by which they are addressed is that of the commemoration. It should be noted that even in such cases, however, it is not a question simply of "calling to mind" persons who were morally outstanding and well-loved by God, or of appealing to their merits

in the confident hope that they may represent a motive for God to protect and assist us. The deeper theological cultic significance of these commemorations lies in the fact that—as is aptly noted by Dom Vagaggini in the passage cited above—the Church Militant, conscious of its communion with the Church Triumphant, intends to live and explicitly realize this bond precisely in order to offer the greatest possible cult, availing herself of the force deriving from the union of all the members of the Mystical Body among themselves. This consciousness of her communion with the Church Triumphant and this deliberate intention to associate herself with it, lead the Church Militant to turn at least implicitly to the members of the Church Triumphant, with the aforementioned commemorations. That the Church Militant's recourse to the Church Triumphant should take this particular form precisely in the Mass is understandable if one considers that the Mass is, by its very nature, the sacrifice which Christ offers to the Father in the Spirit, and that the prayers of the Mass, according to a very ancient Christian tradition, are almost exclusively directed to God the Father (cf. note 61). But just as it would be a methodological error to conclude from this practice that there does not exist—either during the Holy Sacrifice or outside it—a cult directed immediately and explicitly to the Person of the Word Incarnate (cf. note 60), so too it would be erroneous to conclude that the cult of the Saints is exercised solely in the form of a commemoration without a direct recourse to them. Such a conclusion would moreover be in open contradiction with the teaching and practice of the Church which assembles her children and encourages them to pray publicly with prayers directed to the Saints themselves during the course of the solemn liturgical functions; for example, the chanting of the Litanies during the Paschal Vigil, the Mass of Ordination, Rogation days, etc.

109. C. Vagaggini, O.S.B., *op. cit.* (in Note 46), pp. 187–188 (English abridged translation). In the Mass according to the Roman Rite, such references to the Saints are found in the following parts: Confiteor, Oramus te Domine, Suscipe sancta Trinitas, Communicantes, Nobis quoque peccatoribus, Libera nos, and, in those Masses celebrated in honor of one or more Saints, also in the Oratio, Secreta (Preface), and Postcommunio. For the history of the introduction of these references to the Saints in each part and the implications thereof, cf. J. Jungmann, S.J., *Missarum Sollemnia. Eine genetische Erklärung der römischen Messe,* Vienna, 1958, respectively: I, 390–392, 407; II, 62–63, 214–225, 314–320, 353–354; I, 481; II, 118, (149), 526–527, tr. by Francis Brunner and revised by Charles Riepe, *The Mass of the Roman Rite, Its Origins and Development,* New York, Benziger, 1959. For the commemoration of the Saints in the Oriental liturgy, cf. H. Dalmais, O.P., "Les Commémorations des Saints dans l'office quotidien et hebdomadaire des liturgies orientales," *Maison Dieu* n. 52 (1957) pp. 98–108.

110. In the first part of this study, we tried to explain why the Church, according to God's providential design, in addition to her relations with the

entire Church Triumphant in general, must and actually does have special relations with certain Saints (cf. particularly pp. 18f.). The theological reasons adduced at that point to explain the liceity, suitability, and necessity of the canonization of some Saints, seen in the light of subsequent observations we have made, indicate that the full and perfect realization of what is intended by these canonizations necessarily demands the exercise of special acts of public cult in honor of these Saints. It should be noted, however, that we are speaking here purposely of the full and perfect realization of those relations between the Church Militant and the canonized Saints, relations which are officially acknowledged by solemn canonization; and, secondly, that we are not specifying the concrete form of the acts of cult. It is up to the Church to specify further what are her relations with a canonized Saint, and to determine in what concrete form public cult of the Saint is to be practiced, continued, promoted, and eventually restricted in the course of centuries. In this context, it will suffice to indicate the historical development of the liturgy—in particular the various reforms of the Church's sanctoral cycle—and to recall briefly that the special terrestrial and posthumous providential function of the canonized Saints can vary in importance for the history of humanity according to time and circumstance. It is certain, however, that the full and perfect realization of the special relations existing between the Church Militant and a canonized Saint, such as are recognized and proclaimed by canonization, demands and implies the performance of special acts of public cult. The Church moreover, throughout the course of history, must actuate fully and perfectly her relations not only with the Church Triumphant in general, but also with those particular Saints whom divine Providence indicates as having a perennial or passing significance of special moment for the life of the Church.

111. In addition to the texts referred to in note 101 and elsewhere, we would like to indicate several other passages particularly relevant to our topic, inasmuch as they emphasize the necessity of mediation by the Saints precisely because willed by God. St. Bonaventure, *In IVum Sent.*, d. 45, a. 3, q. 1, concl.; St. Peter Canisius, *Commentariorum de Verbi Dei corruptelis* . . ., t. I, *De venerando Christi Domini praecursore Ioanne Baptista*, c. 14, ed. cit., p. 209; and F. Suárez, who clearly explains the principles of this necessity: *De virtute et statu Religionis*, tract. 4, lib. 1, c. 10, n. 21, ed. cit. t. XIV, p. 43. In our own times, the noted German theologian Karl Rahner has emphasized this point: "The Church's veneration of the Saints is an indispensable part of her life, something truly belonging to her as a religious and Christian reality. . . ." (R. explains this assertion in a footnote) "whether this or that person is honored as a Saint by the Church or by an individual Christian, may (apart from the absolutely central figures in the history of salvation: Mary, the Baptist, the Apostles) be a matter for free choice. But this freedom cannot be simply extended to the veneration of Saints in general and as a whole. Apart from other considerations, Lk 1.48, Acts 7.54–60, Heb. 11—12, Apoc. 21.14 forbid

such an extension." K. Rahner, S.J., *Die Kirche der Heiligen, Schriften zur Theologie,* III, (1957) 113.

112. It is obvious that among the Saints to whom the Church must always direct her cult specifically and individually are those who occupy a particularly important position in salvation history. In addition to the Mother of God, whose case is altogether singular and privileged, John the Baptist and the Apostles, there is one we would like to mention in particular: St. Joseph, who was so appropriately proclaimed Patron of the Universal Church by Pius IX (Decretum *Quemadmodum Deus,* Dec. 8, 1870), and whose name has recently been inserted into the Canon of the Holy Mass by John XXIII (Decretum issued by the Sacred Congregation of Rites, *Novis hisce temporibus,* Nov. 13, 1962, *AAS* 54 [1962] 873), thereby acknowledging at this late date in the devotional life of the Church his particular importance in the life of Our Lord and of His Mystical Body. We are by no means saying that the Church can rest content to pay special veneration only to the Saints whom we have mentioned. As the Church's history attests, it is evident that God continues not only to raise up new Saints in her midst, but also to reveal, by means of miracles, those who, according to God's providential design, have a special mission to fulfill in the life of the Church even after their death. These Saints also deserve special veneration. It seems that we can say that this enables us to understand why it is possible for the cult of certain Saints to be intense as long as those circumstances for which God specially singled them out continue to exist, and then afterwards to diminish. It also accounts for the fact that the cult of other Saints, whose mission was not linked to special circumstances, not only does not fade away but retains its vitality and full richness; for example, the cult of the more famous Martyrs, the Doctors of the Church, famous Missionaries, Founders, and others.

113. In this light we can understand why the Church, through the course of the centuries, constantly proposed to her persecuted children the example of the Martyrs, encouraging them to turn to those brave souls and implore their assistance so that they might receive in their time of trial strength to bear valiant witness to their faith and love for Christ, a witness similar to that given by the Martyrs. For this same reason, the Church continues to propose other Saints who are not Martyrs, exhorting the faithful to follow their example in their ordinary daily lives, according to the diverse circumstances in which they live. Among the most recent documents of Pope Paul VI, see particularly the Allocutions pronounced on the occasion of the beatification of Bishop John Nepomucene Neumann, C.SS.R. (*AAS* 55 [1963] 915–918), and of Nunzio Sulprizio (*AAS* 56 [1964] 25–30).

Such exhortations were repeated in all the official Acts promulgated on the occasion of Beatifications and Canonizations, and in discourses delivered by the Supreme Pontiffs at various stages in the examination of their Causes. In addition to the documents and acts published in the *Acta Summorum Pontificum (Acta Sanctae Sedis,* 1865–1908, *Acta Apostolicae*

Sedis from 1909 till the present), consult also the collected discourses of the more recent Pontiffs: Pius XI, *Inviti all'eroismo. Discorsi di S.S. Pio XI nell'occasione della lettura dei Brevi per le Canonizzazioni, le Beatificazioni, le proclamazioni dell'eroicità delle virtù dei Santi, Beati e Servi di Dio*, Rome, vol. I, 1941; vol. II, 1942; vol. III, 1942. Pius XII, *Discorsi e Radiomessaggi di Sua Santità Pio XII*, Milano-Città del Vaticano; Vita e Pensiero-Tipografia Poliglotta Vaticana, I, 1940–XX, 1959; (Index of first fifteen volumes available). John XXIII, *Discorsi Messaggi Colloqui del Santo Padre Giovanni XXIII*, Città del Vaticano, Tipografia Poliglotta Vaticana, I, 1960 and following.

114. On this question, cf. J. Löw, C.SS.R., "Calendario della Chiesa universale," *Enciclopedia Cattolica* 3, 364–372. The author concludes his exposition with these words: "Anyone who reads through these lists, with the continual addition of feasts, ranks or rites, will readily conclude that the liturgical year, in its predominant orientation, is now almost completely occupied with feasts of the Saints. The increase in canonizations in our times aggravates the situation. It is clear from what we have written that at the time of Pius V there was a fine balance between the sanctoral and the temporal cycles. Clement VIII opened the door to an unlimited number of feasts of the Saints. During the reign of Clement X, the Sacred Congregation of Rites was concerned with this state of affairs and formulated the decree of June 20, 1671, which prohibited the introduction of any feast during the subsequent fifty years. The decree was renewed for another fifty years by Clement XI (May 4, 1714), but it was impossible to enforce it rigorously. Owing to continual canonizations —especially of founders of religious Orders—the pressure exerted by Catholic rulers for the insertion of new feasts, and other peculiar circumstances, the decree was not very often observed. Benedict XIV recognized that the continual increase in Saints' feasts was detrimental to the good order of the liturgy, and the reform of the Breviary instituted by him was intended to put a stop to this. But it was especially from the second half of the past century that new growth and variation in the rites occurred. This gave rise to a strong desire for a definitive liturgical reform, already begun by Pius X, which would include a revision of the Calendar" (columns 371–372). Cf. also the articles of: A. Bugnini, C.M., "Verso una riforma del Martyrologium Romanum?" *Ephemerides Liturgicae* 61 (1947) 91–99; Id., "Per una riforma liturgica generale," *ibid.* 63 (1949) 166–184, in which the author lists, synthesizes, and comments on the results of a questionnaire circulated among the contributors and readers of the periodical. (A digest of this article, authorized by the author himself, was published in *La Documentation Catholique* 47 [1950] 1098–1116); see esp.: 3. Calendario, B. Santorale, pp. 171–173 (cc. 1102–1104). O. Heiming, O.S.B., "Réflexions sur la réforme du calendrier liturgique," *La Maison-Dieu*, n. 30 (1952) 104–124, esp. "Le Sanctoral," pp. 117ss., "Détermination de la date," pp. 117–119; "Un Saint par jour," pp. 119–120; "Pour un choix entre les Saints," pp. 120–123. D. R. Van Doren, "La réforme du calen-

drier des Fêtes," *Les questions liturgiques et paroissiales* 37 (1956) 173–
178. Amongst the vast amount of literature on this subject we call special
attention to the following articles in the well-known review of the Centre
de Pastorale et Liturgie in a recent issue devoted to the sanctoral cycle:
A. Chavasse, "Sanctoral et année liturgique," *La Maison Dieu,* n. 52
(1957) 89–97; P. Jounel, "La réforme des propres diocésains," *ibid.*, 134–
140; Id., "Le Sanctoral romain du 8e au 12e siècles," *ibid.*, 59–88. An excellent historical synthesis can be found in the chapter "Der liturgische
Wochenzyclus," of Jungmann's *Liturgisches Erbe und pastorale Gegenwart,
Studien und Vorträge,* Innsbruck, 1960, pp. 332–365 (published originally
in *Zeitschrift für Katholische Theologie* 79 [1957] 45–68). In the mean-
while, the Church has already effected some reforms: cf. "Decretum generale de rubricis ad simpliciorem formam redigendis," die 23 martii 1955,
AAS 47 (1955) 218–224; "Litterae Apostolicae motu proprio datae 'Rubricarum instructum,'" die 25 iulii 1960, *AAS* 52 (1960) 593–595, and
"Decretum generale quo novus rubricarum Breviarii ac Missalis Romani
Codex promulgatur," die 26 iulii 1960, *AAS* 52 (1960) 596–740. Further
reforms have been announced in the Constitution on the Sacred Liturgy
of the Second Vatican Council, ch. V, "The Liturgical Year" (n. 108).

115. In fact, such is the prudential attitude of many bishops and priests
laboring in mission lands. On the other hand, the presentation of the
reality of the "Communion of Saints" and the nurturing of the consciousness of the bonds existing between the members of the Church Militant
and those of the Church Triumphant is a precious element in preaching
and pastoral ministry precisely in mission lands and must not be underestimated. With good reason does J. Hofinger make this observation: "In
speaking to human hearts, feasts promote the spirit of community in an
eminent manner. During the ceremonies, the small community of a remote outpost feels itself not only united and associated fraternally in the
solemn confession of one and the same faith but also assisted by the
immense community of the Saints in heaven and on earth. Together with
this vast assembly, it celebrates the same feasts, professes the same ideas.
Thanks to this profession of faith, countless millions of our brothers have
attained their full development in the Church Triumphant. . . . Missionary
practice, it would seem, must accord a greater prominence to the Feast
of All Saints. Celebrated in a favorable time, it has an especially rich content (Christian life—the consummation of Christian living). The heavenly
harvest festival at the end of the autumn reaping." "La célébration des
fêtes liturgiques," in J. Hofinger, S.J., J. Kellner, S.J., P. Brunner, S.J., J.
Seffer, S.J., *Pastorale liturgique en chrétienté missionnaire,* Cahiers de
"Lumen Vitae" XIV, Brussels, etc., 1959, pp. 148, 150–151 (originally
published in German: *Liturgische Erneuerung in der Welt-Mission,* Innsbruck, etc., 1957, p. 185 and p. 189).

116. The opinion of F. Suárez on the point is relevant: cf. *Defensio
Fidei Catholicae adversus anglicanae sectae errores,* lib. 2, c. 9, nn. 21–22,
ed. cit., t. XXIV, pp. 166–167.

117. In the work of Benedict XIV, a basic text for the Process of Beatification and Canonization, we find the following passage from which it is evident that the cult of the Saints is considered as one of the elements in the heroic exercise of the virtue of faith: "At, ut clare procedatur in re, de qua nunc agitur, hoc est in exponendis regulis necessariis, utque tutum feratur iudicium de heroicitate virtutum Servorum Dei, et signanter Fidei, dicimus, habitum communem Fidei Theologicae dignosci primo ab externa confessione eorum quae in corde per Fidem creduntur . . . secundo, dignoscitur ex observantia praeceptorum: tertio, ex oratione ad Deum: quarto, ex cordis demissione et oboedientia erga Deum, Ecclesiam Catholicam, et eius visibile caput Romanum Pontificem in omnibus, quae pertinent ad credendum et operandum propter salutem aeternam: quinto, ex Fidei dilatatione, aut saltem eius desiderio: sexto, ex timore Dei: septimo, ex cultu Dei et Sanctorum. . . ." Benedictus XIV, *De Servorum Dei beatificatione et Beatorum canonizatione*, lib. III, c. 23, n. 4, ed. cit, t. III, p. 310. Commentators take up this concept and explain that in the interrogations it must be made evident whether and to what extent the Servant of God practiced this cult: "En vero quae potissimum notitiae requirantur oportet: . . . (3) Quod attinet ad virtutem Fidei. . . . Requiratur an D.S. peculiari honore prosequutus fuerit Sanctos Coelites; quos ex eis patronos sibi elegerit, quae in eos ostenderit cultus indicia. . . ." *Codex pro Postulatoribus Causarum beatificationis et canonizationis*, Romae, 1929 (4a), p. 11. See also: S. Indelicato, *Il Processo Apostolico di Beatificazione*, Roma, 1945, Parte Seconda, art. 4, 1, "La fede eroica," p. 79; D. J. Blaher, O.F.M., *The Ordinary Processes in Causes of Beatification and Canonization. A historical synopsis and a commentary.* The Catholic University of America, Canon Law studies, No. 268, Washington, 1949, Part II, Canonical Commentary, ch. 5, art. III, A. 2, Life and Virtues of the Servant of God, XI, Faith, p. 88. The practice of the S. Cong. of Rites is a further confirmation: certainly if in the evaluation of the heroic virtue of a Servant of God, it could be established that he had been opposed to the cult of the Saints or even that he had failed to practice it according to the mind of the Church, such a fact would constitute a peremptory obstacle.

118. We might note in passing that analogous arguments are proposed with disconcerting frequency in our day as difficulties against other forms of Catholic cult; for example, especially the cult paid to the Mother of God, but also that surrounding the Sacred Humanity of our Lord, His Sacred Heart, and His Most Precious Blood. It is sad to observe how in certain places the consequence of such an attitude is a notable decrease in the exercise of these enriching forms of cult. On this subject, cf. I. N. Zorè, "Recentiorum quaestionum de cultu SS. Cordis Iesu conspectus (Utrum crisis an evolutio cultus praevideatur)," *Gregorianum* 37 (1956) 104–120, esp. pp. 105–109. See also the work: *Cor Salvatoris. Wege zur Herz-Jesu Verehrung*, edited by J. Stierli, Freiburg i. Br., 1956[2] (tr. by Paul Andrews, S.J., *Heart of the Saviour. A Symposium on Devotion to the Sacred Heart*, New York, 1958[2]), esp. the chapter of R. Gutzwiller,

"The Opposition," pp. 1–14 (Eng. trans.). If the reader will follow our line of argument, he will not wonder at the fact that it is precisely the same type of objection which is advanced in all these related cases.

119. Cf. M. Viller, S.J., "Martyre et perfection," *RAM* 6 (1925) 3–25; Id., "Le martyre et l'ascèse," *ibid.*, 105–142; Id., *La spiritualité des premiers siècles chrétiens*, Bibliothèque catholique des Sciences religieuses, n. 35, Paris, 1930, ch. II, Le Martyre, pp. 15–24; M. Viller, S.J.—K. Rahner, S.J., *Aszese und Mystik in der Väterzeit, Ein Abriss*, Freiburg i. Br., 1939, pp. 29–40; L. Bouyer, *La spiritualité du Nouveau Testament et des Pères. Histoire de la spiritualité chrétienne*, I, Paris, 1960, ch. VIII, Le Martyre, pp. 238–261 (tr. by Mary P. Ryan, *The Spirituality of the New Testament and Fathers*, London, 1963). Th. Camelot, O.P., "L'engagement chrétien du baptême au martyre," *Nova et Vetera* 24 (1949) 226–348; K. Baus, "Das Gebet der Märtyrer," *Trierer Theologische Zeitschrift* 62 (1953) 19–32; M. Pellegrino, "L'imitation du Christ dans les Actes des Martyrs," *La Vie Spirituelle* 98 (1958) 38–54; P. Hartmann, S.C.I., "Origène et la théologie du Martyre d'après de PROTREPTIKOS de 235," *Ephemerides Theologicae Lovanienses* 34 (1958) 773–824; M. Pellegrino, "Cristo e il Martire nel pensiero di Origene," *Divinitas* 3 (1959) 144–170; J. Capmany, "San Cipriano de Cartago, maestro y pastor en la persecución," *Estudios Eclesiásticos* 33 (1959) 275–302; Id., *"Miles Christi" en la espiritualidad de San Cipriano*, Dissertatio ad Lauream in Fac. Theol. Pont. Univ. Gregorianae, Barcinone 1956, esp. c. 2, El Miles-Christi ante la persecución, pp. 69–126.

120. In addition to the literature already cited in note 119, see in particular: H. Delehaye, S.J., *Les origines du culte des Martyrs*, Subsidia Hagiographica 20, Brussels, 1933²; Id., *Sanctus. Essai sur le culte des Saints dans l'antiquité*, Subsidia Hagiographica 17, Brussels, 1927, esp. c. 3, "Le culte" pp. 122–161; B. de Gaiffier, S.J., "Réflexions sur les origines du culte des Martyrs," *La Maison-Dieu*, n. 52 (1957) 19–43; Card. A. I. Schuster, O.S.B., *Liber Sacramentorum*, vol. IX, Turin-Rome, 1932, pp. 1ss.; J. A. Jungmann, *The Early Liturgy to the Time of Gregory the Great*, Univ. of Notre Dame Press, 1959, ch. 14, "The Veneration of the Martyrs," pp. 175–187; P. A. Frutaz, "Martirio e martire, II. Culto dei m. e iconografia antica," *Enciclopedia Cattolica* 8, 236–243; Id., "Märtyrer," *Lexikon für Theologie und Kirche* 7 (1962²) 127-132. Among the many works on aspects of this subject, see: G. Jouassard, "Le rôle des chrétiens comme intercesseurs auprès de Dieu dans la chrétienté lyonnaise au second siècle," *Revue de Sciences Religieuses* 30 (1956) 217–229, esp. pp. 217–222; P. Jounel, "L'été 259 dans le calendrier romain," *La Maison-Dieu* n. 52 (1957) 44–58; G. Zulli, S.D.B., *S. Ambrogio e il culto dei Santi. Culto dei Martiri e delle loro reliquie*. Excerpta ex dissertatione ad lauream in Fac. Theol. Pont. Univ. Gregorianae, Romae, 1945.

121. On this point, cf. H. Delehaye, S.J., *Les Origines du culte des martyrs*, pp. 24–49.

122. For a synthetic view of the historical development of devotion to

the Saints cf. P. Séjourné, O.S.B., "Saints (culte des)," *DTC* 14, 870–978.

123. Cf. C. Lambot, O.S.B., "Les sermons de S. Augustin pour les fêtes de martyrs," in *Analecta Bollandiana* 67 (1949) 249–266.

124. St. Augustine, *Sermo in Natali Martyrum Fructuosi episcopi, Augurii et Eulogii diaconorum,* Sermo CCLXXIII, vii, 7, *PL* 38, 1251.

125. It happens at times in contemporary discussions on the cult of the Saints that reference is made to the text of St. Augustine referred to in note 124; but in such a way that it is torn from its context and presented as if it contained a reprobation of cult to the Saints. This rather dishonest technique naturally creates the impression among the uninformed that St. Augustine was opposed to the cult of the Saints. To offset this error, we have referred to the passage from St. Augustine as an example, although many other Fathers and Ecclesiastical writers could have been cited. The passage cited can be more readily understood if we bear in mind that in Sermon 273, the holy Doctor is commenting on a few excerpts from the "Proconsular Acts," the official accounts of the process that preceded the martyrdom of Fructuosus, Augurius, and Eulogius. During the interrogation, the presiding judge, Emilian, directed this question to Eulogius in order to induce him to participate in the pagan sacrifices: "Numquid et tu Fructuosum colis?" and the holy deacon replied: "Ego Fructuosum non colo, sed ipsum colo quem et Fructuosus," alluding to the reply previously given by Fructuosus to the judge, "Ego unum Deum colo, qui fecit caelum et terram, mare et omnia quae in eis sunt." In his sermon, St. Augustine took as his point of departure, Eulogius' reply and endeavored to explain to his hearers the difference between cult of adoration which the pagans paid to certain men deemed by them to be divine, and the veneration shown the Martyrs by Christians: "Quid ergo, fratres mei, quid vobis dicam de hominibus illis quos pagani pro diis coluerunt, quibus templa, sacerdotia, altaria, sacrificia exhibuerunt?" (*loc. cit.*, vi, 6, *PL* 38, 1250). The controversial passage which we cited in the preceding note follows immediately upon these words. Seen in context, it contains nothing against the cult of the Saints; on the contrary, it offers a clear exposition of the practice. That the passage in question could not have the negative meaning attributed to it by some, is also evident from the concluding words of the sermon: "Ideo, carissimi, veneramini martyres, laudate, amate, praedicate, honorate; Deum martyrum colite" (*loc. cit.*, ix, 9, *PL* 38, 1252).

126. H. Delehaye, S.J., *Les Origines du culte des martyrs,* pp. 113–114. In this chapter, the renowned Bollandist adduces many witnesses from both Greek and Latin Fathers, who confirm in full our statement concerning the ideas which were prevalent during the first centuries with respect to the cult of the Martyrs.

127. St. Augustine, *In Natali martyrum Perpetuae et Felicitatis,* sermo CCLXXX, vi, 6, *PL* 38, 1283.

128. St. Augustine, *In Natali martyrum Mariani et Jacobi,* sermo CCLXXXIV, 5, *PL* 38, 1291.

129. St. Augustine, *In Natali Cypriani martyris*, sermo CCCXIII, ii, 2, *PL* 38, 1423.

130. St. Augustine, *In die Natali martyrum Casti et Aemilii*, sermo CCLXXXV, 5, *PL* 38, 1295–1296.

131. On this point, cf. what we said at the end of Part Two, pp. 99f.

132. Cf. L. Malevez, S.J., "Liturgie et prière privée," *NRT* 83 (1961) 914–942; H. A. P. Schmidt, S.J., *Introductio in Liturgiam Occidentalem*, ed. cit., V. "Liturgia et Perfectio christiana," pp. 88–130, with a fine bibliography. See also: Cardinal Franz König, "Liturgiereform des Vatikanischen Konzils und persönliche Frömmigkeit," in: *Der grosse Entschluss* 19 (1964) 389–392; J. A. Jungmann, S.J., "Liturgie und geistliches Leben. Die Spiritualität der Constitutio de Sacra Liturgia," *Geist und Leben* 37 (1964) 91–98.

133. Such generalizing evaluations are almost always superficial. By concentrating attention on certain exterior forms, at times assuredly exaggerated, they fail to explain that behind this exterior a wealth of religious spirit is often concealed. They fail to take into consideration that every race and people has its own distinctive traits and qualities, and no race or people has all conceivable characteristics worth having. There is a tendency to feel that anything diverging from one's own peculiar qualities is by that very fact inferior and to be disdained. It would be much wiser and more balanced to recognize how all these gifts and qualities must be integrated (because willed by God for His greater glorification) and, consequently, how we must render one another mutual assistance in living our peculiar style of religious life without falling into exaggerations and abuses. Setting aside this observation the implications of which are quite evident, we would like to raise a question: With what justification is it alleged by some that non-Latin peoples are averse, by nature and temperament, to devotion to the most holy Humanity of our Lord, to the cult of the Sacred Heart and Most Precious Blood, of the Blessed Virgin Mary and the Saints? The history of spirituality demonstrates that there is no foundation for such assertions. On this point see the profound observations of: L. von Hertling, S.J., *Geschichte der Katholischen Kirche*, Berlin, 1949, Elftes Kapitel, "Die Reformation, Gründe für den Abfall," pp. 249–251 (tr. by Anselm G. Biggs, *A History of the Catholic Church*, Westminster, Md., Newman, 1957, pp. 368–372. Is it not actually the universality and catholicity of these devotions that strike the historian? Even if practiced with different nuances and in diverse forms these devotions are found among all peoples of Christendom. Rather than dwell at length on things already well known, we will merely cite by way of example a little-known medieval devotion, namely, that directed to God viewed also as a mother. This devotion, rich in affective warmth and exquisite delicacy, was initiated by St. Anselm and spread throughout the whole of Europe. It was in fact practiced, with slight variations, by Margaret d'Oyngt, Mechtilde of Hackenborn, Julian of Norwich, and by many others (cf. A. Cabassut, O.S.B., "Une dévotion médiévale peu connue," *RAM* 25 (1949) 234–245; P. Molinari, S.J., *Julian*

of Norwich, The Teaching of a 14th Century English Mystic, London, etc., 1958, esp. III, 3: A further aspect of God's "homely loving": the concept of God as our Mother, pp. 169–176. Coming down to our own day, with respect to the cult of the Saints, where can one find a movement of such deep interest, devotion, and truly religious feeling comparable to that which exists in England towards the Forty Holy Martyrs, or in Germany towards Rupert Mayer? For a calm and balanced evaluation of this entire problem, consult the discourse delivered at Genoa, Nov. 20, 1961, by His Eminence Cardinal Frings, "Il Concilio Ecumenico Vaticano II di fronte al pensiero moderno," published in: *Concilio Ecumenico Vaticano II,* Edizioni del Columbianum, Genoa, 1962, pp. 145–176.

134. For obvious reasons, we have purposely refrained from giving names and citations of Catholic authors; but we feel obliged to make an exception to this mode of procedure and to direct the reader's attention to a rather unfortunate expression which appeared in a recent work of high theological value and wide circulation. If we depart from our customary restraint, we certainly do not do so with the intention of censuring an author who otherwise—as is clear from the content of the article—is far from depreciating the cult of the Saints, and whom we certainly do not wish to include among the incompetent. Rather we are led to do so solely by the fact that we think it will be useful to rectify and counter the negative influence which a single expression could arouse—contrary to the very intention of the author and the editors of the work—in the minds of many of its readers. We are referring to the following passage of H. Vorgrimler, in the article "Heiligenverehrung," in the *Lexikon für Theologie und Kirche,* 5 (1960²) 106: "Resistance to veneration of the Saints arises primarily (1) from the distaste of religious man for created reality because it is not the Absolute. Against such a tendency it must be realized that a religious act reaches its fulfillment only when it can find *in* God the creature itself, for the creature's value increases rather than diminishes with its increasing nearness to God; (2) from the misunderstanding accompanying popular piety, which often thinks of God simply as *one* reality *alongside* others (the reason for the Protestant rejection of the veneration of the Saints) and frequently in its preference for certain Saints, fails to be guided objectively by their concrete value as models."

Even if we recognize that this paragraph contains some excellent observations, what Vorgrimler says with respect to the "reformator. Ablehnung der Heiligenverehrung" (the Protestant rejection of the veneration of the Saints), seems inaccurate to us. In fact, this "misunderstanding of popular piety" certainly was not the reason—much less the sole reason—why the Protestants rejected the cult of the Saints. At most, it was one of the reasons, or rather one of the occasions, for the attitude of the Reformers and was later exploited to the utmost, even after the reaction on the part of Catholic theologians (cf. the works cited in note 49). But even prescinding from the purely historical question, such an assertion seems to ignore the fact that the divergence between Catholics and Protestants concerning the cult of the Saints rests, in the last analysis, on basic differences regarding dogmatic questions. The same phenomenon occurs in this field as in that of the Holy Sacrifice. (On this point, cf. F. Clark, S.J., *Eucharistic Sacrifice and the Reformation*, London 1960, ch. 4, "Practical abuses and superstitious observances connected with the altar in the pre-reformation period," pp. 56–72.) Concerning the condition of the liturgy on the eve of the Reformation, consider the opinion expressed by J. A. Jungmann, S.J., "Der Stand des Liturgischen Lebens am Vorabend der Reformation," in his *Liturgisches Erbe und pastorale Gegenwart*, Studien und Vorträge, Innsbruck, 1960, pp. 87–107.

135. It is common knowledge that this thought was dear to John XXIII, and that he often expressed it in documents and allocutions referring to the coming Ecumenical Council, Vatican II. The most authoritative personalities of the Catholic world, following in the footsteps of His Holiness, have expressed similar opinions. It would be superfluous to substantiate these statements with numerous references; we will simply refer the reader to some of the articles of His Eminence Cardinal Bea, among which we call special attention to those which appeared in the *Civiltà Cattolica*. In these articles the learned Cardinal, with his customary depth and clarity enhanced by the authority conferred on him in his capacity as President of the Secretariate for the Union of Christians, explains at length what ought to be our attitude towards the separated brethren. These articles have been translated in the work: *The Unity of Christians*, ed. by Bernard Leeming, S.J., with an introduction by Archbishop Gerald P. O'Hara, New York, 1963. See esp. ch. 1: "The Catholic Attitude towards the Problem," pp. 19–37; and cc. 9 and 10: "Protestants and the Council. I. Agreements and Disagreements, II. Possible Contributions to Church Unity," pp. 129–153.

136. "Communi consilio decrevimus, memoriam illius, id est sancti Udalrici episcopi, affectu piissimo, devotione fidelissima venerandam: quoniam sic adoramus et colimus reliquias martyrum et confessorum, ut eum, cuius martyres et confessores sunt, adoremus; honoramus servos, ut honor redundet in dominum, qui dixit: qui vos recipit, me recipit [Mt 10. 40]: ac proinde nos qui fiduciam nostrae iustitiae non habemus, illorum precibus et meritis apud clementissimum Deum iugiter adiuvemur, quia divina saluberrima praecepta, et sanctorum canonum ac venerabilium Patrum instabant efficaciter documenta omnium ecclesiarum pio considerationis intuitu, immo apostolici moderaminis annisu, utilitatum commoditatem atque firmitatis perficere integritatem, quatenus memoria Udalrici iam praefati venerabilis episcopi divino cultui dicata exsistat, et in laudibus Dei devotissime persolvendi semper valeat proficere" (Pro canonisatione Sancti Udalrici), Concilium Romanum (non oecumenicum), anno 993, *Denz*. 342. The reader should note how in this text the finality of canonization and of the cult of the Saints in general is clearly expressed: "ut eum, cuius martyres et confessores sunt, adoremus; honoramus servos, ut honor redundet in dominum, etc." (in order to adore Him to Whom they bear witness and

Whom they confess; we honor the servants, so that the honor may redound to the glory of the Master).

137. Consult the documents listed in the systematic index of the *Enchiridion Symbolorum* of Denzinger, under XI, and in the 32nd edition, edited by A. Schönmetzer, S.J., see Index systematicus, K 2dc; also notes 56 and 57 above.

138. *Errores Michaelis de Molinos,* damnati in Decreto S. Officii, 28 Aug., et in Constit. "Coelestis Pastor," 20 Nov. 1687. *Error* 35: "Non convenit animabus huius viae internae, quod faciant operationes, etiam virtuosas, ex propria electione et activitate; alias non essent mortuae. Nec debent elicere actus amoris erga beatam Virginem, Sanctos aut humanitatem Christi: quia cum ista obiecta sensibilia sint, talis est amor erga illos." *Denz.* 1255. *Error* 36: "Nulla creatura, nec beata Virgo nec Sancti sedere debent in nostro corde: quia solus Deus vult illud occupare et possidere." *Denz.* 1256.

139. As is known, the Council of Trent was concerned with the cult of the Saints in two different sessions, the XXIIth and the XXVth. In Session XXII, "Doctrina . . . de sanctissimo Missae Sacrificio," the Council also treated "De Missis in honorem Sanctorum," devoting a chapter to this subject: "Cap. 3. Et quamvis in honorem et memoriam Sanctorum nonnullas interdum Missas Ecclesia celebrare consueverit, non tamen illis sacrificium offerri docet, sed Deo soli, qui illos coronavit. Unde 'nec sacerdos dicere solet: Offero tibi sacrificium, Petre et Paule' [S. Augustinus, C. Faustum, 20–21, *PL* 42, 384], sed Deo de illorum victoriis gratias agens, eorum patrocinia implorat, ut ipsi pro nobis intercedere dignentur in coelis, quorum memoriam facimus in terris [Missale]." *Denz.* 941; to which there corresponds the Canon: "Can. 5. Si quis dixerit, imposturam esse, Missas celebrari in honorem Sanctorum et pro illorum intercessione apud Deum obtinenda, sicut Ecclesia intendit: A.S." *Denz.* 952. In Session XXV, the cult of the Saints was treated more directly. For this reason, we included the wording of its text in the body of our work.

140. Session XXV (3 and 4, Dec. 1563), *Denz.* 984 (cf. note 19 above). In conformity with this doctrine in the *Professio Fidei Tridentina,* promulgated by Pius IV in the Bull "Iniunctum nobis" of Nov. 13, 1564, we read: "Constanter teneo [purgatorium esse, animasque ibi detentas fidelium suffragiis iuvari]; similiter et Sanctos una cum Christo regnantes venerandos atque invocandos esse, eosque orationes Deo pro nobis offerre, atque eorum reliquias esse venerandas." *Denz.* 998.

We wish to emphasize how in the text of the Council of Trent cited above, attention is drawn to both the union of the Saints with Christ and the christocentric and theocentric character of the cult directed to them: "bonum atque utile esse, suppliciter eos [scil. Sanctos una cum Christo regnantes] invocare et ob beneficia impetranda a Deo per Filium eius Jesum Christum Dominum qui solus noster Redemptor et Salvator est, ad eorum orationes, opem auxiliumque confugere, etc." The Second Ecumenical Vatican Council has wished to express this doctrine in its entirety,

especially in view of its great pastoral value: "The Church has also included in the annual cycle days devoted to the memory of the martyrs and
the other saints. Raised up to perfection by the manifold grace of God,
and already in possession of eternal salvation, they sing God's perfect praise
in heaven and offer prayers for us. By celebrating the passage of these
saints from earth to heaven, the Church proclaims the paschal mystery
achieved in the saints who have suffered and been glorified with Christ;
she proposes them to the faithful as examples drawing all to the Father
through Christ, and through their merits she pleads for God's favors" *Constitution on the Sacred Liturgy,* ch. 5, #104 (NCWC translation).

141. An authoritative confirmation of what we have been saying about
the timeliness of not concealing or disguising our beliefs is the fact that
John XXIII, who frequently exhorted us in his allocutions to imitate the
example of the Saints and invoke their aid, wished to proclaim St. Joseph
as Protector of the current Vatican Council from which such high hopes
are entertained for the reunion of Christians—a unique procedure in the
history of Ecumenical Councils. Cf. "Epistula Apostolica ad locorum Ordinarios et christifideles catholici orbis: de pietate erga S. Ioseph, univer-
salis Ecclesiae Patronem, cuius praesidium ob cogendum Concilium
Vaticanum II imploratur," of March 19, 1961, *AAS* 63 (1961) 205–213.

142. Assertions of this type are of no help in clarifying the problem;
moreover, by diverting attention from the central issue they can—by making use of an ambiguous concession and consequent compromise—create
the illusion that there is no reason for thinking that the position of Catholics is essentially different from that of Protestants. The opposition which
non-Catholics express towards the cult of the Saints does not in fact
derive from the particular question of whether or not the Church maintains its necessity as a condition for salvation. Rather, it is based on the
conviction that it is illicit in so far as it is in opposition to the Word of
God and to the doctrine of Christ's mediation and the honor due to Him.
Now it is precisely this conviction that is in conflict with our Catholic
faith. Consequently, to limit ourselves to saying simply that the cult of the
Saints is not, according to our faith, a necessary condition for salvation
tends to obscure and in fact does disguise the real conflict which exists
between the two positions. It means that we are concealing a part of the
truth for fear of its not being accepted. Such a procedure is illegitimate
and in fact contrary to true charity towards our brothers.

143. We meet frequently in the writings of some authors the tendency to
speak of the *veneration* of the Saints rather than of their *cult,* so that this
latter term might be reserved to designate the religious acts of worship
(latria) directed to God. This tendency is justified by the assertion that
it is necessary to adapt ourselves to the use of such words in different
languages, especially Nordic languages. A secondary aim, however, is the
desire to avoid misunderstandings and discussions with non-Catholics. In
opposition to this tendency and the reasons adduced, we offer the following reply: It is a frequent phenomenon that with the passage of time the

original meaning of a term undergoes modification, becomes more extensive or restricted, acquires a greater or lesser precision. We know that such has actually occurred with respect to the terminology in our particular field of study; for example, the term "adoration" has become more restricted in meaning, much to the advantage of clarity of expression. The question we are raising is whether it is legitimate to pretend that a similar process has occurred with regard to the term "cult," as if this term had a current significance so delimited and restricted that it must be considered synonymous with the word "adoration" and consequently whenever there is no question of religious acts directed to God, the word "veneration" must be substituted for it. We feel obliged to reply in the negative and duty-bound to emphasize that the term "veneration," which some would like to reserve for designating the religious attitude proper towards the Saints, is rather colorless and inappropriate for expressing what Catholic doctrine and practice mean by the technical phrase "cult of the Saints" or *dulia*. Whenever one wishes to insist on the use of the term "veneration" it would be appropriate to complete it with the qualification "religious veneration" or "veneration and invocation." By so doing we would avoid the misunderstanding which leads persons not conversant with our doctrine to think that our cult of the Saints is nothing more than an attitude of veneration, respect, and esteem which we entertain towards all those who, for some reason or other, are worthy of honor and reverence, such as, for example, our beloved dead.

144. Despite the abundance of material and writings in which various aspects of the cult of the Saints are treated, not a single one of the authors whom we studied presented a speculative theological synthesis of the entire problem.

145. "Illud procul dubio hominibus praecipuum officium est, ut se quisque vitamque suam ad Deum dirigat. Ipse enim est cui principaliter alligari debemus tamquam indeficienti principio, ad quem etiam nostra electio assidue dirigi debet, sicut in ultimum finem, quem etiam negligentes peccando amittimus, et credendo et fidem praestando recuperare debemus" (St. Thomas, *Summa Theologica*, IIa–IIae, q. 81, a. 1). "Man turns properly to God when he acknowledges His supreme majesty and supreme authority; when he accepts divinely revealed truths with a submissive mind; when he scrupulously obeys divine law, centering in God his every act and aspiration; when he accords, in short, due worship to the One True God by practicing the virtue of religion," (Pius XII, *Mediator Dei, AAS* 39 [1947] 525, NCWC trans. #13). As is commonly known, the foundation for St. Thomas' entire teaching on religion (IIa–IIae, q. 81ss) is the fact that all the acts of worship of God, and especially the most important of them, adoration, are based on the knowledge and consciousness of the transcendent majesty of God and of His fatherly goodness. See esp. q. 81, a. 1–6; q. 82, a. 1–3; q. 83, a. 3; q. 84, a. 1, in which St. Thomas recapitulates, integrates, and develops the doctrine of revelation and tradition. The reader is referred also to the classic commentators on St. Thomas, and among the modern authors, above all to O. Lottin, O.S.B., J. Lecuyer,

C.S.Sp. and I. Mennesier, O.P., already cited in note 46. Cf. St. Robert
Bellarmine, *De Ecclesia Triumphante* . . ., lib. 1, c. 12, ed. cit. t. II, pp.
440–441, and the excellent clarifications of F. Suárez, *De virtute et statu
Religionis*, esp. tract. 2, lib. I, cc. 1–2, ed. cit. t. XIII, pp. 77–87, and
Commentaria ac disputationes in Tertiam Partem D. Thomae, q. 25, ed.
cit., t. XVIII, pp. 538ss. Modern syntheses and ample bibliographical data
can be found in: B. Häring, *Das Gesetz Christi*, Moraltheologie, Freiburg
i. Br., 1956³ (tr. by Edwin G. Kaiser, C.PP.S., *The Law of Christ*, Westminster, Md., 1963, II, 111–137); A. Molien, "Adoration," *DS* I (1937)
210–222; P. Molinari, S.J., "Adoration," *A Catholic Dictionary of Theology*,
London, I (1962) 38–41.

146. As we stated above, we are limiting our discussion to the cult of the
Saints, prescinding from the privileged case of the Blessed Virgin Mary.
Naturally, since she also is a mere creature, the theological argument concerning the Catholic cult directed to her develops along the same principles we have indicated. There can never be question of a cult of
adoration, *latria*. By reason of the unique excellence of the Mother of
God, new reasons are introduced which are not present in the case of the
Saints and elevate her cult above that of the Saints (in technical language,
her cult is termed *hyperdulia*). The basis for this distinction is the fact
that she enjoys an altogether unique union with Christ (Mother of God,
Immaculate, Full of grace, Coredemptrix, Mediatrix, Mother of the Faithful, Queen of all the Saints).

147. Cf. St. Thomas, *Summa Theol.*, IIa–IIae, q. 103, a. 1 c; *ibid.* a. 2 c;
III, q. 25, a. 1 c; St. Robert Bellarmine, *De Ecclesia Triumphante* . . . lib. 1,
c. 12, ed. cit., t. II, p. 440. That this excellence is of a religious nature, can
be seen from F. Suárez, *De virtute et statu Religionis*, tract. 1, lib. 1, c. 5,
n. 5, ed. cit., t. XIII, pp. 54–55; *De Incarnatione*, disp. 52, sect. 2, n. 2,
ed. cit., t. XVIII, p. 567; *ibid.* sect. 3, n. 2, ed. cit., p. 568; *Defensio Fidei
Catholicae adversus anglicanae sectae errores*, lib. 2, c. 8, n. 4, ed. cit.,
t. XXIV, p. 157. Besides, it is enough to consider the fact that the investigation which the Church carries out before elevating a person to the honors of the altar turns essentially on his heroic exercise of supernatural
virtues; cf. Benedict XIV, *De Servorum Dei Beatificatione et Beatorum
Canonizatione*, lib. 3, c. 21 ss, ed. cit. t. III, pp. 273–811.

148. We do not deny that even a person who does not have the gift of
faith can still discern in the person and life of the Saint an altogether
special excellence: extraordinary intelligence and other intellectual gifts,
character, conduct, maturity and balance, goodness, industry and influence,
etc. But we wish to emphasize that we can have an adequate understanding
of the greatness of the Saints, that is, an appreciation that penetrates to its
deepest roots, only when we comprehend, in the light of faith, that the
Saints are pre-eminent members of Christ's Mystical Body and that it is
from their union with Him that they derive their excellence. We might
note in passing that it is precisely in the lives of the Saints that we find a

clear illustration of the famous theological axiom: grace presupposes, elevates, and perfects nature.

149. Peter Lombard, summing up the tradition before him, drew attention to this fact centuries ago, in: *Lib. III Sententiarium*, d. 9, c. un., n. 62, ed. cit. t. II, p. 591, a classic text which serves as a basis for the comments and further developments of the Scholastics.

150. F. Suárez, *De virtute et statu Religionis*, tract. 4, lib. 1, c. 10, n. 6, ed. cit., t. XIV, p. 37. See also the clear formulation of this same principle in St. Thomas, *Summa Theol.*, IIa–IIae, q. 83, a. 4 c. and ad 1; and in St. Robert Bellarmine, *De Ecclesia Triumphante* . . ., lib. 1, c. 17, ed. cit., t. II, p. 448; St. Peter Canisius, *Catechismus Maior* [post-trid.], c. III, 1, viii, n. 49, pp. 100–101; Benedict XIV, *De Servorum Dei Beatificatione et Beatorum Canonizatione*, lib. 1, c. 12, nn. 2–4, ed. cit. I, 92–94. Citing the text of St. Thomas mentioned above, Pope Leo XIII expressed this doctrine in these words: "Catholica fide enim docemur, non ipsum modo Deum esse precibus exorandum, sed beatos quoque caelites, licet ratione dissimili, quod a Deo, tamquam bonorum omnium fonte, ab his tamquam ab intercessoribus, petendum sit. Oratio, inquit S. Thomas, porrigitur alicui dupliciter, etc." Epistola Encyclica SS.mi D. N. Papae Leonis XIII de Rosario Mariali, "Augustissimae Virginis," 12 Sept. 1897, *ASS* 30 (1897–1898), p. 132.

151. We distinguish purposely between the attitude of adoration or the cult of *latria* and that of *dulia*, inasmuch as this terminology corresponds more accurately to modern usage and precludes the danger of confusion. But we wish to note that even those ancient authors who used the term "adoration" in its original wider and more generic sense (speaking indiscriminately of adoration of God, the Blessed Virgin Mary, the Angels, and the Saints) left no doubt as to the essential difference between the *latreutic* adoration owed to God, and that of dulia or hyperdulia owed to outstanding creatures. For examples of this, cf.: St. Robert Bellarmine, *De Ecclesia Triumphante*, lib. 1, c. 12, ed. cit., t. II, pp. 440–441; F. Suárez, *De Incarnatione*, disp. 52, sec. 2, n. 1, ed. cit., t. XVIII, pp. 566ss., *Defensio Fidei Catholicae* . . . lib. 2, c. 8, n. 3, ed. cit. t. XXIV, pp. 156–157; Benedict XIV, *De Servorum etc.*, lib. 1, c. 1, n. 15, ed. cit., t. I, p. 9. In the same way are we to interpret the few contemporary authors who continue to use this term "adoration" in the generic sense corresponding to "cult" (e.g. J. A. de Aldama, S.J., *Sacrae Theologiae Summa,* III, tract. II, Mariologia seu de Matre Redemptoris, BAC 62, Madrid, 1961[4], nn. 233ss, pp. 472ss).

152. As is known, even the technical term dulia was further clarified in the course of history. It has been observed that present usage of the term owes much to the holy doctor Robert Bellarmine: "With respect to cult, he distinguished the cult of latria (by which we honor the divine excellence alone), civil cult (by which we recognize natural excellence), the cult of dulia (by which we honor an excellence which occupies the region between the divine and the human by reason of supernatural gifts such as the grace

and glory of the Saints). A special cult of hyperdulia is due to creatures who had a more intimate union with the Word of God, namely, the humanity of Christ considered in itself, and the Virgin Mother of God, loc. cit., c. 12, p. 168. We see how much contemporary theology owes to Bellarmine." P. Séjourné, O.S.B., "Saints (culte des)," DTC XIV, 968. Cf. St. Robert Bellarmine, De Ecclesia Triumphante, lib. 1, c. 12, ed. cit. t. II, pp. 440–442.

153. One of the typical characteristics of the liturgy is that it directs the attention of the faithful to the hierarchy of supernatural values. It expresses and emphasizes the difference between the cult of God on the one hand, and the cult of the Blessed Virgin Mary and the Saints on the other, not only using prayers which have clearly distinct formularies in each case but also prescribing diverse actions and gestures according to the dignity of the one to whom the cult is being exteriorly manifested (prostrations, genuflections, inclinations, etc.).

154. We refer the reader to the texts listed above in notes 149, 150, and to those below in notes 156, 157; esp. cf. St. Thomas, In IVum Sent., d. 45, q. 3, a. 2, c. and ad 1; St. Peter Canisius, Commentariorum de Verbi Dei corruptelis, tomus Alter de Maria Virgine incomparabili . . ., lib. 5, c. 15, ed. cit., p. 698; St. Robert Bellarmine, De Ecclesia Triumphante, lib. 1, c. 20, ed. cit., t. II, p. 436; F. Suárez, De virtute et statu Religionis, tract. 1, lib. 3, c. 5, n. 6, ed. cit. t. XIII, p. 55; Id., De Incarnatione, disp. 52, sect. 2, n. 4, ed. cit. t. XVIII, pp. 567–568; Benedict XIV, De Servorum Dei etc., lib. 1, c. 13, n. 1, ed. cit., t. I, pp. 98ss, where the author comments on the meaning of the traditional formula of solemn canonization: "Ad honorem Sanctae et Individuae Trinitatis, ad exaltationem Fidei Catholicae et Christianae religionis augmentum . . ." ibid., pp. 100–112.

155. St. Robert Bellarmine, De Ecclesia Triumphante . . ., lib. 1, c. 20, ed. cit., t. II, p. 457.

156. Ibid., c. 17, pp. 448–449, and c. 20, p. 457. Also: Id., Apologia . . . ad librum Jacobi . . . cuius titulus est Triplici Nodo triplex cuneus, c. 8, ed. cit., t. IV, altera pars, p. 376; F. Suárez, De virtute et statu Religionis, tract. 4, lib. 1, c. 10, n. 11, ed. cit., t. XIV, p. 39, and n. 12, p. 40.

157. St. Peter Canisius, Catechismus Maior [ante-trid.], c. III, n. 44, ed. cit., pp. 15–16; cf. also Catechismus Minor [post-trid.], c. III, 1, VIII, n. 49, ed. cit., p. 101. That christocentrism and theocentrism underlie the thought of the great theologians of the Counter-Reformation when they write of the cult of the Saints is evident to anyone who reads their writings on this subject. For example: St. Robert Bellarmine, De Ecclesia Triumphante, lib. 1, c. 16, ed. cit., t. II, pp. 447–448; c. 17, p. 448; F. Suárez, De virtute et statu Religionis, tract. 4, lib. 1, c. 10, n. 5, ed. cit., t. XIV, pp. 36–37; n. 12, p. 40; n. 13, p. 40; n. 17, p. 41; n. 18, p. 41; Defensio Fidei Catholicae . . ., lib. 2, c. 9, n. 15, ed. cit., t. XXIV, p. 164; n. 18, p. 165. From this last-mentioned work, we quote a compendious text from which it is evident that these great doctors from a century which is too

readily underestimated today drew upon Catholic tradition and explained the rich treasures of the cult of the Saints precisely in theocentric and christocentric terms: "Multo ergo magis orationes nostrae cum Sanctorum intercessionibus coniunctae efficaciores fiunt, ac subinde utiliores. Neque propterea Dei, vel Christi cultus minuitur, sed augetur, quia dum Sanctos invocamus, divinam maiestatem magis reveremur, nostramque indignitatem recognoscimus, et per Sanctos Deum magis honorare et glorificare cupimus, eique gratias pro tot beneficiis agimus," *ibid.* n. 25, p. 168.

158. K. Rahner, S.J., "Die ewige Bedeutung der Menschheit Jesu für unser Gottesverhältnis," in *Schriften zur Theologie*, Band III, Einsiedeln, etc. 1957[2], 47–60, 54–56. (This was originally published in *Geist und Leben* 26 [1953] 279–288.) For a theological exposition of the Christian attitude towards the world, cf. the richly documented study of C. V. Truhlar, S.J., *Antinomiae Vitae Spiritualis*, III. "Transformatio mundi et fuga mundi," Romae 1961[3], pp. 76–123 (originally published in *Gregorianum* 38 [1957] 405–455; cf. *Theology Digest* 8 [1960] 154–158, "Transform the world and relinquish it"). For scriptural teaching on this subject as contained in the New Testament, cf. R. Schnackenburg, *Die Kirche im Neuen Testament,* Quaestiones disputatae 14, hrsg. von K. Rahner, S.J. und H. Schlier, Freiburg i. Br. etc. 1961, esp. IV, 5: "Kirche und Welt," pp. 156–165.

159. We direct the reader's attention to an observation made by K. Rahner in the passage cited above, concerning the necessity of reconsidering, in a more profoundly theological manner than has hitherto been done, precisely what is the relationship between the cult of latria and that of dulia. There is a certain difficulty and discomfort in presenting the cult of dulia as a part of religious cult; for example, consider these passages from the articles on "cult" and "dulia" in the *Enciclopedia Cattolica* 4 (1950) 1040, 1041: "By religious cult we mean to designate all those excellencies which either have God as their direct term or refer directly to God (God, Jesus Christ, the Saints, relics, ecclesiastical authority . . .); by secular cult we mean to acknowledge all those other forms of excellence which are not God and are not directly referred to God (our country, parents, national heroes, famous men, civil authority . . .). Religious cult is then the concrete expression of the duties connected with the moral virtue of religion, while secular cult is the expression of the duties associated with the virtue of piety and obedience." "Dulia. In the Saints we find sanctity, that is, martyrdom or the heroic practice of all the Christian virtues; since this is the fruit of supernatural grace, there is reflected in the Saints the essential holiness of God the Creator in a special manner. By reason of this divine life which is eminently revealed in them the Saints will be the objects of a cult which has its raison d'être in the cult of latria, because the excellence venerated in them is the particular manifestation of the divine perfection and therefore a cult subordinate to the cult of latria, which came to be called the cult of dulia (can. 1255 #1; 1276). The cult of hyperdulia and of dulia directed to our Lady and the Saints is, so to say, a special form of religious cult, either because religious cult

as such is due to God alone, or because the Blessed Virgin and the Saints are venerated only inasmuch as they are united to God and God manifests His power in them. Accordingly, it is a cult which does not terminate ultimately in the Saints or our Lady but in God, precisely as the Liturgy expresses it: 'Sanctorum memoriam colimus, Domine, Te magnificamus . . .' " (L. Oldani). In view of the explanation we have given in the course of this present study, there is no need to repeat why we consider this presentation theologically incomplete. It is evident that this approach fails to provide an harmonious and distinct synthesis of the relations between the cult of latria and that of dulia. This deficiency, in our opinion, derives from a too rigid adherence to the classic scholastic division of virtue, which presents, as is known, notable difficulties, especially in regard to the virtue of religion. On this point, cf. E. Amann, "Religion (Vertu de)," *DTC* 13 (1937) 2306–2312.

160. This can be seen with particular clarity from a comparison between the spirituality of the Martyrs and their first admirers and that of subsequent centuries, a time in which legends cropped up abundantly (cf. notes 119–120, and 169). Similar observations can explain certain aspects of the devotional life of the late Middle Ages, of the period preceding the Reform, of the Baroque period, and of the nineteenth century. Unfortunately, to the best of our knowledge there do not as yet exist historical studies which systematically demonstrate how the rise of exaggerated and unwholesome forms of devotionalism is always associated with an increasing ignorance of basic religious truths, with the subsequent obscuring of theocentrism and christocentrism.

161. We know, for example, that not long ago a pastor in a large European city on the day of Pentecost celebrated a solemn Mass in honor of the Saint to whom the parish church was dedicated and whose feast occurred in that year on Pentecost Sunday. Another, during Passiontide, continued to conduct afternoon devotions for the "month of St. Joseph" with great pomp (sermons, hymns, etc.), interrupting this program on Holy Thursday and then resuming it on Easter Sunday, without making even the least reference to the central feast of Our Lord's resurrection. Sad to say, the list of such incidents could be extended at length. These incongruities are well known to those with pastoral experience, which reveals that such exaggerations are frequently linked to unrestrained forms of cult of local patrons, supported and promoted, unfortunately, by some members of the clergy, both diocesan and regular.

162. The profound influence which the cult of the Saints has exercised on the customs, practices, and even the language of peoples can be seen from the numerous notes which the *Enciclopedia Cattolica* has appended to the articles which treat of the better-known Saints of antiquity and of the Middle Ages. On this topic, see the article of: P. Charles, S.J., "Essai de Folklore Théologique," *NRT* 68 (1946) 745–765, and the fascinating study of H. Schauerte, *Die volkstümliche Heiligenverehrung*, Münster,

1948. See also L. Veit–L. Lenhart, *Kirche und Volksfrömmigkeit im Zeit-alter des Barock*, Freiburg i. Br., 1956, esp. pp. 58–74.

163. In one of the works of the famous liturgist J. A. Jungmann, S.J., who has contributed so much to scientific research on the liturgy and to the progress of the liturgical movement, we find the following passage which deserves deep reflection: "We honor our *saints* and we have every reason to do so. From time to time we see veneration for a particular saint reach the point of vigorous enthusiasm among the Christian people. So it once was for Anthony, and so it is today for Theresa of the Child Jesus. Votive pictures and statues, novenas, special prayers are to be found everywhere. Even were all this to show that men are specially looking for a helper in their need, we would not disapprove of it. There is no more worthy object of our veneration and trust, and a moral ideal is being pursued at least concomitantly with it. We can, as a matter of fact, go a step further. For the ordinary piety of simple people it matters little if they are so taken up with their saints that all the other chapters of Catholic doctrine fade somewhat in their consciousness. With St. Anthony they also hold fast to the Catholic faith and they fulfill their Christian duties. But this only applies in the simplest circumstances—a pious old mother or a servant girl who, without question or criticism, lives in a situation where the supporting and strengthening function of an integrated consciousness of the faith can be dispensed with. For the pastoral guidance of a community, however, we can no longer neglect the integration of the veneration of the saints into the larger whole of Catholic doctrine" (*Die Frohbotschaft und unsere Glaubensverkündigung*, Regensburg, 1936, p. 201; tr. and ed. by Wm. A. Huesman, S.J., *The Good News Yesterday and Today*, New York-Chicago, 1962, pp. 139–140). In a footnote to this passage [in the German edition], Jungmann refers to a work of P. Lippert, S.J.: "Why should we be so impudent as to force upon every soul the entire realm of the Christian world of ideas and the inexhaustible depths of the Christian experience in their entirety? We should leave the solitary adorer in his cell and not drive him into the maelstrom of activity under the pretext that the harvest is great but the laborers are few! And then the quiet, simple, heavily bur-dened working women who make themselves capable of carrying their burdens through the assistance of an 'effective little prayer' culled from a simple book and attendance at Mass with prayers to St. Anthony on their lips! Let us respect even their unliturgical manner of praying! They need not climb up to the heights of eucharistic theology and liturgy in their thoughts; it suffices that they be a sacrificial lamb in their wills and lives, integrated into the sacrificial offering of the mystical body of Christ." P. Lippert, S.J., *Von Seele zu Seele. Briefe an gute Menschen*. Freiburg, 1937[33-34], pp. 130–131.

It should be evident from the content of our entire study that, in adduc-ing these texts, we in no way intend to condone any comfortable inertia on the part of those who have the grave responsibility of educating the people in their faith and initiating them in the riches of our liturgy. We have cited these authors simply to counter, within proper limits, the occasional attitude which looks with disdain and an ironic intellectual superiority—hardly justifiable—on the forms of piety which may well be unsophisticated if measured by objective norms, but at the same time are inspired by a sublime religious simplicity which is certainly dear and acceptable to God.

164. We do not understand how anyone can disparage or look with disdain upon certain gestures and exterior manifestations of interior dispositions (e.g. the use of flowers, candles, etc.), when these are dictated by a deep and sincere interior feeling and discreetly maintained within proper limits. This is all the more puzzling if we consider that even those who assume an attitude of superiority when confronted by the practices of the simple faithful have recourse in their daily lives to these and other external means of expressing their affections to others, or to externalize the respect they feel for their deceased relatives.

165. St. Jerome, *Liber contra Vigilantium*, 7, PL 23, 345–346.

166. Numerous are the articles written in this vein; but since it would be odious to mention names, we will refrain from documenting our statement with specific references. This is in no way to deny the existence of the many abuses, deviations, and errors which have been pointed out. But we feel obliged to emphasize that such abuses are exaggerated, at times, and often criticized in such a derisive and sarcastic tone that hardly any good can come of it. In this field as in all others, there is need for calm, constructive criticism, characterized by suggestions and guiding rules based on an harmonious vision of theological, ascetical, and liturgical principles, which serves to build up the Body of Christ.

167. Precisely with this intent in mind, John XXIII paternally and affectionately reproached those priests who, instead of undertaking the laborious task of instruction based upon fundamental religious truths, were preoccupied with the "anxious concern to cultivate certain practices and devotions which are excessive in their cult of our Lady, the dear Mother of Jesus—who is not in the least offended by our words—and of certain Saints, with the result that the external expression of the religious spirit of our good people is at times impoverished." And to explain his thought more clearly, His Holiness went on to say: "Please try to understand what we are saying. It is the priest's duty to be cautious and to warn his flock. Certain pious practices are calculated exclusively to gratify feeling, but by themselves fail to fulfill perfectly our religious obligations and are far from corresponding perfectly with the first three precepts of the Decalogue, which bind us so seriously" (*Allocutio ad Romanum utriusque ordinis Clerum, postquam primae Romanae Synodi leges vim obligandi habere inceperunt*, 24 Nov. 1960, *AAS* 52 [1960] 969).

168. No one can deny that in some churches the attention of the faithful is distracted from the tabernacle and directed instead to a forest of statues and portraits of Saints, which are often of questionable artistic value and

contribute little towards directing piety and devotion along proper lines. It is not surprising that such a sad state of affairs has been recognized in recent discussions on sacred art, in the course of which, however, there have been manifested certain theological attitudes with respect to the cult of the Saints which cannot be totally justified. Our problem has two aspects: (1) In what measure representations of the Saints ought to occupy a place within our churches; and (2) what theological, liturgical, and artistic norms ought to be observed. On this topic we should recall the words of Pius XII cited above (note 14) and consult the following: *Instructio ad locorum Ordinarios, De arte sacra*, issued by the Holy Office on June 30, 1952, *AAS* 44 (1952) 542–546, esp. p. 545, "De arte figurativa"; the well-known document issued by the *Commission Episcopale de Pastorale et Liturgie* on April 28, 1952, and approved by the Assembly of Cardinals and Bishops of France. See the text in *La Croix*, 18–19 May 1952, "De quelques principes directeurs en matière d'Art sacré," and in the appendix of the article of J. Streignart, S.J., "Au-dessus d'une querelle. Deux documents ecclésiastiques en matière d'art religieux," *NRT* 74 (1952) 944–959. See also: G. Mariani, *La legislazione ecclesiastica in materia d'arte sacra*, Pontificia Commissione Centrale per l'arte sacra, 8, Rome, 1945, esp. c. IV, a. II, n. 31 A, pp. 65–68; L. Kuppers, *Kirche und Kunst in zeitgenössischen Dokumenten*, Religiöse Quellenschriften, 5, Düsseldorf, 1955; T. Klauser, *Richtlinien für die Gestaltung des Gotteshauses aus dem Geiste der römischen Liturgie, Im Auftrage und unter Mitwirkung der Liturgischen Kommission*, Münster, 1955. Useful explanations can be found in G. Rovella, S.J., "Posizioni e Premesse della Istruzione sull'Arte Sacra," *Civiltà Cattolica* 103 (1952–III) 337–346; Id., "Prescrizioni e Norme dell'Istruzione sull'Arte Sacra," *ibid.*, 609–618; Id., "Commento a commenti circa l'Istruzione del Sant'Ufficio sull'Arte Sacra," *ibid.*, 104 (1953–I) 517–529; 654–665; R. M. de Hornedo, S.J., "Arte y imagen sacra," *Razón y Fé* 168 (1963) 295–306; H. A. P. Schmidt, S.J., "De arte sacra moderna," *Periodica* 42 (1953) 139–151, included and enriched with a bibliography in the author's work already cited, *Introductio in Liturgiam Occidentalem*, Rome, etc., 1960, cap. XXIV, Ars Sacra, pp. 686–702; R. Egenter, *Kitsch und Christentum*, Ettal, 1958[2].

169. It is very instructive to recall what befell the cult of the Martyrs in the centuries which followed the trying period of the persecutions. Chiefly because of panegyrics filled with rhetoric and devoid not only of historical value but often even of religious content, and also because of the legends which took their rise from such panegyrics, the authentic christocentric spirituality of the Martyrs and of those who venerated them gradually shifted its focal point, frequently assumed distorted forms, and lost much of its spiritual vigor and richness. Cf. H. Delehaye, S.J., *Les Passions des Martyrs et les genres littéraires*, Brussels, 1921, esp. ch. II. "Les panégyriques," pp. 183–235; ch. III. "Les Passions épiques," pp. 236–315; Id., *Les Légendes hagiographiques*. Subsidia hagiographica, n. 18a, Brussels, 1955[4].

Unfortunately, even today, despite the appearance of numerous fine works, the majority of popular lives of Saints leave much to be desired. Cf. what we wrote above at the end of Part One (pp. 32f.), and M. Carrouges, "Le scandale de l'hagiographie," *La Vie Spirituelle* 83 (1950) 307–310; Id., "L'avenir de l'hagiographie," *Maison-Dieu* n. 52 (1957) 121–133; Apostolus, "Des pécheurs et des saints . . ." *La Vie Spirituelle* 98 (1958) 281–284.

170. E. Moureau, "Actes liturgiques et dévotions populaires," *Revue Ecclésiastique de Liège* 38 (1951) 134–140, 135–137.

171. Cf. John XXIII, "Epistula Apostolica 'De cultu pretiosissimi Sanguinis D. N. Iesu Christi promovendo,'" *AAS* 52 (1960) 546.

172. See above, esp. pp. 86f.

173. The only aspect of the problem which seems to have been treated with some degree of adequacy is that of how the Saints can know and, in fact, are aware of the prayers which wayfarers on earth address to them. For the classic authors on this question, see notes 95–101; for more modern theologians, consult the article of the *DTC* (cited in note 101) and the manuals, esp. I. F. Sagüés, S.J., *De Novissimis,* lib. i, cap. iii, a. 8, in *Patres Societatis Iesu Facultatum Theologicarum in Hispania Professores, Sacrae Theologiae Summa* IV, BAC 73, Madrid, 1962[4], nn. 132–135, pp. 904–906.

The expositions of these authors, however, fail to offer a complete and integrated treatment of the entire problem, and of its place in the theology of the cult of the Saints. Modern writers of manuals concern themselves with the question not under the aspect of the cult of the Saints, but in the treatise *de Novissimis,* when they raise the question of the extent of the knowledge of the blessed. The pastoral aspects of this problem are ignored and, as a consequence, no use is made of one of these most precious themes for reinforcing in the faithful their belief in the immortality of the soul and in the eschatological character of our Christian life.

174. On this precise point, see the study of H. Zeller, S.J., "Corpora Sanctorum, Eine Studie zu Mt. 27, 52–53," *Zeitschrift für katholische Theologie* 71 (1949) 385–465.

175. Although it is evident from the context, nevertheless we wish to emphasize that when we use the expression "direct personal contact," we do not mean to assert without qualification that there is no difference in form and modality between our contacts with the Saints and our contacts with wayfarers. We use the expression in an analogous sense. Nor do we wish to give the impression that our contacts with the Saints are less direct and personal than those which we have with our fellow wayfarers. On the contrary, we know by faith that the Saints are closer to us than persons who are corporeally present to us; that the knowledge they have of us and the love they exercise towards us are much deeper than the knowledge and love which any wayfarer can have. Consequently, the contact we establish with them in Christ has a dimension and a degree of intimacy which surpass by far the intimacy possible among persons living on earth.

176. We refer the reader to what we stated above, pp. 16f.

177. Cf. the text of the Encyclical *Mystici Corporis, AAS* 35 (1943) 209–210, quoted and commented upon (cf. pp. 20f.).

This same principle obviously serves as a basis for the procedure followed by the Church in the processes of Beatification and Canonization. The spontaneity of the *fama sanctitatis*, renown for holiness, and its widespread diffusion are considered as a typical sign of God's will; that is, as an indication that it is God Himself who is eliciting such devotion in the hearts of the faithful because He is seeking to unite them to Himself by utilizing the influence and attractive charm which a person dear to Him can arouse in them.

INDEX

Abraham, the Patriarch, 133
Adam, K., 182
Agel, H., 180
Agnes, St., 180
Aigrain, R., 178, 182
Albert, F. E., 200
Aldama, J. A. de, S.J., 225
Alphonsus Liguori, St., 183
Alszeghy, Z., S.J., 196
Altaner, B., 190
Amann, E., 228
Ambrose, St., 216
Anger, J., 182
Anne, St., Mother of Our Lady, 195
Anouilh, J., 180
Anrede, 196
Anselm, St., 218
Antonelli, F., O.F.M., 186
Anthony, Abbot, St., 183
Anthony Claret, St., 177
Anthony of Padua, St., 229
Aparicio, F., S.J., 180
"Apostolus," 232
Archbishop of Canterbury, 193
Augurius, St., 114, 217
Augustine, St., 51, 68, 113, 114, 115, 131, 186, 217, 218, 221
Ayfre, A., 180
Azevedo, E. de, S.J., 185, 191

Bacchelli, R., 179
Bacht, H., S.J., 199
Balthasar, H. U. v., 200
Baragli, E., S.J., 180
Bardy, G., 182
Barth, K., 199
Basil, St., 183
Baum, Gregory, 165, 172
Baumann, F., S.J., 177, 187
Baus, K., 216
Bazin, A., 180
Bazin, R., 179
Bea, A. Cardinal, 220
Behr-Sigel, E., 188
Benedict, St., 179, 183
Benedict XIV (Prosper Lambertini), viii, 34, 185, 186, 191, 194, 205, 213, 215, 224, 225, 226
Benedict XV, 177
Bernanos, G., 179
Bernard, P., 208
Bernadette Soubirous, St., 177, 179, 180
Bernard of Clairvaux, St., 183
Blaher, D. J., O.F.M., 186, 215
Bolt, R., 180
Bon, H., 187
Bonaventure, St., 191, 204, 205, 211
Bonduelle, J. F., O.P., 209

Boros, L., S.J., 200
Bouyer, L., 216
Boyer, C., S.J., 192
Braga, C., C.M., 195
Brillant, M., 184
Brosch, J., 192
Browning, C., C.P., 204
Brunet, R., S.J., 182
Brunner, E., 199
Brunner, P., 214
Bruylants, P., O.S.B., 203
Bugnini, A., C.M., 208, 213
Bultmann, R., 200
Buomberger, F., 179

Cabassut, A., O.S.B., 218
Calvin, John, 199
Camelot, P. Th., O.P., 216
Cano, M., O.P., 34
Capmany, J., 216
Carinci, A., 177
Carrouges, M., 232
Carter, J. C., S.J., 187
Castus, St., 218
Catherine of Siena, St., 180
Cavallera, F., S.J., 183
Cerfaux, L., 182
Cesbron, G., 179
Charles, P., S.J., 228
Chavasse, A., 214
Chesterton, G. K., 179
Chollet, A., 190
Cioppa, G. della, 186
Claeys Boùùaert, M., S.J., 189
Clark, F., S.J., 220
Claudel, P., 179, 180
Clement VIII, 213
Clement X, 213
Clement XI, 213
Cochlaeus, J., 193
Congar, Y., O.P., 182, 190, 199
Coppola, R., 185, 191
Cornelius a Lapide, S.J., 188
Cuenca, C. Fernández, 180
Cyprian, St., 98, 216, 218
Cyril of Jerusalem, St., 99

Daeschler, R., S.J., 182
Dalmais, I. H., O.P., 210
David, the Prophet, 133
Deinhardt, W., 208
Delehaye, H., S.J., 114, 181, 182,
   183, 216, 217, 231
Delooz, P., S.J., 176, 184
Denzinger, H., 183, 194, 221
Dhanis, E., S.J., 187
Dionysius, the Pseudo-Areopagite,
   207
Dominic, St., 179, 183
Dörfler, P., 179
Douillet, J., S.J., 192
Doyé, F.v.S., 208
Dürig, W., 208
Dunne, W. P., 209

Ebneter, A., 193
Eckius, J., 193
Egenter, R., 231
Eliot, T. S., 179, 180
Emilian, Roman judge, 217
Emilius, St., 218
Eulogius, St., 114, 217

Faber, J., 193
Fabri, D., 179, 180
Faustus, 221
Feckes, C., 182
Federer, H., 179
Fernández Cuenca, C., 180
Flick, M., S.J., 196
Ford, Ch., 180
Fort, G. von le, 179
Francis of Assisi, St., 179, 180, 183
Francis de Sales, St., 183
Frank, H., 208
Frings, J. Cardinal, 163, 219
Fructuosus, St., 114, 217
Frutaz, P. A., 216

Gagna, F., 185
Gaiffier, B. de, S.J., 216
Garate, F., S.J., Servant of God, 178
Garrigou-Lagrange, R., O.P., 184

Garrone, Gabriel, Archbishop, 162, 163
Gemma Galgani, St., 173
Gemmeke, M., O.C., 177
Ghéon, H., 179
Giordani, I., 179
Gleason, R. W., S.J., 200
Görres (Coudenhove), I. F., 179
Goyau, G., 180
Gregory the Great, St., 196, 216
Gregory XVI, 176
Grillmeier, A., S.J., 199
Grumel, V., 195
Guérard de Lauriers, M. L., O.P., 190
Guibert, J. de, S.J., 183, 203
Gummersbach, J., S.J., 209
Gutzwiller, R., S.J., 215

Halkin, L. E., 193
Handel-Mazzetti, E.v., 180
Hanssens, I., S.J., 194
Hardon, J., S.J., 186
Häring, B., C.SS.R., 224
Hartmann, P., S.C.J., 216
Hausherr, I., S.J., 182
Heiming, O., O.S.B., 213
Héris, Ch.-V., O.P., 182
Hertling, L.v., S.J., 33, 176, 182, 186, 189, 218
Hessels, J., 193
Hild, J., O.S.B., 192
Hillig, F., S.J., 180
Hoffmann, G., 190
Hofinger, J., S.J., 214
Hofmann, R., 186
Hoogstraeten, J., O.P., 193
Hornedo, R. M. de, S.J., 231
Huby, J., S.J., 188
Hunter, L., 194

Ignatius Loyola, St., ix, 179, 180, 183, 184
Indelicato, S., 185, 215
Innocents, the Holy, 195
Isaac, the Patriarch, 133

Jacob, the Patriarch, 133
James, St., 217
Jay, E. G., 207
Jedin, H., 183, 194
Jeremias, the Prophet, 133, 206
Jerome, St., 143, 204, 230
Jerphanion, G. de, S.J., 179
Joachim, St., father of Our Lady, 195
Joan of Arc, St., 180
John, the Apostle, 118, 131
John the Baptist, St., 193, 195, 211, 212
John Bosco, St., 177, 180, 183, 186
John of the Cross, St., 183
John Baptist de La Salle, St., 183
John Marie-Baptiste Vianney, St., 177, 180
John XXIII, 42, 149, 160, 161, 162, 165, 181, 209, 213, 220, 222, 230
Jombart, E., S.J., 190, 192, 208
Joseph, St., spouse of Our Lady, 171, 195, 212, 222, 228
Joseph Cottolengo, St., 183
Jouassard, G., 216
Jounel, P., 192, 214, 216
Journet, C., 182
Judas Maccabeus, 206
Julian of Norwich, 218
Jungmann, J. A., S.J., 190, 196, 209, 210, 214, 216, 218, 220, 229
Jürgensmeier, F., 182

Kaiser, E. G., 224
Kapitel, E., 218
Kellner, J., S.J., 214
Kemp, E. W., 186
Kempf, K., S.J., 176, 185
Klauser, Th., 231
Knabenbauer, J., S.J., 188
Koch, A., S.J., 179
Kolbe, M., O.F.M., Servant of God, 177
Konig, F. Cardinal, 163, 218
Krane, A.v., 180
Kremer, J., 202

Künstle, K., 178
Kuppers, L., 231

Lagrange, M. J., O.P., 187, 188
Lamalle, E., S.J., 179
Lambertini, Prospero; see Benedict XIV
Lambot, C., O.S.B., 217
Lansemann, R., 180, 193
Lanz, A., S.J., 186
Larrañaga, V., S.J., 187
Larraona, A. Cardinal, 162, 163
Lawrence, St., 195
Lebreton, J., S.J., 196
Leclercq, H., O.S.B., 208
Lecuyer, J., C.S.Sp., 190, 223
Ledit, J. H., S.J., 189
Leeming, B., S.J., 200
Lengeling, E. J., 190, 193
Lenhart, L., 229
Léonard, E. G., 193
Leo XII, 176
Leo XIII, 176
Leprohon, P., 180
Leturia, P., S.J., 184
Leuret, F., 186
Lippert, P., S.J., 229
Lottin, O., O.S.B., 190, 223
Louis Gonzaga, St., 179
Löw, G., C.SS.R., 186, 208, 213
Luke, St., the Evangelist, 130
Luther, Martin, 193, 199

Maldonatus, G., S.J., 188
Mâle, E., 195
Malevez, L., S.J., 198, 218
Malmberg, F., S.J., 198, 201
Manacorda, G., 180
Margaret of Cortona, St., 180
Margherita d'Oyngt, 218
Maria Goretti, St., 177, 180
Mariani, G., 231
Marianus, St., 217
Martimort, A. G., 192
Martini, C., S.J., 185
Martyrs, Carmelite, Blessed, 180

Martyrs, Canadian, Saints, 177
Martyrs, Jesuit, of China, 180
Martyrs of England and Wales, Forty Blessed, 178, 219
Mary Michael of the Blessed Sacrament, St., 177
Mary, Mother of Jesus, 8, 52, 98, 130, 152, 163, 165, 171, 180, 189, 193, 198, 211, 212, 221, 224, 225, 226, 227, 230
Massarelli, 194
Matt, L.v., 179
Matteucci, B., 189
Mauriac, F., 180
Mayer, R., S.J., Servant of God, 177, 219
Meersch, M.v.d., 180
Mechtilde of Hackenborn, 218
Meester, P. de, O.S.B., 188
Menessier, I., O.P., 190, 224
Mersch, E., S.J., 182, 198
Michel, A., 192, 202, 208
Mitterer, A., 182
Molien, A., 192, 224
Molinari, P., S.J., 218, 224
Molinos, M. de, 124, 221
Molle, A., Servant of God, 178
Monden, L., 29, 187, 188, 189
Monica, St., 180
Moretti, G., O.F.M., 179
Moureau, E., 147, 232

Napoli, G. de, 190
Neumann, John, 212
Nied, E., 209
Nigg, W., 180

O'Flynn, J. A., 188
Oldani, L., 190, 228
Origen, 205, 207, 216

Pacomius, Abbot, St., 183
Palazzini, P., 183
Paul, the Apostle, St., 49, 66, 69, 70, 118, 144, 168, 169, 195, 221

Paul of the Cross, St., 183
Paul VI, 163, 164, 165, 212
Papini, G., 180
Pascher, J., 192
Paschini, P., 190
Peeters, P., S.J., 188
Pellegrino, M., 216
Pemán, J. M., 180
Peter, the Apostle, St., 67, 115, 116, 195, 221
Peter Canisius, St., 193, 204, 211, 225, 226
Peter Lombard, 191, 204, 207, 225
Philip Neri, St., 183
Piolanti, A., 192
Pius IV, 194, 221
Pius V, St., 213
Pius VII, 176
Pius VIII, 176
Pius IX, 176, 212
Pius X, St., 176, 177, 180
Pius XI, 177, 213
Pius XII, viii, 3, 7, 20, 41, 147, 149, 177, 181, 182, 194, 195, 196, 203, 213, 223, 231
Pohle, J., 209
Polycarp, 36, 98
Poulpiquet, P. de, O.P., 182
Pourrat, P., 182
Pro, M. A., Servant of God, 177

Quadrio, G., S.D.B., 192
Quasten, J., 190
Queffélec, H., 180

Racioppi, S., 189
Rahner, K., S.J., 19, 136, 162, 181, 182, 183, 191, 200, 201, 205–206, 211, 216, 227
Raphael, the Archangel, 206
Richstätter, K., S.J., 176, 184
Righetti, M., 208
Robert Bellarmine, St., 191, 204, 205, 224, 225, 226
Roberti, F., 192
Rodewyk, A., S.J., 179

Rouët de Journel, M. J., S.J., 190
Rovella, G., S.J., 231

Sackville-West, V., 180
Sagüés, I. F., S.J., 232
Salaverri, S., S.J., 182, 184
Santos, R. Cardinal, 163
Sara, 206
Sauras, E., O.P., 182
Schamoni, W., 178, 179
Schauerte, H., 192, 228
Schmidt, H. A. P., S.J., 190, 192, 218, 231
Schnackenburg, R., 199, 227
Schneider, R., 180
Seitz, A., 187
Séjourné, P., O.S.B., 192, 217, 226
Semmelroth, O., S.J., 182
Servière, J. de la, S.J., 191
Soiron, Th., O.F.M., 198
Sorokin, P. A., 3
Spedalieri, F., S.J., 183
Staehlin, C. M., S.J., 180
Stanislaus Kostka, St., 179
Stephen, St., 195
Stenzel, A., S.J., 190, 209
Streicher, F., S.J., 193
Streignart, J., S.J., 231
Suárez, F., S.J., 191, 204, 205, 207, 211, 214, 224, 225, 226

Teresa of Avila, St., 183
Theresa of Lisieux, St., 177, 180, 229
Ternus, J., S.J., 199
Thils, G., 22, 23, 24, 184, 187
Thurian, M., 193
Timmermans, F., 180
Tobias, 206
Thomas Aquinas, St., 65, 66, 190, 191, 198, 204, 205, 207, 223, 224, 225
Tóth, J. B. de, 194
Troisfontaines, R., S.J., 200
Tromp, S., S.J., 182, 192, 196
Truhlar, K., S.J., 189, 227
Tyszkiewicz, S., S.J., 183

Umberg, J. B., S.J., 192, 195

Vagaggini, C., O.S.B., 190, 192, 208, 210
Valentini, E., 184
Van Doren, D. R., 213
Vansteenberghe, G., 204
Vernet, F., 182
Vigilantius, 134, 204, 230
Viller, M., S.J., 182, 190, 191, 216
Vincent de Paul, St., 179, 180, 183
Volk, H., 199
Vorgrimler, H., 192, 205, 219

Walsh, M., 180

Walz, J. B., O.P., 183
Warszawski, J., S.J., 179
Waugh, E., 180
Weiser, F. X., S.J., 192
Weismantel, L., 180
Werfel, F., 180
Wissing, A., 195
Witte, J. L., S.J., 199
Wright, J. H., S.J., 207
Wulf, F., S.J., 180, 200

Zapelena, T., S.J., 182
Zeller, H., S.J., 232
Zorè, I. N., S.J., 215
Zulli, G., S.D.B., 216